Peter Jordens (Ed.)
Language Development and Developmental Language Disorder

Studies on Language Acquisition

Series Editors
Peter Jordens
Luke Plonsky
Martha Young-Scholten

Responsible Editor
Peter Jordens

Volume 62

Language Development and Developmental Language Disorder

Edited by
Peter Jordens

DE GRUYTER
MOUTON

ISBN 978-3-11-135572-6
e-ISBN (PDF) 978-3-11-071202-5
e-ISBN (EPUB) 978-3-11-071210-0
ISSN 1861-4248

Library of Congress Control Number: 2022930250

Bibliographic information published by the Deutsche Nationalbibliothek
The Deutsche Nationalbibliothek lists this publication in the Deutsche Nationalbibliografie;
detailed bibliographic data are available on the Internet at http://dnb.dnb.de.

© 2023 Walter de Gruyter GmbH, Berlin/Boston
This volume is text- and page-identical with the hardback published in 2022.
Typesetting: Integra Software Services Pvt. Ltd.
Printing and binding: CPI books GmbH, Leck

www.degruyter.com

Peter Jordens
Preface

Language development in children learning their mother tongue and in adults learning a second language is a stepwise process. As argued by Peter Jordens and Dagmar Bittner in Chapter 1 (*Developing language: Driving forces in children learning Dutch and German*), this developmental process can be characterized as progressing from a simple, basic learner system to a more complex, target-like system. The relevant study shows that this stage model holds not only for children learning Dutch (Jordens 2012) but also for children learning German. That is, initially, these children appear to use a learner system based on types of verb-argument structure that are either agentive or non-agentive, as in Dutch: *kannie* **losmake** 'cannot loose-make' and German: *magnich* **nase putzen** 'like-not nose clean' vs. Dutch: *popje* **valt** *bijna* 'doll falls nearly' and German: *ente fällt* 'duck falls'). At the relevant stage, agentive utterances, i.e. utterances with an agent in initial position, refer to situations that are under control, while non-agentive utterances, i.e. utterances with a theme in initial position, refer to situations that happen to occur. This initial stage is called 'the lexical stage'. Developmental progress towards 'the functional stage' is driven by the acquisition of the structural means to express the functional features of finiteness. 'Finiteness' is a concept of information structure which is central to the acquisition of 'the functional stage'. It indicates that the utterance serves as an assertion, meaning "that the situation described by the utterance indeed obtains" (Klein 1998). In Dutch and German, finiteness is expressed by the verbal element in 'verb-second' (V2) position. In the present Chapter, it is argued that the acquisition of this V2 position projects a 'functional prefield' for both verbal elements in V2 position to express the functional features of finiteness and for constituents such as NPs and ADVs in initial position to express the functional features of 'topicality'. Moreover, it is stated that it is these elements in the prefield of the utterance that are fit to achieve contextual cohesion. That is, it is the function of these elements to constitute a close relationship in meaning between the assertion and the situation that it applies to. More specifically, it is this informational function that accounts for the acquisition of the linguistic features of functional morphology (auxiliary verbs, subject-verb agreement, tense, gender), function words (determiners, question words, pronominal anaphora) and word order variation (inversion).

The present volume takes the language acquisition process in typically developing (TD) children as a point of reference for the study of developmental language disorder (DLD). Furthermore, it takes DLD as the reason for 'persisting linguistic difficulties' (Fletcher 1999) leading to 'a significant delay' (Leonard 2014) in language development.

Empirical investigations on DLD have traditionally focused on linguistic difficulties in the area of morpho-syntax. In a seminal study, Clahsen (1999) has put forward his 'missing agreement hypothesis'. It is believed to account for the fact that German speaking children with DLD have difficulty with the linguistic feature of control agreement, playing a role in, for example, subject-verb agreement (*ich bleibe* vs. *du bleibst* vs. *er bleibt*.- I stay vs. you stay vs. he stays) and case marking (*sie vertraut **ihm*** vs. *sie mag **ihn***. – she trusts him vs. she likes him), while they do not have problems with linguistic features such as noun plurals (*Wiese* vs. *Wiesen* – meadow vs. meadows; *Buch* vs. *Bücher* – book vs. books) and past-participle inflection (*gesucht* vs. *gefunden* – searched vs. found) where control agreement does *not* play a role. Linguistic difficulties in the area of morpho-syntax have also been studied for English speaking children with DLD. Leonard (2014) has categorized a range of grammatical elements that are associated with 'the notion of functional categories' such as articles (*a* and *the*), prenominal determiners (*this, that, these, those*), third singular *-s* (agreement), regular past *-ed* (tense), the use of the complementizers *that, if,* auxiliary inversion and *wh-*questions.

As pointed out before, our present research is based on the idea that language acquisition in TD children is a two-stage developmental process in which at some point the initial, lexical system will be given up in favour of a targetlike, functional system. As opposed to Clahsen (1999), Peter Jordens argues in Chapter 2 (*Developmental language disorder and the functional category system*) that the relevant developmental process in children with DLD is subject to an overall delay. This should account for the typically functional linguistic difficulties that these children are facing. However, this leaves us with the question of the cause of this delay. It seems our findings can adequately be interpreted in terms of the computational demands of language processing at the functional stage, more specifically, the computational problem in DLD children to establish contextual cohesion. In fact, it will be argued that this computational problem is due to an underdeveloped working memory.

Evidence of the aforementioned two-staged process of language development in DLD children comes from Bastian, a DLD child learning German as his mother tongue. In Chapter 3 (*Language acquisition in a German DLD child*), Dagmar Bittner and Peter Jordens show that at the initial, lexical stage, Bastian's language system, as is the case in TD children, is based on two types of utterance structure: utterances with an agent in initial position referring to situations that are under control vs. utterances with a theme in initial position referring to situations that happen to occur. Unlike TD children, language development with Bastian is subject to a delay of about 2 years. Given that this developmental delay is not a specific linguistic deficit such as 'missing agreement', it seems that Bastian has problems with the use of the linguistic features that serve to establish contextual cohesion. So, it is argued, following Kolk (1998), that this is caused by an underdeveloped working memory which prevents Bastian from dealing with the relevant computational demands.

Nevertheless, it should be noted that Bastian is cognitively more mature than younger TD children, who have reached the same level of language development. So, it is claimed that it is this cognitive ability that allows Bastian, while he is still at the lexical stage, to accommodate linguistic features of the target language such that they meet the constraints of a limited working memory. This holds for the expression of some functional features of finiteness and for the positioning of constituents used to express topicality. Thus, verbal elements, such as *hab(e)* (have-1^{st}sg) and *hat* (has-3^{rd}sg), that are used as auxiliary verbs at the functional stage, as in *ich* **hat** (*=habe*) *stulle aufgegessen* (I have bun up-eaten. 3;8), are adapted as verbal elements used to express lexical aspect. Furthermore, the use of constituents in initial, topic position to establish the relation between the utterance and the situation that it applies to, is going to be adapted with a left-dislocated position for adverbials and objects as in **hier**, *eisenbahn wegfahr(e)* (here, railway away-move. 3;6); **da**, *Charly teddy (sch)mutzig machen* (there, Charly teddy dirty make. 3;6); **viele brötchen**, *papa eingekauft* (many buns, daddy bought. 3;6); **haus**, *Teddy haben* (house T want-have). Finally, the use of intonation or stress to indicate which element is in focus, is adapted with a right-dislocated position for any element as, for example, the object in *muss dleiden (=schneiden),* **brötchen** (must cut, buns. 3;6) or the verbal partical in *omi fahren,* **weg** (grandma drive, away. 3;6).

The relevant phenomena of the auxiliary used to express lexical aspect and of both left- and right-dislocation to reduce the grammatical complexity of the target system confirm our claim that with DLD children, it is the computational limitations of their working memory that causes the delay in language development at the lexical stage.

The grammatical feature of 'verb second' is a typological characteristic of adult Dutch and German. It accounts for the variable position of the lexical verb in main clauses. While in the default case the lexical verb occurs in final position with non-finite morphology, i.e. as infinite (Vinf) or past-participle (Vpp), it may occur in V2 position with finite morphology (Vfin) provided this position has not been taken by a modal or auxiliary verb. This accounts for the distributional opposition between non-finite vs. finite verb forms as in *er will einen Turm* **bauen** (he wants a tower build-Inf) and *er hat einen Turm* **gebaut** (he had a tower built-Vpp) vs. *er* **baut** *einen Turm* (he builds-Vfin a tower). Evidence of verb second is the presence of morphologically finite verb forms in second-constituent position. However, in order for children to be in the position to acquire verb second the relevant V2 position has to be instantiated first. As long as this has not been the case both TD and DLD children may produce utterances such as *er Turm bauen* (he tower build-Vinf) instead of *er baut einen Turm* (he builds-3^{sg} a tower). Under the assumption that at the initial stage of language acquisition both options occur in free variation, the relevant phenomenon has been used to characterize the initial stage in Dutch and German as the optional infinitive (OI) stage. For DLD children, however, it has been argued for an EOI stage, i.e. for the claim that in these children this OI stage might extend (E) further up the MLU range than for TD children. Nonetheless, in Chapter 4 (*Testing the Extended Optional Infinitive Hypothesis in a German child with DLD*), Charleen List argues for an input-driven Dual factor model for DLD children, which in addition to the OI hypothesis should also explain the use of infinitives as in *Tierpark **bauen** ich wieder gleich* (wildlife-park build-Vinf I again now) and *Auto **gehen** nicht* (car go-Vinf not). According to this Dual factor model, DLD children are assumed to have a general preference for the infinitive instead of the finite verb form. Their use of the infinitive as the default form is claimed to be due to the fact that the finite form is only weakly represented in the system. In addition, the Dual factor model also provides for the observation that at the initial stage, agentive finite verb forms, such as *baut* (builds-3^{sg}) in, for example, *er baut einen Turm* (he builds-3^{sg} a tower), are absent. The reason for this, as has also been shown in Chapter 1–3, is the fact that at the relevant stage, lexical verbs are used in complementary distribution such that eventive verbs that are used to express desired or intended actions occur as infinitives, while verb forms referring to states and changes-of-state are used as finite verb forms.

In her study presented in Chapter 5 (*The acquisition of finiteness in auch- and aber-clauses in DLD. A case study*), Damaris Bartz investigates the early production of *auch-* and *aber-*clauses in the longitudinal data of a child with DLD. She focuses on the interaction of the acquisition of functional finiteness with the particles *auch* and *aber*. The results are compared with the acquisition of *auch-* and *aber-*clauses in typically developing children (Bartz & Bittner 2018). The present study shows that the use of finite verb forms in V2 position in the *auch-* and *aber-*clauses of this DLD child is comparable to that in TD children. That is, in both cases the rare use of finite verb forms in *auch-*clauses compared to simple main clauses is mainly restricted to *auch-*clauses produced prior to the acquisition of functional finiteness. Furthermore, in both populations, *auch-*clauses tend to omit the verb more frequently after the acquisition of functional finiteness. In *aber-*clauses, however, the use of finite verb forms is supported once functional finiteness is acquired. This suggests that the informational function of finiteness serves as the driving force. Moreover, deviations from the acquisition of *auch-* and *aber-*clauses in TD children seem to be in line with the assumption of limited working memory capacities in children with DLD. For example, the particularly long delay in the realization of OVS word order and separated particle verbs in the *aber*-clauses of the DLD child supports the assumption of a computational problem in DLD. The higher demands by these structures on the working memory seems to add to the complexity of *aber*-clauses.

References

Bittner, Dagmar & Damaris Bartz. 2018. Finiteness in early *but*-clauses in German L1-acquisition. *First Language*, 38(4), 337–358.

Clahsen, Harald. 1999. Linguistic perspectives on specific language impairment. In W.C. Ritchie & T.K. Bhatia (eds.), *Handbook of child language acquisition*, 675–706. San Diego: Academic Press.

Fletcher, Paul. 1999. Specific language impairment. In Martyn D. Barrett (ed.), *The development of language*, 349–37. Hove: Psychology Press.

Jordens, Peter. 2012. *Language acquisition and the functional category system*. Berlin/Boston: Walter de Gruyter.

Klein, Wolfgang. 1994. *Time in language*. London/New York: Routledge.

Kolk, Herman. 1998 *Compenseren voor een taalstoornis. Een neurocognitief model*. Radboud Universiteit: Nijmegen.

Leonard, Laurence B. 2014, *Children with specific language impairment. Second edition*. Cambridge, Mass.: The MIT Press.

Acknowledgements

The present research started with a grant from the Netherlands Organization for Scientific Research (NWO) entitled *The development of finiteness. From a lexical to a functional category* (365-70-019). Originally, it was carried out at the Department of Applied Linguistics at Amsterdam VU University. It continued both at the Max Planck Institute for Psycholinguistics (MPI) at Nijmegen and the Leibniz-Zentrum Allgemeine Sprachwissenschaft (ZAS). At MPI Nijmegen, it was carried out in connection with the Max Planck Research project 'The Acquisition of Finiteness' and the European research group 'The Structure of Learner Varieties'. We want to express our thanks to Prof. Wolfgang Klein who made it possible to accomplish the Dutch part of the project at the MPI Nijmegen and to Prof. Manfred Krifka for the opportunities made available at ZAS Berlin to enhance this project with a German extension. We would also like to thank the ESRC for the grant ES / L008955 / 1, awarded to Charleen List as part of a studentship from the ESRC International Centre for Language and Communicative Development (LuCiD). Special thanks go to Julian Pine from the University of Liverpool.

Contents

Peter Jordens
Preface —— V

Acknowledgements —— XI

Peter Jordens and Dagmar Bittner
Developing language. Driving forces in children learning Dutch and German —— 1

Peter Jordens
Developmental language disorder and the functional category system —— 55

Dagmar Bittner and Peter Jordens
Language acquisition in a German DLD child —— 89

Charleen List
Testing the extended optional infinitive hypothesis in a German child with DLD —— 137

Damaris Bartz
The acquisition of finiteness in *auch-* and *aber-*clauses in DLD. A case study —— 165

Index —— 211

Peter Jordens and Dagmar Bittner
Developing language. Driving forces in children learning Dutch and German

Abstract: Spontaneous language acquisition in children learning their mother tongue shows that language development proceeds in a stage-wise manner. Given that a developmental stage can be defined as a coherent linguistic system, this paper is a study on the early language systems of children learning Dutch and German as their mother tongue. Initially, these child learner systems appear to be lexical systems based on types of verb-argument structure that are either agentive (as in Dutch: *kannie losmake* 'cannot loose-make', or German: *magnich nase putzen* 'like-not nose clean') or non-agentive (as in Dutch: *popje valt bijna* 'doll falls nearly', or in German: *ente fällt* 'duck falls'). This initial stage is referred to as 'the lexical stage'. For Dutch and German children, it is claimed that developmental progress is driven by the acquisition of the structural means to express 'semantic finiteness'. Semantic finiteness is a concept of information structure which is central to the acquisition of 'the functional stage'. It indicates that the utterance functions as an assertion, meaning "that the situation described by the utterance obtains" (Klein 1998, 227). It is expressed by the syntactic feature of 'verb second' (V2). Verbal elements in V2 position serve as carrier for the functional category (F) which projects an initial, topic position for elements to express 'topicality'. Elements in topic position are used to refer to the situation that the utterance applies to. It seems the function of both the elements in V2 and in initial, topic position, i.e. the elements in the prefield of the utterance, to achieve contextual cohesion. That is, these elements should constitute a close relationship in meaning between the assertion and the situation that it applies to. It is argued that it is this informational function that accounts for the acquisition of the linguistic features of functional morphology (auxiliary verbs, subject-verb agreement, tense, gender), function words (determiners, question words, pronominal anaphora) and word order variation (inversion).

Keywords: child language development, learner varieties, Dutch and German, semantic finiteness, topicality, contextual cohesion

---

Peter Jordens, Amsterdam VU University, The Netherlands; Max Planck Institute for Psycholinguistics, Nijmegen, The Netherlands; e-mail: jorde074@planet.nl
Dagmar Bittner, Leibniz-Zentrum Allgemeine Sprachwissenschaft, Berlin, Germany; e-mail: bittner@leibniz-zas.de

1 Introduction

Researchers studying spontaneous processes of language acquisition, either in children learning their mother tongue or in adults learning a second language, have noted that in early language development particular linguistic features are systematically missing (Selinker 1972; Corder 1978; Klein and Perdue 1997; Clark 2003). Language development in children learning Dutch and German is no exception (De Haan 1987; Jordens 1990; Hoekstra and Jordens 1994; Bittner 2003; Gillis 2003; Jordens 2012). That is, in the early stages of the acquisition of Dutch and German, grammatical function words such as auxiliary verbs, determiners, anaphoric pronouns and question words are absent, there is no variation in word order and morphology is often not used productively. Hence, the early language systems are 'simple systems'. However, they are not just 'simple' in the sense that they are simplified versions of the language system of the adults. They are language systems in their own right: 'interlanguages' (Selinker 1972) or, as Klein (1997, 5) puts it, they are "a genuine manifestation of the human language faculty". Klein has taken this line of thought even a step further in arguing: "In fact, I believe that learner varieties are the core manifestation of the human language faculty and real languages (...) are the borderline cases" (Klein 1997, 5).

In the following, we will first claim that the early language system of children learning either Dutch or German is best described as a *lexical* learner system, i.e. as a language system that is solely based on the lexical projection of types of verb-argument structure. Evidence comes from an analysis of utterances that these children spontaneously produced. A sample of these utterances is given in (1).

(1) Utterances in child Dutch and child German at the lexical stage
    Child Dutch   Child German

  poes bal hebbe.   *du auch malen.*
  kitty ball get   you too draw
  jij opemake.   *tasche mitnehmen.*
  you open-make   bag with-take
  kannie losmake.   *magnich nase putzen.*
  cannot loose-make   like-not nose clean
  nee g(r)as lope.   *willnisch raus.*
  may-not grass walk   want-not it-out
  magwel dat hebbe.   *tann-schon dis (r)eintun.*
  may-indeed that get   can-indeed this it-in-do

ikke g(l)ijbaan (ge)maakt.	*der papa (ge)macht.*
I slide [have] made	daddy [has] made
popje valt bijna.	*ente fällt.*
doll falls nearly	duck falls
poes komt niet.	*hier kommt die mama, hier.*
kitty comes not	here comes mommy, here
Jaja vindt vies deze.	*mama liegt da.*
J finds dirty this	mommy lies there
kanniet zellef.	*du kannst nicht raus.*
cannot self	you can not out
goene aan.	*mund zu.*
shoes on	mouth closed
pop da in.	*hier rum.*
doll there in	here it-around
hoefniet plak op.	*rock an.*
must-not glue on	dress on

Furthermore, we will provide evidence for our claim that developmental progress is driven by the acquisition of the functional expression of contextual cohesion as it refers to a close relationship in meaning between the utterance and the situation that the utterance applies to. Evidence of the functional expression of contextual cohesion is the variable placement of linguistic elements in the prefield of the utterance structure. This concerns, first, placement of verbal elements in verb-second (V2) position to express 'semantic finiteness', meaning "that the situation described by the utterance obtains" (Klein 1998, 227) and, second, placement of non-verbal elements in initial position to express 'topicality', meaning that elements in initial, topic position serve to refer to the situation that the utterance applies to. Finally, it will be shown that the acquisition of variable placement in terms of what is referred to as 'verb movement' and 'topicalization' is prerequisite for the acquisition of the functional category system as a whole.

The functional category system of adult Dutch and German is apparent in morphology, function words and word order variation. Relevant functional categories are presented in Table 1.

As shown in Table 1, the functional category system in Dutch and German consists of the morphological categories finite vs. non-finite and tense, of the function word categories auxiliary verbs, determiners and anaphoric pronouns and, finally, of word order variation as it occurs in verb movement, topicalization, *wh-* and *yes/no-*question formation.

Table 1: Relevant functional categories in adult Dutch and German.

Functional systems	Categories	Examples	
morphology	finite/non-finite	Dutch:	*kom* (come-1SgPres), *komt* (come-2,3SgPres), *kom**en*** (come-1,2,3PlPres) vs. *komen* (Inf).
		German:	*komm(e)* (come-1SgPres), *komm**st*** (come-2SgPres), *komm**t*** (comes-3SgPres), *komm**en*** (come-1,2,3PlPres) vs. *kommen* (Inf).
	tense	Dutch:	*maakt* (bite-3SgPres) vs. *maakte* (bit-3SgPast).
		German:	*macht* (bite-3SgPres) vs. *machte* (bit-3SgPast).
function words	auxiliary verbs	Dutch:	*heb* (have), *heeft* (has); *ben* (am), *is* (is).
		German:	*habe* (have), *hat* (has); *bin* (am), *ist* (is).
	determiners	Dutch:	*de* (the-Sg/Pl), *het* (the-Sg) vs. *een* (a, an).
		German:	*der, die* (the-M/F.Sg), *das* (the-N.Sg,), *die* (the-Pl) vs. *ein* (a, an-M./N.Sg), *eine* (a, an-F.Sg).
	anaphoric pronouns	Dutch:	*hij* (he), *zij* (she), *hem* (him), *haar* (her), *het* (it), *daar* (there), *hier* (here) etc.
		German:	*er* (he), *sie* (she), *ihm* (him), *ihr* (her), *es* (it), *da* (there), *hier* (here) etc.
word order variation	verb movement	Dutch:	We **gaan** straks een glaasje **drinken** (we go later a glass drink) vs. *Straks **drinken** we een glaasje* (later drink we a glass).
		German:	*Wir **wollen** gleich ein Gläschen **trinken*** (we will later a glass drink) vs. *Gleich **trinken** wir ein Gläschen* (later drink we a glass).
	topicalization	Dutch:	***Dat** geloof ik niet* (that believe I not) vs. *Ik geloof **dat** niet* (I believe that not).
		German:	***Das** glaube ich nicht* (that believe I not) vs. *Ich glaube **das** nicht* (I believe that not).
	question formation	Dutch:	***Wie** heeft dat gedaan?* (who has that done?) vs. *Heeft hij dat gedaan? (has he that done?).*
		German:	***Wer** hat das gemacht?* (who has that done?) vs. *Hat er das gemacht? (has he that done?).*

The examples in (1) are evidence that learner utterances at the initial stage are typically lexical. That is, they are used to refer to actions, states and changes of state with persons and objects playing a particular semantic role. Grammatically, these learner utterances are the expression of a predicate-argument structure that consists of lexical constituents such as nouns, deictic pronouns, verbs, verbal particles, adjectives and adverbs.

A comparison of the examples in (1) with the functional elements of adult Dutch and German listed in Table 1 shows that in the relevant children's languages some functional features systematically do not occur. That is, grammatical function words such as auxiliary verbs, determiners and anaphoric pronouns are absent, and so is variation in word order. Morphological categories, however, seem to be present to some degree. So, while the morphological feature of tense marking does not occur, the morphological feature of finite vs. infinite seems to be present. However, it should be noted that morphologically 'finite' and 'infinitival' verb forms are used in complementary distribution. That is, finite verb forms typically refer to states or changes of state as, for example, Dutch *komt* (comes. J 1;10), *zit* (sits. J 1;11), *valt* (falls. A 2;0) and German *liegt* (lies. A 1;11), *passt* (fits. C 2;0), *fällt* (falls. C 2;0), while infinitival verb forms as, for example, Dutch *maken* (make. J. 1,11) and *meeneme* (with-take. A 2;1) and German *malen* (draw. A 1;11) and *mitnehmen* (with-take. C 2;0) typically refer to actions. Furthermore, verb forms referring to states and changes of state occur in second-constituent position, while verb forms referring to actions are placed utterance-finally. This indicates that verb *placement* is based on the semantics of the verb, while verb *forms* are initially used morphologically unanalyzed. Hence, there is reason to believe that in early Dutch and German the inflectional morphology of finite vs. infinite is not a productive feature of the learner system, either.[1]

In sum, at the initial stages of language development, Dutch and German children seem to create a simple, basic language variety which is essentially the same across individuals. Representative of this basic linguistic knowledge system are the examples in (1). They suggest that the children's utterances are initially lexical projections of verb-argument structure. Functional elements, it seems, are systematically missing. Nevertheless, the 'simple' learner systems that these utterances come from should serve the basic communicative needs that young children may have.

In the following, we will investigate the process of language development in children learning Dutch and German focussing on three questions. First, what are the principles that the basic learner system is based on? Second, how do children progress from their basic lexical language system to a more advanced functional system? Finally, what does insight into the acquisition process tell us about the faculty of human language development.

The data of the present study originate from investigations on children learning Dutch or German as their native language. These data come from longitudinal

---

1 With respect to the use of the term 'finite', a distinction is made between 'finite forms' (*morphological finiteness*) and 'finiteness' (*semantic finiteness*) as a concept of information structure (Klein 1998). At the initial, lexical stage of the developmental process finite forms do appear. However, they occur as the reflection of the input and not as the representation of a functional category. Finiteness as a functional category is claimed to be the result of language development.

studies of utterances produced spontaneously. The Dutch data originate from two corpora of diary data: Jasmijn (J) and Andrea (A). The German data come from two corpora of video-recorded data: Anna (A) and Caroline (C). In the examples below a reference such as, for example, 'J 1;9' means that this utterance occurred when Jasmijn was 1 year and 9 months of age. In the following, it will turn out that the data used in this study are representative of two stages of language development, i.e. an initial, lexical stage and a targetlike, functional stage. The relevant data are distributed as in Table 2.

Table 2: Dutch and German child data collected from two stages of language development.

	Dutch		German	
	Jasmijn	Andrea	Anna	Caroline
lexical stage	1;10–1;11	2;0–2;1	1;11–2;0	2;0–2;1
functional stage	2;0–2;2	2;2–2;4	2;1–2;2	2;2–2;5

2 The analysis of early learner data

2.1 Types of utterance

As illustrated in (1), children's utterances in early Dutch and German are evidence of an underlying language system that makes use of lexical elements only. With this lexical learner system children are able to produce types of utterance that are the expression of some kind of predicate-argument structure.

In earlier investigations on the acquisition of child Dutch and German as, for example, in Clahsen (1986), De Haan (1987), Poeppel and Wexler (1993) and Ingram and Thompson (1996), a prominent role is attributed to utterances in which the verbal part of the predicate is an infinitive. These utterances are currently known as 'root infinitives'. They are found to occur relatively frequently at the initial, lexical stage of the acquisition process. Examples from child Dutch and German are given in A1.

A1. Infinite verb form ('root infinitive')
Child Dutch   Child German

*mama dit **geve**.* (J 1;10)   *und der **pieken**.* (A 1;11)
mommy this give   and that-one prick
*deze slagroom **ete**.* (J 1;10)   *du auch **malen**.* (A 1;11)

this-one whipped-cream eat
*poes bal **pakke***. (J 1;11)
kitty ball get
*dit **losmake***. (J 1;11)
this loose-make
*gaag boekje **leze***. (A 2;0)
like booklet read
*deze, jurk **aandoen***. (A 2;0)
this, dress on-do
*jij g(l)ijbaan **make***. (A 2;1)
you slide make
klimme. (A 2;1)
climb

you too draw
*jetzt ei **essen**?* (A 2;0)
now egg eat?
*schok(o)lade nich(t) **haben***. (A 2;0)
chocolate not get
*tasche **mitnehmen***. (C 2;0)
bag with-take
*buch **anschauen***. (C 2;0)
book at-look
*ich tür **aufmachen***. (C 2;1)
I door open-make
*nicht **ab(r)oll(e)n***. (C 2;1)
not down-role

As is evident from the examples in A1, the infinite verb of a 'root infinitive' always appears in clause-final position. The complement precedes the verb, thus the VP of a 'root infinitive' is head-final. Simultaneously with the occurrence of 'root infinitives' there is also a type of utterance with a finite verb form. Although this type of utterance is produced less frequently, it appears systematically in both early child Dutch and German. Examples are given in B1. As shown in B1, finite verb forms occur systematically in second-constituent position. They precede the complement, hence the VP is head-initial.

B1. Finite verb form
    Child Dutch   Child German

*poesje, **heb** jij?* (J 1;10)
kitty, [what] have you?
*uil, zo **komt***. (J 1;10)
owl, so comes
*da **zit** mama*. (J 1;11)
there sits mommy
*da, poes **blijf**(t) hier*. (J 1;11)
there, kitty stays here
***gaat-ie** niet? **gaat-ie** ja*. (A 2;0)
works-it not? works-it yes
*Jaja **valt** niet*. (A 2;0)
J falls not
*Jaja **heef**(t) koud*. (A 2;1)
J has cold

*mama **liegt** da*. (A 1;11)
mommy lies there
*hier **kommt** die mamma, hier*. (A 1;11)
here comes mommy, here
*krokodil **kommt***. (A 2;0)
crocodile comes
*papa **hat** zeitung*. (A 2;0)
daddy has newspaper
***passt** bald*. (C 2;0)
fits soon
*ente **fällt***. (C 2;0)
duck falls
*eina **fehlt** noch*. (C 2;1)
one misses still

Jaja **vindt** vies, deze. (A 2;1)
J finds awful, this
g(r)ote paard **is** hier. (A 2;1)
big horse is here

äh **deht** (=geht) nicht. (C 2;1)
eh works not
die **is(t)** da. (C 2;1)
that-one is there

Looking at the distribution of infinitives as in A1 and finite verb forms as in B1, the similarity between Dutch and German children is striking. In both the Dutch and the German data there is a correlation between form and position of the verb. That is, infinitives always occur in clause-final position, while finite verb forms are found in second position. This observation explains why morpho-syntactic phenomena such as 'agreement' and 'verb movement' play a central role in commonly recognized research on the shape of German child grammar at the initial stage (see Clahsen 1986; Poeppel and Wexler 1993; and Ingram and Thompson 1996). However, the conclusion that placement of the verb is based on its morphological properties becomes less obvious, if we acknowledge that the relevant distributional difference is actually based not on the morphology but on the semantics of the verb, meaning that verbs that occur in one position do not occur in the other.[2]

Furthermore, the set of data as typically presented in terms of 'infinite' vs. 'finite' is not representative at all. It constitutes a selection from the perspective of the target language system. More specifically, it is a selection from the perspective of the phenomenon of 'verb movement' which holds that in the target language the same lexical verb may occur both in final and in second position. However, for a complete picture of the language system of Dutch and German children at the initial stage of language acquisition, there is a variety of data that should be taken into account as well. For example, there is the type of utterance as in A2.

A2. Modal/aspectual element + infinitive
    Child Dutch   Child German

kannie pakke. (J 1;10)
can-not get
ik **wil** mellek **pakke.** (J 1;10)
I want milk get
moet inzitte. (J 1;11)
must in-sit

will kucken **gehen.** (A 2;0)
want see go
willnisch raufsitzen. (A 2;0)
want-not it-on-sit
papa nich(t) **soll** hier **reinkomm**(en). (A 2;0)
daddy not should here it-in-come

---

[2] It should be noted that this analysis in terms of a semantic opposition runs counter to the 'overlap hypothesis' adhered to as in, for example, De Haan (1987) and Poeppel and Wexler (1993).

***doet**-ie alles **opete**.* (J 1;11)
does-it everything up-eat
*Jaja **mag** dop **opdoen**.* (A 2;0)
J may cap on-do
***kan**-ie nie **hope** (=lope).* (A 2;0)
can-it not walk
***kan**wel papa **zitte**.* (A 2;1)
can-indeed [with] daddy sit-down
***gaat**-ie (sl)**ape**.* (A 2;1)
goes-it sleep

***will** kawee **ring**.* (A 2;0)
want coffee drink
***mag**nich nase **putzen**.* (C 2;0)
like-not nose clean
***dann**-t nich **wicken**.* (C 2;0)
can-it not fly
***muss** aba uhu **anmalen**.* (C 2;1)
must however owl on-paint
***tan**-schon dis (r)**eintun**.* (C 2;1)
can-indeed this in-do

Utterances as in A2 occur with a modal or an aspectual element in second-constituent position. The nominal constituent in first position refers to the speaker or another individual in the actual situation. In spontaneous production when the speaker assumes that the hearer is able to infer who he/she is talking about, this individual is often either not explicitly expressed or it may be referred to with an affix attached to the modal/aspectual head (as in *doet-ie* (does-it), *kan-ie* (can-it), *gaat-ie* (goes-it). Utterances as in A2 are used to express that some-one 'wants', 'can', 'may', 'must', 'is going' to do some kind of activity or is 'currently involved in' doing this. What the particular individual actually 'wants to do', 'can do', 'may do' etc. is expressed with the OV-complement of the modal/aspectual head. This OV-complement may serve as a lexical entity as, for example, with target Dutch *handen wassen* (hands wash), *tanden poetsen* (teeth brush) or target German *Kuchen essen* (cake eat) and *Nase putzen* (nose clean).

Utterances as in A1 – the so-called 'root infinitives' – are, regardless of the frequency with which they occur, a special case of type A2. They are a special case in the sense that in root infinitives, the position of the modal head is empty. Their frequent use is due to the fact that in a normal speech situation the relevant modal meaning is often left to be inferred from the context. The examples in (2) are evidence of the variable use of utterances as in A1 and A2. They show that at the relevant stage in Dutch, Jasmijn and Andrea vary between the use of infinitives (Vinf) and modal/aspectual elements + infinitive (Mod/Asp + Vinf) even with the same lexical verbs. The examples in (3) show the same variable use in German with Anna.

(2) Child Dutch: variable use of Vinf and Mod/Asp + Vinf

*dit **losmake**.* (J 1;11)
this loose-make
*glijbaan, **aanmake**.* (J 2;0)

***kan**nie **losmake**.* (J 1;11)
can-not loose-make
***doe**maar **aanmake**.* (J 2;0)

slide, on-make
*poppie **hebbe**?* (A 2;1)
doll get?
*eve **aaie** mette kipje.* (A 2;2)
just caress with-the chicken

do-please on-make
***mag**-ikke ijssie **hebbe**?* (A 2;1)
may-I ice-cream have?
*Jaja **magwel** hondje **aaie**.* (A 2;2)
J may-indeed doggie caress

(3) Child German: variable use of Vinf and Mod/Asp + Vinf

*jetz ei **essen**.* (A 2;0)
now egg eat
*xxx **reinkomm**(en)!* (A 2;0)
it-in-come!
*hand **mitmal**(e)n?* (A 2;1)
hand with-draw?
*du **fah**(re)n?* (A 2;1)
you drive?

***willnisch** was **essen**?* (A 2;0)
want-not something eat?
*papa nich(t) **soll** hier **reinkomm**(en).* (A 2;0)
daddy not must here it-in-come
***kann** der nich(t) **mitmal**(e)n.* (A 2;1)
can he not with-draw
*du **musst** auto **fahren**?* (A 2;1)
you must car drive?

Comparable with the data in A2 are those in A3. In utterances as in A3 however, the complement, when present, is a non-verbal predicate.

A3. Modal + non-verbal predicate³
Child Dutch

***kanniet** goed niet.* (J 1;10)
can-not good not
*mama **kanniet** kusje.* (J 1;11)
mommy can-not kiss
***magniet** oppe dak.* (J 1;11)
may-not on-the roof
***mag**-ikke ook gijbaan?* (A 2;0)
may-I too slide?
***moet**-ie hier?* (A 2;0)
must-it here?

Child German

***muss** lieber.* (A2;0)
must preferably
***kann**-ma(n)!* (A 2;0)
can-one!
*der teddy **will** auch noch.* (A 2;1)
teddy wants too
*du **möchtest** kaffee?* (A 2;1)
you want coffee?
*bei mama, **muss**-ich.* (A 2;1)
with mommy, must- I

---

3 At the relevant stage of acquisition, predicate forms such as *mag-ikke* (may-I) and *moet-ie* (must-it) in Dutch and *kann-ma(n)* (can-one) and *muss-ich* (must-I) in German occur as unanalysed wholes.

Research on spontaneous processes of language acquistion usually does not take into account utterances as in A3. However, the only difference with the examples in A2 is the fact that a complement such as *kusje* (kiss) or *oppe dak* (on-the roof) in Dutch and *auch noch* (too) or *kaffee* (coffee) in German is not a verbal constituent. Nevertheless, these complements have the same meaning as in cases in which they occurred with an infinitive. Thus, *kusje* means *ik kan niet kusje geven* (I cannot kiss give) and *magniet oppe dak* means *hij mag niet op het dak klimmen* (he may not on the roof climb). Similarly in German, *auch noch* (too) means *auch noch haben* (too have) and *kaffee* (kaffee) means *kaffee haben* (coffee get). Thus, at the relevant stage, non-verbal complements are used with the function of a predicate. Being non-verbal predicates they are distributed like 'non-finite' verbal elements.

The utterances as in A1, A2 and A3 are all variants of the same type of utterance structure. They occur with a modal/aspectual element in second position or with a structural position available for it.[4] In this respect, type-A utterances differ from utterances of type B not only semantically, as argued before, but also structurally, i.e. in terms of the presence or absence of a structural position for a modal/aspectual head.

A typical phenomenon in child language is the use of utterances with *in* (in), *op* (on), *aan* (on), *uit* (off), *om* (on, around) in Dutch and with *rein* (it-in), *in* (in), *rauf* (it-on), *auf* (on), *ran* (it-on), *an* (on), *raus* (it-off), *aus* (off), *runter* (it-down), *unter* (under) in German. Initially, these elements may occur as the predicate of one- or two-word utterances. Examples in Dutch are: *toti **in*** (pencil in. A 1;8), *buggy **in*** (buggy in. J 1;8), *dop **op*** (cap on. A 1;8), *deze, paartie **op*** (this, horse on. A 1;11), *jas **aan*** (coat on. A 1;10), *(s)tekker **uit*** (plug out. J 1;11), *tiktak **om*** (watch on. J 1;7). Examples in German are: ***raus*** (it-off. A 2;0), *an(d)ere männer **rauf*** (other men it-on. A 2;0), *alle tiere **rein!*** (all animals it-in! A 2;0), ***runter*** (it-down. A 2;0), ***ran*** (it-on. A 2;0), ***ab*** (off. A 2;0). These predicates are referred to as 'verbal particles'. Utterances with these types of predicate can be categorized as variants of either type A or type B.

---

[4] This is a problem for Ingram and Thompson (1996). Their Modal Hypothesis claims that it is the morphology which serves to carry modality as part of the lexical meaning of the infinitives: "(. . .) the claim is that the infinitives are semantically associated with modality as part of their lexical information" (102).

A4. Verbal particle[5]

Child Dutch

Particle	Particle + infinitive (variant of A1)	Modal + particle (variant of A2)
*Mijnie **in**, tiktak.* (J 1;8) M in, watch	*da [melk] **ingenke**.* (J 1;10) there milk in-pour	***unne** pleister **op**.* (J 1;10) want plaster on
*Mijnie bril **op**.* (J 1;8) M glasses on	*[blaadje] **oplegge**.* (J 1;10) piece-of-paper on-put	***hoeniet** plak **op**.* (A 2;0) must-not glue on
*dop **op**.* (A 1;8) cap on	*dop **opdoen**.* (A 1;11) cap on-do	
*goene **aan**.* (A 1;11) shoes on	*goene **aandoen**.* (A2;0) shoes on-do	
*zak **uit**.* (A 1;11) bag off	*dit **uithale**.* (J 1;11) this off-get	***minne** hoene **uit**.* (J 1;17) want shoes off
*tittat **om**.* (J 1;7) watch on	*[tiktak] **omdoen**.* (J 1;11) watch on-do	***minne** tittat **om**.* (J 1;7) want watch on

Child German

Particle	Particle + infinitive (variant of A1)	Modal + particle (variant of A2)
*[zaunteile] **raus**.* (A 2;0) fence parts it-off	*des hier **rausmachen**.* (A 2;0) that here it-off-take	
*an(d)ere männer **rauf**.* (A 2;0) other men it-on		
*alle tiere **rein**!* (A 2;0) all animals it-in!	*wasser **reinmachen**.* (A 2;0) water it-in-do	
*[zum papa] **runter**.* (A 2;0) to daddy it-down	*papa, **runtergehen**.* (A 2;0) daddy, it-down-go	
*[teile] **ran**.* (A 2;0) parts it-on	*[sich] **ranstellen**.* (A 2;0) oneself it-at-put	

---

5 In these examples, the elements in brackets '[ ]' are added on the basis of contextual information.

[klebriges] ab. *[einen teil]* **abmachen**.
(A 2;0)   (A 2;0)
sticky-stuff off   a part off-take
   [bad] **rausgehen**. (A 2;0)   **willnisch raus**. (A 2;0)
   bath it-off go   want-not it-off

As shown in A4, the type of utterance with a verbal particle as the predicate serves as a variant of type A1. That is, the verbal particle is used with the same function as the infinitive in A1. See, for example in Dutch, the child utterances *goene* **aan** (shoes-on) next to *goene* **aandoen** (shoes on-do) and *tittat* **om** (watch on) next to *[tiktak]* **omdoen** (watch on-do) and in German, the child utterances *alle tiere* **rein**! (all animals it-in!) next to *wasser* **reinmachen** (water it-in-do) and *[zum papa]* **runter** (to daddy it-down) next to *papa,* **runtergehen** (daddy, it-down-go). The claim that particle utterances as in A4 are in fact variants of A1 is, furthermore, confirmed by the fact that, as in the A2, the A4-particles may also occur with a modal element. Examples in child Dutch are **unne** *pleister* **op** (want plaster on), **hoeniet** *plak* **op** (must-not glue on), **minne** *hoene* **uit** (want shoes off), **minne** *tittat* **om** (want watch on) and in child German **willnisch raus** (want-not it-off).

The verbal particles in child Dutch and their German equivalents may also occur as predicates of utterances as in B4.

B4. Verbal particle

   Child Dutch
   Particle   Finite form + particle
      (variant of B1)

   *pop da-**in**.* (J 1;10)   *[popje]* **sit**-*ie da-**in**.* (J 1;10)
   doll there in   doll sit-it there-in
   fiets **in**. (J 1;8)   **kom** *es inne huisje.* (J 2;0)
   bicycle in   come in-the house
   Mijnie buggy **in**. (J 1;8)   **pas**-*sie (= past-ie)* **in**. (A 2;1)
   M buggy in   fits-it in
   mauw **op** *[plaatje].* (A 1;9)   *[paard]* **zit**-*ie oppe dak.* (J 1;11)
   kitty on picture   horse sits-it on-the roof
   *die der-**uit**.* (A 1;9)   **kom**-*ie da-**uit**.* (A 2;0)
   that it-out   comes-it it-out
   *[popje] daar-**uit**.* (J 1;11)   *da* **valt**-*ie* **uit**. (J 1;7)
   doll there-out   there falls-it off

Child German Particle	Finite form + particle (variant of B1)
*Anna **weg**.* (A 1;11) A gone	***weg** ist die!* (A 1;11) gone is it
*ein (k)nopf (d)**ran**.* (A 1;11) a button it-on	***idn** napf **ran**.* (A 1;11) is a button it-on
*der **geht los**.* (A 1;11) it goes loose	
*(d)**rin**, (d)**rin** was. da.* (A 1;11) it-in, it-in something. There	*weg. **rin** is(t).* (A 1;11) gone. it-in is
*ke(r)ze **drin**.* (A 2;0) candle in	*geht gar nicht. **passt** nicht **rein**.* (A 2;0) goes absolutely not. fits not it-in
*kein mütze **auf**.* (A 2;0) no cap on	*Jonas **passt** noch **rauf**.* (A 2;0) J fits also it-on
	*da **rauf geht** der nicht.* (A 2;0) it on goes it not
	*da **geht** der **aus**.* (A 2;0) there goes he out
***runter**.* (A 2;0) it-down	*[ist] löwl (=löffel) **unterfalln**.* (A 2;0) is spoon down-fallen
*(ka)**putt**, bau(e)n.* (A 2;0) kaput, build	*oh, oh, [ist] (ka)**putt**(ge)gang(en).* (A 2;0) oh, oh is kaput-gone

As shown in B4, here the utterances with a verbal particle as the predicate serve as a variant of type B1. That is, the relevant predicates are used with the same function as in utterances with a finite form as in B1. Examples are in Dutch: child utterances such as *pop da in* (doll there in) next to *[popje] sit-ie da in* (doll sits-it there in), *mauw op[plaatje]* (kitty on picture) next to *[paard] zit-ie oppe dak* (horse sits-it on-the roof) and *die der-uit* (that it-out) next to *kom-ie da-uit* (comes-it it-out); and in German: child utterances such as *ein (k)nopf (d)ran* (a button it-on) next to *idn napf ran* (ist-ein knopf dran) and *(d)rin, (d)rin was. da* (it-in something. there) next to *weg. rin is(t)* (away. it-in is).

2.2 Summary

The basic language system of children learning Dutch or German is a lexical system. That is, the relevant learner system makes use of nouns, deictic pronouns, verbs, verbal particles, adjectives and adverbs. Utterance structure, as shown in Table 3a, is determined by a simple predicate-argument structure that discriminates between two types of predicate. So, on the one hand, predicates in utterances of type A occur with an 'infinite' verbal constituent (VP) in final constituent position and may or may not be used with a modal/aspectual element (Mod/Asp) in second-constituent position. On the other hand, predicates in utterances of type B occur with a 'finite form' of V in second-constituent position.

Table 3a: Types of utterance at the lexical stage.

Type of utterance	Predicate
A: agentive	(Mod/Asp) + [X + V_{inf}]$_{VP}$
Child Dutch:	*jij g(l)ijbaan **make**.* (A 2;1) you slide make *kannie **losmake**.* (J 1;11) can-not loose-make
Child German:	*ich tür **aufmachen**.* (C 2;1) I door open-make *du **musst autofahren**?* (A 2;1) you must car drive
B: non-agentive	V_{fin} + X
Child Dutch:	*Jaja **valt** niet.* (A 2;0) J falls not
Child German:	*eina **fehlt** noch.* (C 2;1) one misses still

Furthermore, at the lexical stage, the morphology of V is determined by the input. Hence, when V is part of VP, as in type-A utterances, it occurs in final-constituent position and therefore, as is the case in the input, children use it as a morphologically correct infinitive. When, on the other hand, V occurs in second constituent position, as in type-B utterances, children use it, as is also the case in the input, as a morphologically correct finite form. However, given the fact that at the relevant stage, there is no evidence of a morpho-syntactic regularity according to which *the same verb* can be used systematically with either an infinitive or a finite form, there is no reason to believe that the relevant morphological opposition should represent rule based linguistic knowledge. In other words, there is no reason to believe that independently of the type of verb, infinitives occur in final position while finite verb forms occur in second position. Rather, verbal elements in V are used in complementary distribution, i.e. either in final or in second position on the basis of the semantics of the verb. More specifically, verbal elements in final position are typically 'agentive', while in second position they are typically 'non-agentive'.

Thus, as far as utterance structure is concerned, the verb forms of type A are part of a VP in final position that constitutes an agentive predicate. The verb forms of type B are part of a VP with V in second position that constitutes a non-agentive predicate. This means that, semantically, utterances of type A and B are used in complementary distribution. Furthermore, as shown in Table 3b, the semantics of V in type A and type B depends on the presence or absence of Mod/Asp.

Table 3b: Types of predicate at the lexical stage: agentive vs. non-agentive.

Utterance	Predicate
Type A	Mod/Asp + [X + $V_{agentive}$]$_{VP}$
Type B	[$V_{non-agentive}$ + X]$_{VP}$

Stating that Mod/Asp determines the semantics of V or VP is another way of saying that in utterances of type A, Mod/Asp is 'the head' while VP serves as its 'complement'. Alternatively, when Mod/Asp is absent as in type B, it is the verbal element in the position of V that is 'the head' of a non-V complement X.

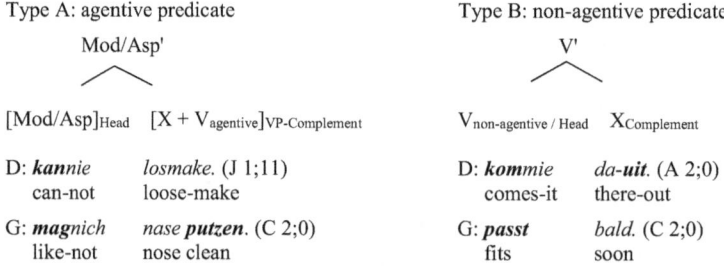

Type A: agentive predicate		Type B: non-agentive predicate	
Mod/Asp'		V'	
[Mod/Asp]$_{Head}$ [X + $V_{agentive}$]$_{VP\text{-}Complement}$		$V_{non\text{-}agentive\,/\,Head}$ $X_{Complement}$	
D: *kannie*	*losmake.* (J 1;11)	D: *kommie*	*da-uit.* (A 2;0)
can-not	loose-make	comes-it	there-out
G: *magnich*	*nase putzen.* (C 2;0)	G: *passt*	*bald.* (C 2;0)
like-not	nose clean	fits	soon

Figure 1: Types of predicate at the lexical stage: [Mod/Asp]$_{Head}$ vs. V_{Head}.

Finally, as shown in Figure 1, in utterances of both typ A and type B the head precedes its complement. Thus, the structure of the predicate at the lexical stage is head-initial.

3 Utterance structure at the lexical stage

3.1 Lexical projections

As pointed out, utterances of type A and B are used in complementary distribution. That is, utterances of type A are typically 'agentive', while utterances of type B are typically 'non-agentive'. Furthermore, utterances of type A may typically be used with an element of Mod/Asp, while utterances of type B may not. Elements of Mod/Asp are used to express the semantics of volition, ability, permission or obligation. In other words, they express the meaning of some kind of 'control'. So, presence or absence of control (CTL) explains why utterances of type A are agentive, while utterances of type B are not. It also explains why the external argument that the predicate applies to is an 'agent' in utterances of type A, while it is a non-agent, i.e. a 'theme', in utterances of type B. Both in type A and type B, this external argument occurs in initial position.

As represented in Figure 2, Mod/Asp elements in CTL serve as the head of utterances of type A. In other words, utterances of type A are a 'projection of CTL'. Similarly, lexical verbal elements in V serve as the head of utterances of type B. Thus, utterances of type B are a 'projection of V'. The configuration of both types of projection shows that the second-constituent position is the position taken by the head of the utterance structure at the lexical stage.

In the agentive utterances (type A), the modal/aspectual verb in the position of the head (CTL) implies an action that is expressed as its complement (VP-Comp). Together these constituents serve as the predicate (CTL') that applies to an external argument being the 'agent' that carries out the action expressed in VP-Comp. This action is either a causal action as in Dutch *dop opdoen* (cap on-do) and German *ei essen* (egg eat) or an agentive motion as in Dutch *oppe dak* (on-the roof [climb]) and German *raufsitzen* (it-on-sit-down). The modal elements, Dutch *wil* (want), *kan* (can), *mag* (may), *moet* (must) and German *will* (want), *mag* (want), *kann* (can), *darf* (may), *muss* (must) are used to express the willingness, the ability, the permission or the obligation of the agent to perform the relevant action.

In the non-agentive utterances (type B), verb forms referring to a state or a change of state occur in the position of the head (V) that may have a complement (X) referring, for example, to a location or a direction. These constituents serve as the predicate V' that applies to an external argument being the 'theme' that either is *in* a state as, for example, in Dutch *zit* (sits), *blijft* (stays), *heeft* (has) and German *liegt* (lies), *passt* (fits), *hat* (has), or *undergoes* a change of state as, for example, in Dutch *valt* (falls), *komt* (comes) and German *fällt* (falls), *kommt* (comes).

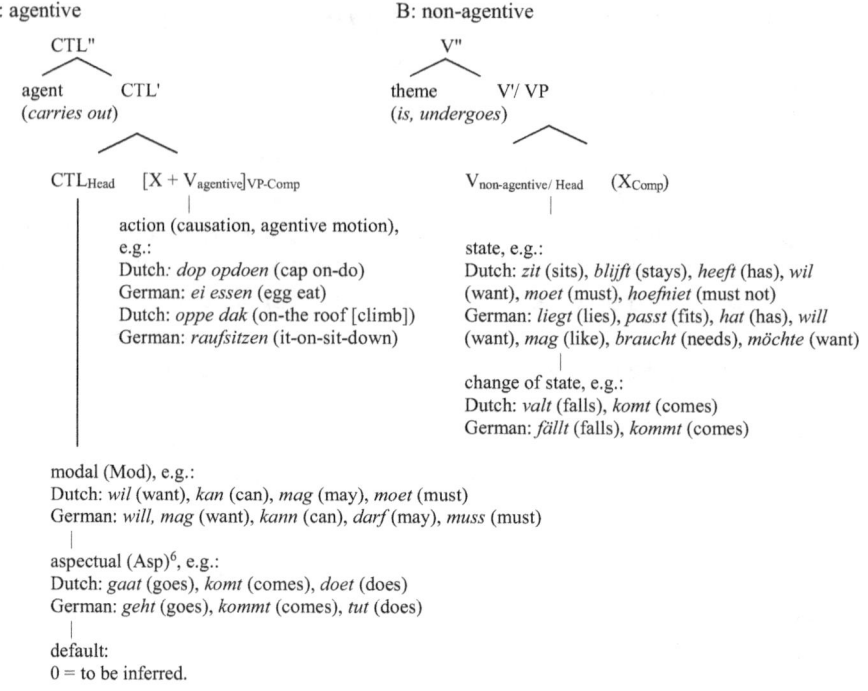

Figure 2: The utterance structure of type A and type B.

Note that in Figure 2, type B modal elements do not express the meaning of 'control'. Rather, they are used to express a possibility, an option or a necessity that holds for the theme.[7] In other words, as shown in (4), they refer to a 'physical state' or a 'state of mind'.

---

[6] As shown in Jolink (2009), Dutch children also produce examples with *is* instead of a modal verb. For example, *die eisje is tieke* (the girl is draw), *paadje is alle biele opete* (horsie is all wheels up-eat), *toen is e vogel da vliege* (then is a bird there fly). It seems that *is* is used with an aspectual meaning such as 'is being'.

[7] In the target language, state and change-of-state predicates are also used with modal verbs. Possible utterances in the target language are *de boom kan omvallen* (the tree can down-fall), *je kunt hier wel zitten* (you can here indeed sit), *dit voorstel mag in de prullenbak* (this proposal may in the waste-paper basket). These modal verbs are not the head of a lexical projection as in Figure 1A. They are the head of a functional projection and, therefore, they function as auxiliary verbs. At the lexical stage, functional projections do not occur. Hence, the relevant utterances should not occur, either. This is precisely what can be observed.

(4) Modality as the expression of a 'physical state' or a 'state of mind'

*Mijnie **kannie**.* (J 1;10)   ***kann*** *ma(n)!* (A 2;0)
[for] M not-possible   [is] possible [for] anyone!
hoefnie *meer.* (J 1;11)   *bisschen noch **brauch** ich.* (A 2;0)
[I] must-not more   a-little more need I
unnie *niet.* (A 2;0)   *so was **möt-sch** nisch.* (A 2;0)
want-I not   like something want-I not
kannie *niet bij.* (A 2;0)   ***will*** *nicht, der bobo **will** nicht.* (C 2;1)
can-I not at   wants not, the bobo wants not
*deze **moet** hier.* (A 2;1)   ***mag*** *nich mehr / **mag** nich.* (C 2;1)
this must here   like not more / like not

The present analysis of learner utterances at the lexical stage should demonstrate that the linguistic categories that are relevant at the initial stages of language development may differ from those that come into play only later in the process. This is particularly true for the morphological properties of the verb. As argued before, morphological properties of the target language system seem to be irrelevant as a feature of the learner language at the initial stage. Hence, if learner data are analyzed in terms of morphological categories of the target language system such as 'finite' and 'infinite', learners are attributed a level of linguistic knowledge for which there is no evidence. This is the case, for example, with Poeppel and Wexler who come to the curious finding that for German children at the initial stage of language development "the best model of the data is the standard analysis of adult German" (1993, 2).

Finally, it should be noted that a morpho-syntactic categorization of the data as in Poeppel and Wexler (1993) and Ingram and Thompson (1996), poses a restriction on the kind of data to be accounted for. That is, a categorization of child utterances in terms of verbs, or verb categories such as 'finite verb', 'infinitive' and 'past participle' tacitly leads to the decision to regard 'verbless' utterances of less or no relevance compared to utterances with verbal elements. Unfortunately, a consequence of this is that a large amount of relevant data is excluded from analysis.

3.2 Testing the model: Particle verbs

Evidence of a basic language system as represented with Figure 2 comes from the children's use of particle verbs. Particle verbs such as Dutch *opdoen* (on-do) and German *rankleben* (it-on-glue) are complex verb forms. They consist of two separable elements such that – in the adult language – *opdoen* may also occur as *doet op* and *rankleben* as *klebt ran*. So, in Dutch this makes *hij wil er een dop* **opdoen** (he wants it a cap on-do) vs. *hij* **doet** *er een dop* **op** (he does it a cap on) and in German *er will das* **rankleben** (he wants that it-on-glue) vs. *er* **klebt** *das* **ran** (he glues that it-on). Interestingly, in adult Dutch and German, there are two types of particle verbs: on the one hand, particle verbs of type A with an agent as its subject, like Dutch *opdoen* (on-do), *losmaken* (loose-make) or *vasthouden* (tight-hold) and German *losmachen* (loose-make), *wegtun* (away-do) or *angucken* (at-look) and, on the other hand, particle verbs of type B with a theme as its subject, like Dutch *omvallen* (down-fall), *thuiskomen* (home-come) or *stukgaan* (kaput-go) and German *losgehen* (loose-go), *runterfallen* (down-fall) or *anhaben* (on-have). At the lexical stage, children are expected to use these types of verb syntactically differently. The agentive type of particle verb should occur in final position and therefore, as in the target language, appear formally 'infinite' as in Dutch *opdoen* (on-do), *losmaken* (loose-make) and *vasthouden* (tight-hold) and in German *losmachen* (loose-make), *wegtun* (away-do) and *angucken* (at-look). On the other hand, the non-agentive type of particle verb should occur with a separated verb form in second-constituent position and, therefore, as in the target language, appear formally 'finite' as in Dutch *valt om* (falls down), *komt thuis* (comes home) and *gaat stuk* (goes kaput) and in German *geht los* (goes loose), *fällt runter* (falls down), *hat an* (has on).

At the lexical stage, Dutch and German children produce particle verbs relatively frequently. These particle verbs provide the empirical evidence confirming the relevant basic language system as represented in Figure 2. Examples are given in A5 (agentive) and B5 (non-agentive), respectively.

A5 vs. B5. Child Dutch: particle verbs at the lexical stage
A5: agentive   B5: non-agentive

Jaja dop **opdoen**. (A 2;0)   ***valtie om***. (J 1;10)
J cap on-do   falls-it down
papa **indoen**. (J 1;11)   *Mijnie* **valt om**. (J 1;11)
daddy in-do   M falls down
vlokke **opdoen**. (A 2;0)   *Tompoes* **komt aan**. (J 2;0)
chips on-do   T comes at
goene **aandoen**. (A 2;1)   ***kom**tie* **daaraan**. (J 2;0)
shoes on-do   comes-it there-at
dit **afdoen**. (J 1;10)   *bokkies* **kome aan**. (A 2;1)
this off-do   goats come at
opemake. (J 1;10)   ***kom**maa* **mee**. (A 2;1)

open-make
*dit **losmake**.* (J 1;11)
this loose-make
***viesmake**.* (A 2;1)
dirty-make
***omslaan**?* (J 1;11)
over-turn?
***openslaan**?* (J 1;11)
open-make?
*punne **aanslijpe**.* (J 1;11)
points on-scharpen
***afdroge**.* (J 1;11)
off-dry
*dit **afhale**.* (J 1;10)
this off-take
*mondje **afvege**.* (J 1;11)
mouth off-wipe
***opdrinke**?* (J 1;11)
up-drink?
*Cynthia **weglope**.* (J 1;11)
C away-run
*dit **vasthoue**.* (J 1;11)
this tight-hold
***uitpakke**.* (A 2;1)
out-pack

come with
*Peter **komt thuis**.* (J 1;11)
P comes home
*gaap **kom** niet Jaja **toe**.* (A 2;1)
sheep come[s] not J to
***kom**-ie da **uit**.* (A 2;1)
comes-it there out
***gaat**-ie **af**.* (A 2;1)
goes-it off
***gaat**ie **inne** garage.* (J 2;2)
goes-it into garage
*poppie **gáát** niet **mee**.* (A 2;1)
doll goes not with
***gaan**ne paarde **toe**?* (A 2;1)
go-we horses to?
***gaan**ne huis **toe**.* (A 2;1)
go-we house to
***vlieg**tie **weg**.* (A 2;3)
flies-it away
*da **valt**ie **uit**.* (J 1;11)
there falls-it out
*zijn niet **thuis**.* A 2;1)
are not home
*ben zo **trug**.* (J 1;11)
am right back

A5 vs. B5: Child German: particle verbs at the lexical stage
A5: agentive

***abmachen** das wieder xx.* (A 1;11)
off-make that again
*ahme **runtermachen**.* (A 2;0)
arms down-make
*des hier **rausmachen**.* (A 2;0)
that here it-out-make
*brötsche **reinmachen**.* (A 2;0)
buns it-in-do
*[weihnachtsmann] **wegtun**!* (A 2;0)
Santa Claus away-do!
*[tur] **zumachen**, schnell.* (A 2;0)

B5: non-agentive

*der **geht, los**.* (A 1;11)
that goes, loose
*da **rauf geht** der nicht, da **rauf geht**.* (A 2;0)
there it-on goes he not, there it-on goes

*da **geht** der **aus**.* (A 2;0)
there goes he out
*geht gar nicht. **passt** nicht **rein**.* (A 2;0)
goes absolutely not. fits not it-in
*los boot **fährt** er.* (A 2;0)

door closed-make, fast
*du soggn **au(s)ziehen**.* (A 2;0)
you socks off-pull
*[hamster]mutter **ankuck**(en).* (A 2;0)
hamster mommy at-look
*[zum] papa, **runtergehen**.* (A 2;0)
to daddy, down-go

loose boat sails he
*Jonas **passt** noch **rauf***. (A 2;0)
J fits still too it-on
passt** nich(t) **durch. (A 2;0)
fits not through

The examples in A5 and B5 show that at the lexical stage particle verbs are used precisely as expected. Agentive particle verbs only occur in utterances that are instantiations of type A. That is, they occur in final position and appear with 'infinite' morphology. Non-agentive particle verbs only occur in utterances that are instantiations of type B. That is, they occur with a separated verb form in second-constituent position and appear with 'finite' morphology.

3.3 Conclusion

Children learning Dutch or German initially create a basic language system that consists of lexical categories only. Utterance structure is determined by the semantics of the predicate. If the predicate refers to an action, there is a modal/aspectual head occurring in second-constituent position, while the agentive V occurs in final position as part of $[X + V]_{VP}$. If, on the other hand, the predicate refers to a state or a change of state, the non-agentive V occurs in second-constituent position as part of $[V + X]_{VP}$. Furthermore, it is the position that determines the form with which V is learned and not vice versa. So, as is the case in the input, if V is in final position, it is learned with an 'infinitival' form, if it is in second position it is learned with a 'finite' form.

The basic language system as represented in Figure 2 is a simple lexical system. Semantically, it is the reflection of situations that can be categorized in terms of the presence or absence of control (CTL). After all, this does not really come as a surprise. In actual life, the notion of control is essential for the assessment of a particular situation. That is, it crucially matters if someone has the possibility to influence a situation or whether he/she is just exposed to it.

It should be noted that as far as their predicate-argument structure is concerned, the two types of utterance as represented in Figure 2 turn out to be structurally similar. Hence, it might not be too difficult for learners to infer that they are in fact variants of the same abstract structure in which a predicate with head-complement structure applies to an external argument. Irrespective of its semantic functioning as either agent or theme, this external argument is referred

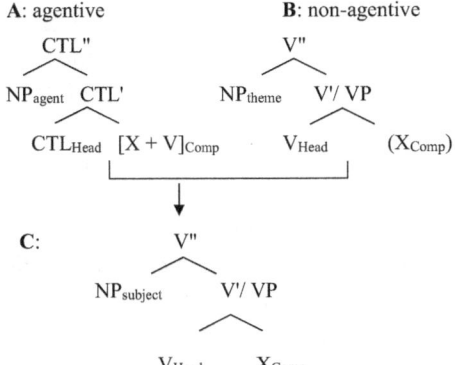

Figure 3: Utterance structure at the lexical stage.

to as 'subject'. Having discovered this, learners have managed to acquire the grammatical knowledge as represented in Figure 3.

To summarize, Figure 3 shows that utterances at the lexical stage are arranged hierarchically at two different levels of semantic structure. At the lower level, as shown in Figure 3A and B, there are two types of utterance structure. In utterances of type A, the head is a modal/aspectual element (CTL). It expresses the willingness, ability, permission or obligation that is exerted by an agent. The complement refers to a causative action or an agentive motion. In utterances of type B, the head (V) is a non-agentive verbal element. It serves to express a state or a change of state. The complement may be an adverbial or a nominal element. Furthermore, due to the similarity between the structural relations as in Figure 3A and B learners are in the position to discover a common utterance structure as shown in Figure 3C. At this higher level of abstraction, the head-complement relation, which constitutes the predicate (V'/VP), holds for an external argument that is referred to as the subject. The hierarchical structure of V" as shown in Figure 3C is well-known in linguistic theory.

Utterances whether they refer to actions, states or changes of state are used for communicative purposes. So, the hearer should be able to comprehend the informational function of an utterance, i.e. whether the utterance is meant to be interpreted as an assertion, a question or an imperative.

As mentioned before, an assertion expresses the claim "that the situation described by the utterance obtains" (Klein 1998, 227). At the lexical stage, this informational meaning of assertion is carried by the lexical head. That is, in agentive utterances it is carried by modal or aspectual elements, while in non-agentive utterances, it is carried by a state or a change-of-state verb (V). At the relevant stage, it seems that lexical means may serve to make the expression of assertion more explicit. So, lexical elements such as *niet* (not) vs. *wel* (indeed) in Dutch and *nicht* (not) in German are used as part of the verbal head. Examples of the use of *niet* vs. *wel* in child Dutch are *wilniet* (want-not), *kanniet* (can-not), *magniet* (may-not), *hoefniet* (must-not) and *lustnie* (like-not) as opposed to *kanwel* (can-indeed), *magwel* (may-indeed) and *luswel* (like-indeed). Similar examples with *nicht* in child German are *mötschnisch* (like-not), *willnicht* (want-not) and *magnich* (like-not). The expression of assertion as a feature of the lexical head explains why it is that at the lexical stage 'object scrambling' does not occur. Hence, children systematically produce utterances such as Dutch **kannie** *losmake* (cannot loose-make. J 1;11), **kanniet** *pakke deze* (can-not get this-one. A 2;1), *Jaja* **magwel** *hondje aaie* (J may-indeed doggie caress. A 2;2), **hoenie** *plak op* (must-not glue on. A 2;0), *Mijnie* **lusnie** *koffie* (M likes-not coffee. J 1;11) and **lusnie** *fles* (like-not bottle. J 1;11) or German **magnich** *nase putzen* (like-not nose clean. C 2;0), while they are unable to produce their targetlike equivalent **kan** *die* **niet** *losmaken* (can that-one not loose-make), **kan** *deze* **niet** *pakke* (can this-one not get), *Jaja* **mag** *hondje* **wel** *aaie* (J may dog indeed caress), **hoef** *plak* **niet** *op* (must glue not on), *Mijnie* **lust** *koffie* **niet** (M likes coffee not), **lust** *fles* **niet** (likes bottle not) and **mag** *nase* **nicht** *putzen* (like nose not clean).

To conclude, the representation given above provides an analysis of our child data in terms of a simple learner system. It makes the claim that at the initial stage of language development without exception *all* learner utterances with a predicate can be accounted for in terms of two types of utterance: agentive utterances with a modal/aspectual lexical head (CTL) and non-agentive utterances with a non-modal lexical head (V). This opposition in terms of types of utterance seems the reflection of a categorization of the outside world in terms of situations that are under control and situations that simply happen to occur.

4 Word order

The analysis of the Dutch and German learner data as presented in Section 2 shows that at the initial stage of language development utterance structure is rather simple. A representation of the semantic relations at two levels of hierarchical structure was given in Figure 3 (Section 3.3). This representation, however, does not yet account for word order.

4.1 Agent first

At the lexical stage, word order rules are very simple, too. They are subject to the semantic principle 'Agent first'.[8] This means that in agentive utterances as in type A, the agent occurs in initial position, while in non-agentive utterances as in type B, this position is taken by the theme. Examples are given (5). At the relevant stage, these two options are the only ones possible. Targetlike utterances with an object or an adverbial in initial position and the subject (agent or theme) in non-initial position typically occur at a later stage of development.

(5) The initial position at the lexical stage: 'Agent first'
    Child Dutch   Child German

   Type A: agentive

   ik *wil mellek pakke.* (J 1;10)   *willnisch raufsitzen.* (A 2;0)
   I want milk get   [I] want-not on-sit
   Jaja *mag dop opdoen.* (A 2;0)   *magnich nase putzen.* (C 2;0)
   J may cap on-do   [I] like-not nose clean

   Type B: non-agentive

   Tompoes *komt aan.* (J 2;0)   ***krokodil*** *kommt.* (A 2;0)
   T comes   crocodile comes
   Jaja *valt niet.* (A 2;0)   ***ente*** *fällt.* (C 2;0)
   J falls not   duck falls

4.2 Topic first

In adult Dutch and German, utterance structure has available an initial, functional position for elements to establish the relation between an utterance and the situation that this utterance applies to (see Figure 4). In cases in which the utterance is an assertion, the initial position is called the topic position. The particular situation that the utterance applies to is called the topic situation TS

---

[8] In Klein and Perdue (1997, 315) this principle is referred to as "SEM1: The NP-referent with highest control comes first."

(Klein 2008, 293). Placement of elements in topic position is accounted for by the functional principle 'Topic first'.

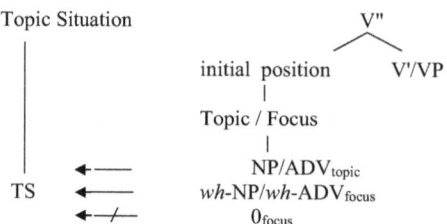

Figure 4: Elements in initial position referring to TS in the target language.

As shown in Figure 4, the element in initial, topic position is either an NP or an ADV that refers to an element in TS. In cases in which the utterance is a *wh*-question or a *yes/no*-question, the initial position is a focus position. This is because the *wh*-element in initial position 'asks' for a referent that should establish a relation to a particular TS. In *yes/no*-questions, finally, the initial, focus position is empty. So, here the formal means to establish a relation to a particular TS are absent.

As opposed to the grammatical system of the target language, learner grammar at the lexical stage, has no functional topic / focus position yet. As shown in Figure 5, it is the subject-NP that serves as a carrier of the topic function.[9] In accordance with the semantic principle 'Agent first', the subject is either the agent or the theme. This accounts for the observation that, at the relevant stage, utterances with an object or an adverbial in initial position and the subject (agent or theme) in non-initial position do not occur, neither do utterances with *wh*-elements in initial, focus position or *yes/no*-questions in which the initial, focus position is empty.

Thus, the linguistic means to establish a relation between the utterance and TS are rather simple. While the subject is used with topic function, the predicate (V') refers to information that is in focus. In other words, at the relevant stage there is a 1:1-correspondence between the syntactic structure of an utterance and its informational, topic-focus structure.

---

[9] Spontaneous child utterances usually apply to topic situations that are linked to the 'here and now' of the moment of speaking. This explains why in child language particularly deictic elements, i. e. proper names, e.g. *Jaja*, and pronouns such as *ik*, *ikke* (I) and *deze* (this-one) are used in first position.

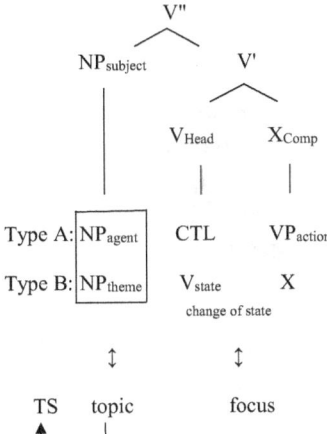

Figure 5: Information structure at the lexical stage.

4.3 Presentatives

So far, utterance structure has been analyzed in terms of utterances with a predicate that holds for its external argument. The external argument in *agentive* utterances is the agent of an action, the external argument in *non-agentive* utterances is the theme of a state or a change of state. Furthermore, the external argument, be it agent or theme, occurs in initial position. At the relevant stage, however, there are also utterances such as Dutch *da zit mama* (there sits mommy. J 1,11) or German *hier kommt die mama* (here comes mommy. A 1;11). Here, the NP *(die) mama* (mommy) does not serve as an external argument. Placement of an NP in utterance-final position is used to express that the referent of the NP is one out of a set of alternatives.[10] Utterances with an NP in final position are called 'presentatives'. They are used to introduce a new participant that is going to be linked to the 'here and now'. This explains the frequent use of linking elements such as *da* (there), *hier* (here), *disse* (these) and *zo* (soon) in child Dutch and *da* (there), *das* (that) in child German as presented in (6a).

---

10 See Klein and Perdue (1997, 317f.):"The argument of one argument verbs has a semantic role, but there is no semantic role asymmetry and, hence, the controller [= semantic] constraints cannot apply. Thus only PR1 [Focus expression last] and phrasal constraints interact: if the referent of the NP is topical, then pattern PH1[NP_T-V] is used; if it is in focus then pattern PH3 [V/Cop-NP_2] is used." Furthermore (see footnote 18, 316): ". . . the semantic relation remains constant whether the argument is preverbal or postverbal . . . ."

(6a) Newly introduced: theme
      Child Dutch   Child German

*da hootie **oma**.* (J 1;11)   *und da wohnt **papi und mami**.* (C 2;1)
there lives-it grandma   and there lives daddy and mommy
*da valtie, da val**tie**, **Oscar**.* (J 1;11)   *da sind-se **alle pup**.* (C 2;1)
there falls-he, there falls-he, Oscar   there are-they all doll
*hier zijn **die**.* (A 2;0)   *da is **die ente**.* (A 2;0)
here are those   there is that duck
*da kanniet **[0]**, hier kanwel **[0]**.* (A 2;1) *da auch **eine ente**.* (A 2;0)
there cannot [it], here can-indeed [it]   there too a duck
*disse zijn **eene**.* (A 2;1)   *das **stroh**.* (A 2;0)
these are ducks   that straw
*uil, zo komt, zo komt **uil**.* (J 1;10)
owl, soon comes, soon comes owl

The examples in (6a) show that in order to serve as contextual linking elements, adverbs such as *da* (there), *hier* (here), *zo* (soon, this-way) or demonstrative pronouns such as *disse* (this-one), *das* (that-one) will do. At the relevant stage, these elements have no particular argument or adjunct function. Hence, the position in which they occur is not yet a constituent position of the utterance.

Contextual linking elements are not only used in presentatives introducing a new participant as in (6a). They also occur in utterances that are used to introduce a new state of affairs. So, utterances as in (6b) use the same type of demonstratives as in (6a) to link a new predicate to the 'here and now'.

(6b) Newly introduced: predicate
      Child Dutch   Child German

*deze **slagroom ete**.* (J 1;10)   *so **hinsetzen**.* (C 2;0)
this-one whipped-cream eat   this-way down-place
*da **sijve**.* (J 1;11)   *das **Lukas malt**.* (A 1;11)
there write   that Lukas draw
*die **oma bed sape**.* (J 1;11)   *da auch noch **Lukas raufmalt**.* (A 1;11)
that grandma bed sleep   that too Lukas drawn
*dit **water indoen**.* (J 1;11)   *da **hinschmissen**.* (A 1;11)
this water in-do   there away-thrown
*deze **jurk aandoen**.* (A 2;0)   *das **auch pieken**.* (A 1;11)
this dress on-put   there too prick
*hier **goed doen**.* (A 2;0)   *da **abmacht**.* (A 2;0)

here good do
*deze **roosvicee indoen**.* (A 2;1)
this-one roosvicee in-do
*hier **toti pakke**.* (A 2;1)
here pencil get
*da **opsappe**.* (A 2;1)
there on-get

there off-taken
*hier auch **hingehen** opa.* (A 2;0)
here too to-go grandpa
*hier **reinkomm**.* (A 2;0)
here in-come
*des hier **rausmachen**.* (A 2;0)
that here out-do

Finally, there is indeed evidence showing that the initial position of linking elements in presentatives is *not* part of a predicate-argument structure. Fact is that at the relevant stage these linking elements may also introduce a new state of affairs expressed by a predicate *with* an external argument as in (6c).

(6c) Newly introduced: predicate with an external argument
      Child Dutch   Child German

*da **poes blijf(t)** hier.* (J 1;11)
there kitty stay here
*dees **baby buggy zitte**.* (J 1;10)
this baby buggy sit
*dit **Cythia maakt**.* (J 1;10)
this C made
*dit **Mijnie vasthoue**.* (J 1 ;10)
this M tight-hold
*da **Goover viege**.* (A 2;0)
there Goover fly

*da, [es] **feht nicht**.* (A 2;0)
there, it misses not
*da, **mei mama war das**.* (A 2;0)
there, my mommy was that
*da [O] **weint**.* (C 2;0)
there O cries

Summarizing, utterances as in (6a) occur with an NP in final position that does not serve as an external argument. As presentatives they are used to express that the referent of the NP is one out of a set of alternatives. Adverbial and pronominal elements may serve as contextual linking elements utterance-initially but with no particular constituent position. This explains why similarly as in (6a) these linking elements may also occur in utterances that consist of predicates with *no* external argument as in (6b) and even in utterances with a predicate *and* an external argument as in (6c).

5 Conflicting constraints

As noted before, at the lexical stage the initial position becomes a subject position, i.e. a position for the constituent that the predicate holds for. According to the semantic principle 'Agent first' this position is taken by the agent in agentive utterances while in non-agentive utterances it is taken by the theme. At the relevant stage, agent and theme in initial position also serve to carry the informational function of the topic. In the target language however, the linguistic system provides the option for an object or an adverbial to be placed in initial, topic position, too. The principle that accounts for this syntactic mechanism of topicalization is the functional principle 'Topic first'. It provides a syntactic position for constituents with topic function regardless their semantic function as either an argument or an adjunct. Acquisition of a syntactic topic position means that at some point there will arise an internal conflict between the semantic principle 'Agent first' and the functional principle 'Topic first'.

The question now is: how does the lexical system solve this conflict such that, for example in agentive utterances, the object or an adverbial may occur in initial, topic position, while at the same time the semantic principle 'Agent first' is still adhered to.

"Contexts of conflicting constraints are very fertile for observing language development" (Perdue 2006: 862). This statement by Perdue also applies to the conflict between 'Agent first' and 'Topic first'. So, a solution to this conflict is initially achieved with a kind of vanishing act. That is, agentive utterances may occur with the object or an adverbial in topic position, while the agent itself is *not* expressed. This form of accommodation ensures that the semantic principle 'Agent first' will not be violated. However, it leads to non-targetlike utterances as in (7).

(7) Agentive utterances: agentless with an object or an adverb in topic position
Child Dutch   Child German[11]

***die** magniet afpakke!* (J 1;11)   ***die mama** anrufen will.* (A 2;0)
that may$_{AG}$-not away-take!   mommy call want$_{AG}$
***da** moet op drukke.* (J 2;1)   ***die** will essen ... die möhre.* (A 2;1)
there must$_{AG}$ on press   that want$_{AG}$ eat ... the carrot
***disse** hoeniet meeneme.* (A 2;1)   ***hase** wollte gucke?* (C 2;3)

---

11 *hier kann-nich raus* (in: Clahsen 1986: 89, 112) 'here cannot out' [The child is pointing to three children who are locked in a room and cannot get out].

this must_AG-not with-take
deze magniet teke. (A 2;2)
this may_AG-not draw
nee losmake. (J 1;10)
[this] want_AG-not loose-make
dit nee afdoen. (J 1;10)
this want_AG-not off-do
da kanwel opzitte. (J 2;0)
there can_AG-indeed on-sit
papa, moet make. (A 2;0)
daddy, [this] must_AG make

die maa hier doen. (A 2;1)
that O_AG-just here do
da kanniet zitte. (A 2;1)
there can_AG-not sit
da kanniet pakke, visie. (A 2;1)
that can_AG-not get, tv
hier moet poesje eve kamme. (A 2;3)
here must_AG kitty just comb

hare wanted_AG look
das kann-schon dis drandrehen? (C 2;3)
that can_AG-just this on-screw
nase anlecken will. (A 2;0)
nose on-lick want_AG
hier auch hingehen, opa. (A 2;0)
here O_AG-also to-go, grandpa
die ansin will. (A 2;0)
that on-put want_AG
nur absteigen soll, du absteigen bloß. (A 2;0)
just off-get must_AG, you off-get just
wolln wir? die xxx reinmach. (A 2;1)
want we? those xxx_AG in-put
der will nicht maln malt. (A 2;1)
that want_AG not draw, drawn
die xx noch ankucken. (A 2;1)
that xx_AG still on-look
trumpf hose näh kann doch nicht. (C 2;3)
pantyhose sew can_AG really not
[O] kann nich hinstellen. (C 2;4)
that can_AG not down-put
wie dürfen machen? (C 2;3)
how may_AG [we] make?
da will .. musik hörn ..., mami. (C 2;3)
there want_AG music listen, mommy

The data in (7) show that at the lexical stage agentive utterances are sometimes used with an object or an adverbial in topic position, while there is no position for the agent.[12] It should be noted however that absence of a position for the agent does not mean that the agent does not play a role. On the contrary, whenever there is an action, there is an agent implied. And precisely because of this the agent-subject (AG) does not have to be expressed explicitly. Hence, utterances as in (7) are evidence of a system-internal solution to express the informational

---

12 See for a similar observation on Dutch child language data Verrips (1996).

function of topicalization while taking into account the constraints of the learner system at the relevant stage.

The same holds for non-agentive utterances as in (8). They may occur with an object or an adverb in topic position, while the theme is not expressed. This is because the semantics of a state or a change of state indicate the implicit role of a particular theme-subject (TH).

(8) Non-agentive utterances with an object or an adverb in topic position
 Child Dutch   Child German

 *nee **tee**, lust nie.* (J 1;11)   *will **nisch**, raufsitzen.* (A 2;0)
 no tea, [that] like$_{TH}$ not   [0] want$_{TH}$ not, on-sit
 ***dit** lus nie.* (J 1;11)   ***hier** noch paßt.* (A 2;0)
 this like$_{TH}$ not   here also fits$_{TH}$
 *mag **die schaar**?* (J 2;0)   ***auf dem fußboden** liegt.* (A 2;0)
 may$_{TH}$ that scissors   on the foor lies$_{TH}$
 ***die** heb ook.* (J 2;1)   ***farbe** brauch.* (A 2;0)
 that have$_{TH}$ too   paint need$_{TH}$
                                          ***kaffee** ham auch noch.* (A 2;1)
                                          coffee have$_{TH}$ too

The learner data in (7) and (8) show the productive use of types of utterance regardless of the fact that there is no evidence in the input. They show that at the lexical stage linguistic knowledge of the relevant language system is used creatively to serve the informational function of topicalization.

Finally, at the lexical stage, there is another way for agentive utterances to provide a topic position while there is no structural position for the agent. This is shown in (9). Here, the function of the agent is served by an affix attached to the verbal head. Given that this affix (for example Dutch *-ie, -se, -e* and German *-isch*) does not require a structural position, using it as a means to refer to the agent is another way to ensure that the semantic principle 'Agent first' will not be violated.

(9) Agentive utterances with a non-agent in topic position and an agent affix

Child Dutch[13]

[0] doetie omdraaie. (J 1;11)
does-he around-turn
[0] doetie alles opete. (J 1;11)
does-he everything up-eat
nou *gaatie weer naar huis toe gaan.*
(J 2;2)
now goes-he again to home to go
[0] doetie viesmake. (A 2;1)
does-he dirty-make
[0] doetie hantie geve. (A 2;1)
does-he hand give
[0] doense same zitte. (A 2;2)[15]
do-they together sit-down
[0] magtie papa zitte. (A 2;2)
may-he [with] daddy sit-down
[0] moete nieuwe make, vokke. (A 2;2)
must-we new-ones make, flakes

Child German[14]

die *wisch auch mal haben, lila.* (A 2;1)
that want-I also once have, lilac
noch eine finden *will-isch* (A 2;0)
more one find want-I

6 Conclusion

For children learning Dutch or German, utterance structure at the initial stage is the expression of a lexical projection of V as represented in Figure 5. Functional categories are not part of the learner system yet despite the fact that ample evidence of the use of functional elements is certainly provided by the input.

Stating that functional categories are not part of the learner system at the lexical stage means that children are claimed not to have at their disposal the functional linguistic means specifically fit to express contextual cohesion. That

---

13 The topic position is often left empty [. . .].
14 Examples with an affix such as *-ma(n)* (one) or *-se* (they) in Dimroth et al. (2003) are: *den damannich essen* (that may-one-not eat. Valle 1;11); *da daman aufmachen* (this may-one open-make. Valle 1;11); *des buch soll'ma / buch anguckn* (the book must-one / book on-look. Valle 1;11); *da hier mussen'se hin* (there here must-they away. Valle 1;11). An example of a non-agentive utterance with a theme-affix and an adverb-topic in child Dutch is: *zo moettet, rije* (this-way must-it drive. A 2;2).
15 *zitten* (sit) meaning 'sit-down' refers to an action.

is, they are not ready to use these functional means to embed an utterance into the context of a larger discourse.

Contextual cohesion in adult Dutch and German can be achieved with the linguistic means to express 'semantic finiteness', i.e. the linguistic means to assert that the situation described by the utterance obtains (Klein 1998, 227, see Section 1). In the system of the target language, there is a structural 'verb-second' (V2) position available for verbal elements to carry this informational function. The relevant features are represented by the functional category (F). Furthermore, in order to express that the assertion holds for a particular situation TS, F projects an initial, topic position. At the lexical stage, both the V2 and the topic position are absent. The consequences of this can be summarized as follows.

First, in absence of a V2 position for a verbal element to express that the utterance serves as an assertion, there is:
– no category of auxiliary verbs (hence, no scrambling, i.e. placement of an element between V2 and the negation),
– no verb movement,
– no inflectional morphology (hence, no agreement and no tense).

Second, in absence of a topic position to express that the assertion holds for a particular topic situation (TS) there is:
– no topicalization (i.e. no subject-verb inversion),
– no focalization (i.e. no *wh*-questions),
– no *yes/no*-questions,
– no determiners (i.e. no elements marking definite vs. indefinite),
– no pronominal anaphora.

Thus, evidence from child learners of Dutch and German shows that the relation between language input and the shape of the learner variety cannot simply be described as "what they hear is what you get" (Ingram and Thompson 1996: 97). Given a particular amount of target language input, learners appear to create a basic language variety that has no functional category system and, hence, no functional projection to express contextual cohesion.

In the following, we will argue that the acquisition of the linguistic means to establish contextual cohesion is the driving force in the acquisition of a functional category F which projects structural positions (a) for a verbal element in V2 position carrying the informational function of semantic finiteness, and (b) for a constituent utterance-initially to express the topic function.

7 Utterance structure at the functional stage

7.1 Developing a functional projection to express 'semantic finiteness'

As argued in Section 5, agentive utterances with an object in topic position such as Dutch *die magniet afpakke!* (that may$_{AG}$-not away-take! J 1;11) or *disse hoeniet meeneme* (this must$_{AG}$-not with-take. A 2;1) and German *das kann-schon dis drandrehen?* (that can$_{AG}$-just this on-screw. C 2;3) or *die will essen, die möhre* (that$_i$ want$_{AG}$ eat, the carrot$_i$. A 2;1) contain the elements of a developmental process that should lead the way to the grammatical system at the functional stage. This process is claimed to be triggered by the reanalysis of the lexical predicate V'/VP as in Figure 6a and b.

As displayed in Figure 6a, the agent (AG) is *implicitly* present as a feature of the modal head (CTL) of the lexical projection of V. Under pressure of the input, AG becomes *explicitly* expressed so that it will serve as the NPagent of the lexical projection of V in Figure 6b. As a consequence of this, the lexical head (**V**$_{Head}$) in Figure 6a becomes a functional head (**F**$_{Head}$) in Figure 6b.

This representation of the developmental process shows that the conflict between the principles 'Agent first' and 'Topic first' has been solved with the creation of two types of 'first positions'. A functional, first position utterance-initially for an element with topic function and a lexical, first position for the agent utterance-internally. It also shows that as a result of this process, the lexical modal verb in **V**$_{Head}$ (Figure 6a) is reinterpreted as a functional auxiliary verb in **F**$_{Head}$ (Figure 6b) that is used as a carrier of semantic finiteness.

So, with **F**$_{Head}$ a position has been created that provides the speaker with the linguistic means particularly geared to express the informational function of assertion. This means that from now on, as shown in Figure 7, learners are in the position to acquire the functional category of non-modal auxiliary verbs, too. This holds for Dutch *heb* (have) or *heeft* (has) and *ben* (am) or *is* (is) in utterances such as *ikke he dit pakt* (I have this taken. J 2;1) and *da is-ie varre* (there is-it fallen. A 2;2) and German *hab* (have) or *hat* (has) and *bin* (am) or *ist* (is) in utterances such as *ich hab das schon aufeheben* (I have that already up-picked. A 2;1) and *das ist ausetunkn* (that is empty-drunk. A 2;1).

Furthermore, as a consequence of the reinterpretation of **V**$_{Head}$ as **F**$_{Head}$, X$_{Comp}$ becomes reanalyzed as a lexical category with a lexical head V (**V**$_{Head}$) which projects a position utterance-internally for the agent (AG) as the external argument of the predicate V$_{Head}$ + X$_{Comp}$.

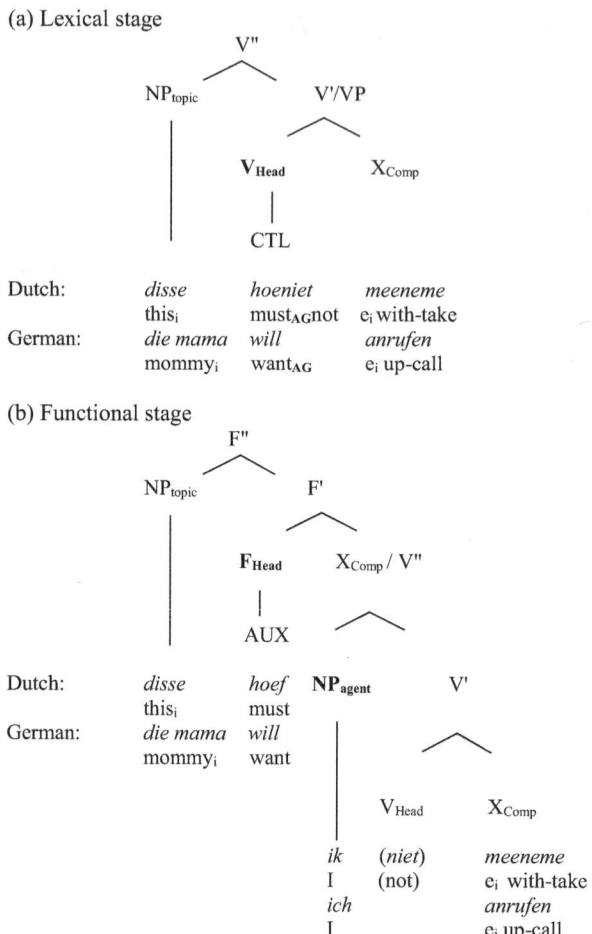

Figure 6: Reanalysis of type-A utterances.

Finally, as shown in Figure 7, the newly created F_{Head} in verb-second (V2) position makes it possible not only for functional verbal elements such as modal and non-modal auxiliary verbs to serve as carrier of *semantic* finiteness but also for lexical verbs, e.g. Dutch *nemen* (take) or German *rufen* (call). Moreover, as soon as these lexical verbs occur in this (V2) position they are going to be used with *morphological* finiteness as is the case in the input, e.g. Dutch *neem* (take-1Sg) and German *rufe* (call-1Sg). Finally, reinterpretation of the initial position as a topic position makes it possible for any constituent XP, i.e. not only for NPs but also for adverbials (ADV), to occur in this functional position, too.

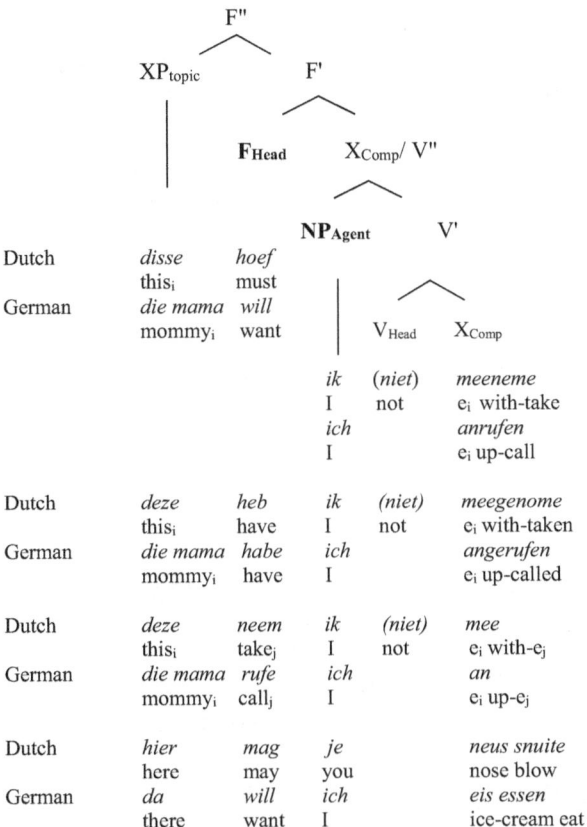

Figure 7: Utterance structure at the functional stage: the functional projection of F.

7.2 Evidence of a functional V2 position

With F_{Head}, as shown in Figure 7, a position has been created that enables children to acquire the use of verb forms as carrier of semantic finiteness. These verb forms may be either auxiliary verbs (modal and non-modal) or lexical verbs. Non-modal auxiliary verbs such as Dutch *heb, heeft, ben, is* (have, has, am, is) and German *habe, hat, bin, ist* (have, has, am, is) occurring in utterances with a past participle are the first words with no lexical meaning that children are able to learn. They are the clearest evidence that the child has reached the functional stage.

Given the fact that the grammatical system at the lexical stage has no position available for non-modal auxiliary verbs, there should be a distributional difference between the use of past participle structures *without* an auxiliary verb at the lexical stage and past participle structures *with* an auxiliary verb at the functional stage. Thus, evidence for the use of past participles with *no* auxiliary verb is expected to occur with Jasmijn (1;10–1;11) and Andrea (2;0–2;1) in Dutch and with Anna (1;11–2;0) and Caroline (2;0–2;1) in German, while evidence for the use of past participles *with* an auxiliary verb is going to occur with Jasmijn (2;0–2;2) and Andrea (2;2–2;4) in Dutch and with Anna (2;1–2;2) and Caroline (2;2–2;3) in German. Examples are given in (10) and (11).[16] These data show that the use of non-modal auxiliaries can indeed be taken as a criterion to identify the developmental stage that the children are in.

(10) Child Dutch: past-participle structures *without* and *with* auxiliary verb

The lexical stage	The functional stage
Jasmijn (1;10–1;11)	Jasmijn (2;0–2;2)
*bal weg. **topt**.* (J 1;10) ball gone. hidden	*ikke **hè** dit **pakt**.* (J 2;1) I have this taken
*dit Cynthia **maakt**.* (J 1;10) this C made	***heb** niet broekie **plast**.* (J 2;2) have not pants peed
*poppie haartie **wast**.* (J 1;10) doll hair washed	*ik **heb wonne**.* (J 2;1) I have won
*dit Cynthia **weest**.* (J 1;10) this C been	*ik **heef afspoeld**.* (J 2;2) I have down-washed
*chicken little **valle**.* (J 1;10) chicken little fallen	*nou's weer **aflope**.* (J 2;2) now is again finished
*poes **opgete**.* (J 1;11) kitty up-eaten	*die **is** altijd opde televisie **geweest**.* (J 2;2) that-one is always on-the tv been
Andrea (2;0–2;1)	Andrea (2;2–2;4)

---

16 A past participle can be preceded by a finite form of the auxiliary verb *hebben* (have) or *zijn* (be) in Dutch and *haben* (have) or *sein* (be) in German. However, due to the fact that the use of a finite form of the Dutch auxiliary verb *zijn* and the German auxiliary verb *sein* is restricted to a relatively small category of mostly intransitive verbs, it occurs rather infrequently. Nevertheless, the available data are in line with what has been found for the use of the auxiliaries *hebben* and *haben*. That is, at the lexical stage the Dutch children Jasmijn and Andrea and the German children Anna and Caroline produce utterances in which the auxiliaries *zijn* and *sein* are typically absent.

*ikke ook boot **hees**.* (A 2;0)
I too boat been
*Jaja **kamd**.* (A 2;0)
J combed
*papa **potmaakt**.* (A 2;0)
daddy kaput-made
*nog niet? **afberope**?* (A 2;0)
not yet? finished?
*Jaja óók gijbaan **hees**.* (A 2;0)
J too slide been
*mama lekker **aapt**?* (A 2;1)
mommy nice slept?
*jou **hege**, dees.* (A 2;1)
you got this

*aap **goonmaakt**.* (A 2;1)
monkey clean-made

*Jaja **hemme** al **goonmaakt**.* (A 2;2)
J has already clean-made
*Jaja **heefe doend**.* (A 2;2)
J has-it done
*da **issie varre**.* (A 2;2)
there is-it fallen
*ikke **hemme** deze **tekend**.* (A 2;3)
I have this drawn
*Jaja **heef** da **puugd**.* (A 2;3)
J has there spit
*isse Barnies **affehope**, mam?* (A 2;4)
is B finished, mommy?
*Jaja **heef** met de haartjes zo **doet**.*
(A 2;4)
J has with the hairs so done
*ik **heef** óók appel **gete**.* (A 2;4)
I have too apple eaten

(11) Child German: past-participle structures *without* and *with* auxiliary verb
The lexical stage   The functional stage

Anna (1;11–2;0)   Anna (2;1–2;2)

*oh, oh **puttgang**.* (A 2;0)
oh, oh kaput-gone
auffressen (=aufgefressen). (A 2;0)
up-eaten
*da **abmacht**.* (A 2;0)
that off-made
*kuck mal, **runterkullert**.* (A 2;0)
look, down-rolled
reinlegt. (A 2;0)
in-put (I)
wegpustet. (A 2;0)
away-blown
*dok (=doch) **schafft**.* (A 2;0)
still made
*löwl (=löffel) **runterfallen**.* (A 2;0)
spoon down-fallen

*das **ist ausetunkn**.* (A 2;1)
that is empty-drunk
*ich **hab** das schon **aufeheben**.* (A 2;1)
I have that already up-picked
*hast das **puttemacht**.* (A 2;1)
[you] have that kaput-made
*das, Lukas **hat** das **mitbracht**.* (A 2;1)
that, L has that with-taken
*hab alles **ausekippt**.* (A 2;1)
have everything out-thrown
*der **hat auseschlafen**.* (A 2;1)
he has out-slept
han möhre essen. (A 2;1)
[we] have carrot eaten
hat tschüss sagt. (A 2;1)
[he] has good-bye said

Caroline (2;0–2;1)

*ente **wall** (=gefallen).* (C 2;0)
goose fallen
*eine **weglauft** (=weggelaufen).*
(C 2;1)
one away-run
*nicht unter **weglauft**
(=weggelaufen).* (C 2;1)
not under away-run
***spukt** voll wasser, mit wasser.*
(C 2;1)
spit full water, with water

Caroline (2;2–2;4)

*da man bun **fallen ist**.* (C 2;2)
there man tree fallen is
*gucken papi **einnekauft hat**.* (C 2;3)
look daddy purchased has

*mich wieder **stosst hab**.* (C 2;3)
myself again hit have

*und autos **sind** da **fahrn**.* (C 2;4)
and cars are there driven

*ich des **gemacht habe**.* (C 2;4)
I that made have
*mal **weggeräumt haben** . . .* (C 2;4)
once away-done have

7.3 Evidence of a functional topic position

As represented in Figure 7, at the functional stage, not only objects but also adverbials may be used in initial, topic position. Evidence in children learning Dutch and German is given in (12) and (13). The Dutch data occur with Jasmijn (2;0–2;2) and Andrea (2;2–2;4), the German data occur with Anna (2;1–2;2) and Caroline (2;2–2;4).

(12) Child Dutch: utterances with objects or adverbials in initial, topic position

Jasmijn (2;0–2;2)
agentive   non-agentive

***die** mag ik lekker opete.* (J 2;2)   ***da** ben ik weer.* (J 2;0)
that may I nicely up-eat   there am I again
***die** mag **boze wolf** niet potmake, de   **dit** heeft **Cynthia**.* (J 2;0)
muts.* (J 2;2)   this has C.
that may bad wolf not kaput-make, the
cap

mag jij hebbe. (J 2;2)
[this] may you have
hier mag je neus snuite. (J 2;2)
here may you nose blow

dan moet Cynthia weer make. (J 2;2)
then must C again make
daa kan ik niet meer lope. (J 2;2)
there can I not anymore walk
mag poekie niet meer aankome. (J 2;2)
[this] may kitty not anymore touch

daar zit jij? (J 2;1)
there sit you?
koppie thee vindt papa wel lekker.
(J 2;2)
cup-of tea finds daddy indeed nice
die wilt ik. (J 2;2)
that-one want I
nou bent mama weer terug. (J 2;2)
now am mommy again back
weer ponypaard heb ik. (J 2;2)
that may again pony-horse have I

Andrea (2;2–2;4)
agentive

nou mag Jaja peenie in. (A 2;2)
now may J pacifier in [do]
mag jij lekke opete mette ei. (A 2;2)
[this] may you nicely up-eat with-the egg
da mag papa wel doen. (A 2;3)
that may daddy indeed do
zo kan ikke Jaja wel niks zien. (A 2;3)
this-way can I J indeed nothing see
hier wilt Jaja ook denkik naa toe.
(A 2;4)
here wants J also think-I to [go]
da kanne kindere inzitte. (A 2;4)
there can children in-sit
broodje mag Cynthia wel opete. (A 2;4)
bun may C indeed up-eat

non-agentive

vogel hoort ik. (A 2;2)
bird hear I
da wone wij. (A 2;2)
there live we
da wus ik wel. (A 2;3)
that like I indeed
die vin Jaja hekker, fokomel. (A 2;3)
hat finds J nice, chocolate-milk
zefde heef Jaja. (A 2;3)
same has J

da valt stoel wel om. (A 2;3)
there falls chair indeed flat
zo doet Cynthia. (A 2;4)
so does C

(13) Child German: utterances with objects or adverbials in initial, topic position

Anna (2;1–2;2)
agentive

diese wir aber lesen. (A2;1)
this we however read
tür müssen wir das aufhängen. (A 2;1)
door must we that up-put

non-agentive

xxx wollen wir aber nicht. (A 2;1)
xxx want we however not
noch was haben wir. (A 2;1)
else something have we

*daf **du** nich rausnehm.* (A 2;1)
[that] may you not out-take

***so** kommt **der** nicht.* (A 2;1)
then comes he not
***löffel** hab **ich** hier.* (A 2;1)
spoon have I here
***das** kann **ich** gar nicht.* (A 2;1)
that can I absolutely not
***blättern** hab **ich**.* (A 2;1)
sheets have I
***das** tüm hab **ich** nich an.* (A 2;1)
that costume have I not on
***sprochen** hab **ich**.* (A 2;1)
spoken have I

Caroline (2;2–2;5)
agentive

*ein dach musst **du** malen.* (C 2;3)
a roof must you draw
*(al)**leine** kann **ich** angucken, selber.* (C 2;3)
only can I at-look, self
***die** möchste haben.* (C 2;4)
that want-you get
***rummachen** macht # wollt **ich** machen.* (C 2;4)
around-make made wanted I do
***da** will **ich** eis essen.* (C 2;5)
there want I ice-cream eat
*darfst **du** nicht machen.* (C 2;5)
[this] must you not do
*brauchst **du** nich # zu helfen.* (C 2;5)
[that] must you not to help

non-agentive

***ausschneiden** ... wollt **ich**?* (C 2;2)
out-cut .. wanted I
***drehen** wollt **ich**.* (C 2;3)
turn-around wanted I
***fressen** könn **die**.* (C 2;4)
swallow can they
***bischen#mitnehm** wollte **der** hase.* (C 2;4)
somewhat with-take wanted the hare
*# mh guckst **du** mal.* (C 2;5)
[allright] look you
***wieder einsteige** willst **du**.* (C 2;5)
again into-go want you

Furthermore, at the functional stage, the initial position serves both the function of topicalization and focalization. So, at the relevant stage, Dutch and German children may not only use utterances with objects and adverbials in initial, *topic* position, but also utterances with *wh*-elements in initial, *focus* position. This focus position remains empty in *yes/no*-questions. Examples are given in (14) and (15).

(14) Utterances with *wh*-elements in initial, focus position
    Child Dutch   Child German

    Jasmijn (2;0–2;2); Andrea (2;2–2;4)   Anna (2;1–2;2); Caroline (2;2–2;4)

    *doet **papa** nou voor mij doen?* (A 2;4)   *wo **kann** das sein?* (A 2;1)
    [what] does daddy now for me done?   where can that be?
    ***waar** ben je nou geweest?* (J 2;2)   *wo **ist** es hier aufgelegt?* (A 2;1)
    where are you now been?   where is it here on put?
                                                 *wo **kann** man de reinstecken?* (C 2;4)
                                                 where can one this in-put?

(15) Utterances with empty focus position in *yes/no*-questions
    Child Dutch   Child German

    Jasmijn (2;0–2;2)   Anna (2;1–2;2)

    zulle lego spele? (J 2;1)   *will**st** haben?* (A 2;1)
    shall-we lego play?   want-you have?
    *mag **ik** wel uit bedje klimme?* (J 2;2)   *auch **du** aufräumen?* (A 2;1)
    may I indeed out-off bed climb?   also you up-clean?
    *mag **ik** die plakke?* (J 2;2)   *wo(llen) **wir** bauen?* (A 2;1)
    may I that glue?   want we build?

    Andrea (2;2–2;4)   Caroline (2;5)

    *mag **ik** ook doen?* (A 2;2)[17]   *willst **du** einsteigen?* (C 2;5)
    may I too do?   want you enter?
    *mag **kikker** ook mij vasthoue?* (A 2;2)   *darf **ich** da drücken?* (C 2;5)
    may frog also me tight-hold?   may I there push?
    *mag **Jaja** kaas ete?* (A 2;3)   *darf **ich** dis mit spieln?* (C 2;5)
    may J cheese eat?   may I this with play?
    *één, tee, zum**me** terre?* (A 2;3)   *kann **man** da musik hörn?* (C 2;5)
    one, two shall-we draw?   can one there music hear?

---

[17] At the lexical stage, Andrea uses utterances with *mag-ikke* as in *mag-ikke paartie rije?* (may-I horsie ride? A 2;0) relatively frequently. They function as phrasal expressions which give way to the analysed structures at the functional stage.

7.4 Conclusion

The observations in Section 7.2 and 7.3 indicate that with the development of a functional projection (F) there are two structural positions in the prefield of the utterance. The V2 position (F_{head}) makes it possible for verbal elements to serve as carrier of semantic finiteness i.e. as the linguistic means to express the informational function of assertion. The initial, topic/focus position (XP_{topic}) makes it possible for objects and adverbials to serve as the linguistic means to establish the relation between the assertion and the particular situation TS (i.e. topic situation) that the assertion is about. This explains why simultaneously with the use of auxiliary verbs in second position as in (10) and (11), non-subjects occur in initial position as in (12), (13) and (14). Furthermore, it should be noted that, given the reanalysis as shown in Figure 6a and b, the instantiation of the functional topic position is also tied to a subject position after the non-modal auxiliary verb. Evidence for this is given in (16).

(16) Topicalization/focalization with the subject after the non-modal auxiliary verb

Child Dutch	Child German[18]
Jasmijn (2;0–2;2)	Anna (2;1–2;2)
*heef **Cynthia** maakt.* (J 2;0) [that] has C made	***gestern** hab **ich** zuguckt.* (A 2;1) yesterday have I at-looked
*die heef **mama** maakt.* (J 2;1) that-one has mommy made	***kaffee** hat **mama** kocht.* (A 2;1) coffee has mommy cooked
*heb **je** visje gehad?* (J 2;1) have you fish had?	*das, **kaffee** hast **du** ausetrunkn.* (A 2;1) that coffee have you empty-drunk
*die heef **Cynthia** gemaakt.* (J 2;2) that has C made	*zeigen, **dort** hab **ich** was malt.* (A 2;1) show, there have I something drawn
***waa** ben **je** nou geweest?* (J 2;2) where are you now been?	*hat **Daggi** mir mitgebracht.* (A 2;1) [that] has D me with-taken
***waa** heb **je** chocola gelate?* (J 2;2) where have you chocolate left?	***dein kaffee** hast **du** aus.* (A 2;1) your coffee have you empty

---

[18] For Caroline the relevant corpus has no data available.

Andrea (2;2–2;4)

*heb **ik** oppegete.* (A 2;2)
[that] have I up-eaten

*hem**me** nogge fippo vonne?* (A 2;2)
have-we more flippo found?

*da ben **ikke** ook wees.* (A 2;3)
there am I too been

*die hem **ik** van Jasmijn kege.* (A 2;4)
that-one have I from J got

***gestern** hab **ich** schon mal arbeit.* (A 2;1)
yesterday have I already worked

***das** (hab) **ich** macht.* (A 2;1)
that have I made

***kaffee** hat **mama** heiß macht.* (A 2;1)
coffee has mommy hot made

Finally, looking at the timespan during which the children are able to restructure their basic lexical system, it seems noteworthy that with all four children the developmental process from a lexical system to a functional system takes place within a month. That is, for Jasmijn between 1;11 and 2;0; for Andrea between 2;1 and 2;2; for Anna between 2;0 and 2;1 and for Caroline between 2;1 and 2;2.

8 Discussion: Organic Grammar

In their book entitled *The acquisition of German. Introducing Organic Grammar*, Vainikka and Young-Scholten (2011) studied, inter alia, the spontaneous language development among children learning German as their mother tongue. The authors characterize their investigation as "a foray into a syntax-driven explanation of transitions from one stage to another in children's acquisition of their first language as well as in children's and adult's acquisition of a second language (L2), primarily in naturalistic (uninstructed) settings (2011, 3)." The so-called syntax-driven explanation is stated to account for language acquisition as a developmental process within the framework of Chomsky's Minimalist Program (Chomsky 1995). More specifically, it is Vainkika and Young-Scholten's Theory of Organic Grammar that attributes a central role to the notion of the Master Tree, being the representation of the end-state syntactic structure. Given that this Master Tree provides the syntactic stepping stones relevant for the process of language development, Organic Grammar claims that a projection that is located at a lower level of hierarchical structure is going to be acquired prior to a projection that is located higher up. This means, for example, that lexical projections are predicted to become acquired before functional projections (Vainikka and Young-Scholten 2011, 13).[19]

Although the notion of a Master Tree may also *account for* our finding that for German – and evidently for other languages, too – there is a lexical stage of acquisition that precedes the functional stage, it is our claim that there is empirical evidence that serves to *explain why* this is the case. Focusing on how children make sense of the input to acquire a grammatical system for the purpose of communication, we argued that the use of contextual information is crucial. So, in the early stages, the relevant situation is restricted to the here and now. As long as this is the case, i.e. as long as contextual cohesion with a situation outside the actual context does not yet play a role, lexical projections are used. Functional projections, on the other hand, are specifically designed to establish contextual cohesion with a situation different from the actual one. Given this to be true, the acquisition of lexical projections before functional projections is a matter of cognitive development. More specifically, it is a developmental process that depends on the presence of a fully developed working memory (see Bittner and Jordens, this volume).

Furthermore, while the notion of the Master Tree entails the general claim that language development occurs as "actual instantiations of the tree [that] are projected from bottom up" (Vainikka and Young-Scholten 2011, 13), we specifically argued for a *two-stage* model of language development. This two-stage model is cognitively based, too. That is, developmental progress from the lexical stage to the functional stage occurs as soon as children become less egocentric, i.e. as soon as children become aware of the fact that for other people the present contextual situation is different from the one that is relevant for themselves. In order to be able to cope with this, children have to develop their current language system such that they have access to the functional linguistic means that are fit to express contextual cohesion. Empirically, it can be shown that the relevant process of language development, which occurs rather suddenly, provides the template for the acquisition of the functional category system as a whole. Thus, while the acquisition of the position of the finite verb serves as a condition for the acquisition of verb movement and subject-verb agreement, the acquisition of the topic position serves as the condition for the acquisition of word order variation and definiteness at the same time. Finally, as shown in Bittner and Jordens (this volume) further independent, empirical evidence for the psycholinguistic adequacy of this two-stage model is the fact that the main developmental

---

19 The notion of the Master Tree, being both the result of the acquisition mechanism (i.e. the end-state syntactic structure) as well as its goal of language development, seems circular in a way.

problem that children with DLD have to deal with is giving up their initial, lexical system in favour of a targetlike, functional system that is fit to express contextual cohesion.

9 Summary

Language development in children learning Dutch and German proceeds in a stage-wise manner. Initially, at the lexical stage, Dutch and German children appear to create a basic language system that consists of lexical categories only. At this initial stage, utterance structure is determined by the semantics of the predicate. So, if the predicate refers to an action, there is a modal/aspectual lexical head (CTL) in second-constituent position, while the agentive predicate (V) is in final position as part of a complement $[X + V]_{VP}$. In contrast, if the predicate refers to a state or a change of state, there is just a non-agentive predicate (V) in second-constituent position serving as the head of $[V + X]_{VP}$. At the relevant stage, this learner system seems the reflection of situations that can be categorized in terms of the presence or absence of control (CTL). Although the two types of utterance are structured syntactically differently, they are similar as far as their predicate-argument structure is concerned. That is, they are both variants of the an abstract head-complement structure that applies to an external argument.

Furthermore, at the lexical stage, word order is constrained by the semantic principle 'Agent first'. This principle accounts for the fact that in lexical structures in which an agent plays a role, the agent is in initial position as, for example, in child Dutch *Jaja mag dop opdoen* (J may cap on-do. A 2;0) or in child German *papa nich(t) soll hier reinkomm(en)* (daddy not should here in-come. A 2;0). Only in lexical structures in which there is no role for an agent, the theme may occur in initial position as, for example, in child Dutch *Jaja valt niet* (J falls not. A 2;0) or in child German *krokodil kommt* (crocodile comes. A 2;0). Both types of utterance, referred to as type A (agentive) and type B (non-agentive) respectively, are lexical structures that specify the relation between the predicate and a constituent (agent or theme) that it holds for. Generalization of this 'hold-for' relation enables children to establish a grammatical category 'subject' that comprises both agent and theme.

The lexical stage is the initial stage of language development. At this stage, the learner grammar does not have the structural means of the target language to establish contextual cohesion. This means that the relevant linguistic categories of information structure are absent. Later, at the functional stage, the basic lexical system is restructured towards a functional category system that has two constituent positions in the prefield of the utterance to express 'semantic finiteness' and 'topicality'. Both these functional categories provide the linguistic means to express contextual cohesion. Semantic finiteness serves as a linguistic means to express that the relevant utterance has to be understood as an assertion, i.e. as a means to express that a particular state of affairs is the case (see Klein 1998, 227). Topicality serves as a linguistic means to establish the relation between the assertion and a particular situation TS (topic situation) that the assertion is about (see Klein 2008, 293). While semantic finiteness is carried by a verbal element in verb-second (V2) position, topicality is expressed by any constituent in utterance-initial position.

At the lexical stage, conflicting constraints are the driving force for language development. As a preliminary move, the initial position in agentive utterances is made available also for topicalized objects, as in Dutch *die magniet afpakke!* (that may$_{AG}$-not away-take! J 1;11) or *disse hoeniet meeneme* (this must$_{AG}$-not with-take. A 2;1) and German *das kann-schon dis drandrehen?* (that can$_{AG}$-just this on-screw? C 2;3) or *die will essen, die möhre* (that$_i$ want$_{AG}$ eat, the carrot$_i$. A 2;1). Even with an object in initial position, these agentive utterances still adhere to the principle 'Agent first'. This is due to the fact that the agent (AG) is *implicitly* present as a feature of the modal/aspectual head of the lexical projection of V. In other words, this agentive utterance allows an object or an adverbial in initial, topic position, provided the agent is *not* expressed. However, this solution is just a provisionary one as long as there is no structural position for the agent. As shown in Figure 6a and b, the conflict between 'Agent first' and 'Topic first' is solved such that the lexical head V (**V$_{Head}$**), fit for modal/aspectual verbs (CTL), becomes reanalyzed as a functional head F (**F$_{Head}$**). F, then, accommodates the category AUX while it projects a functional, topic position utterance-initially. At the same time, as a consequence of this reanalysis, X$_{Comp}$ becomes reanalyzed as a lexical category with a lexical head V (**V$_{Head}$**) which projects a position utterance-internally for the agent (AG) as the external argument of the predicate V$_{Head}$ + X$_{Comp}$.

This developmental process has the following consequences. First, with F$_{Head}$ a position has been created for the auxiliary verb to serve as a carrier of the functional features of semantic finiteness, i.e. the informational function of assertion. As a carrier of semantic finiteness, the auxiliary verb accommodates both modal *and* non-modal auxiliary verbs. The non-modal auxiliary verbs, i.e. Dutch *heb, heeft, ben, is* (have, has, am, is) and German *habe, hat, bin, ist* (have, has, am, is), are the first words with no lexical meaning that children are able to learn. As shown in (10) and (11), they are the clearest evidence that the child has reached the functional stage. Furthermore, given that the V2 position is a functional position for verb forms to express semantic finiteness, *lexical* verbs can be placed in this position, too. However, realization of the morphological feature 'finite' systematically with lexical verbs in V2 position "may at this point still be too complex a process. Therefore, for the time being [auxiliary verbs] are used as a periphrastic means to get a finite verb into second [V2] position while leaving [the nonfinite lexical] verb at the end of the sentence (Jordens 1990, 1434)." Yet, as soon as lexical verbal elements are going to be placed in V2 position, learners are also ready to acquire the morphological features of agreement and tense.

Second, as soon as the new functional head F projects a topic position, any constituent no matter its grammatical function, i.e. subject, object or adverbial, may occur in initial position in order to establish the relation between the assertion and the particular situation (topic situation: TS) that the assertion is about. Examples are given in (12) and (13). In contrast to this, utterances with an empty topic position can*not* serve to express an assertion because there is no element to relate the utterance to a topic situation. Hence, as illustrated in (15), they provide the means to express a *yes/no*-question. Furthermore, as shown in (15) too, at the functional stage, the initial position serves not only the function of topicalization but also of focalization. So, at the relevant stage, Dutch and German children may not only use utterances with objects and adverbials in initial, *topic* position, but also utterances with *wh*-elements in initial *focus* position.

Finally, as already pointed out, auxiliary verb forms are the first functional, verbal elements to occur in V2 position. They appear together with the non-finite lexical verb in final position. As noted before, it is only later in the acquisition process that lexical verbs are placed in V2 position, too.

Particle verbs are a special case as they consist of a verbal element and a particle. In adult Dutch and German the verbal element of a particle verb is subject to 'verb fronting'. That is, the verbal part may occur in V2 position while the particle remains in final position. At the lexical stage, as shown in A5 (Section 3.2), agentive particle verbs such as Dutch *opeten* (up-eat), *(ka)potmake* (kaput-make) and German *aufhängen* (on-hang), *rausnehmen* (it-out-take) are systematically used in final position. Verb fronting with agentive particle verbs, at the functional stage, will be acquired as the result of the input the child is going to receive. A few examples are given in (17) and (18) to illustrate how this may occur in actual interaction.

(17) German: interaction between Anna (child: 2;1) and D (Dagmar: investigator)

    Anna: *du, du, du machst das.*
                  you, you, you do that
    Anna: *du, du, du* **machst** *die kiste* **aufräumen**.
                  you, you, you do the trunk up-clean

> D: *die kiste **räumst** du **auf**.*
> the trunk clean you up
>
> [...]
>
> Anna: *das rein?*
> that it-in
>
> D: *ja, alles rein.*
> yes everything it-in
>
> Anna: *ich, ich **räum** alles **auf**.*
> I, I clean everything up
>
> [...]
>
> Anna: *das auch rein? das kommt auch hier.*
> that too it-in? that comes also here?
>
> D: *klar, **mach** du auch da **rein**.*
> allright, do you also there it-in
>
> Anna: ***aufräumen. räumt** das **auf**.*
> up-clean. cleans that up
>
> [...]
>
> Anna: *ich **räume** alles **auf**.*
> I clean everything up

As shown in (17), the use of the verb *machst* (do-2Sg) together with the particle verb *aufräumen* (up-clean) is evidence that the child is already familiar with the fact that her current language system has the V2 position available to express finiteness. However, due to the complexity of the process of 'verb fronting', the child uses the dummy auxiliary verb *machst* for a periphrastic construction in which the lexical verb is still in final position. However, the moment the investigator (D) has responded using the same particle verb with 'verb fronting', the child feels comfortable to use this structural device, too. Another example showing the relevance of the input that the child receives, is given in (18).

(18) German: interaction between Anna (child: 2;1) and D (Dagmar: investigator)

> D: *welche geschichte **liest** denn die mama **vor**?*
> what story reads now mommy aloud
>
> Anna: *so ne schichte **liest** mama **vor**.*
> such a story reads mommy aloud

Examples as in (17) and (18) enable the child to acquire the linguistic feature of 'verb fronting'. After she has internalized this operation of verb movement, the child will produce utterances as in (19) and (20) on a regular basis.

(19) German: interaction between Anna (child: 2;1) and D (Dagmar: investigator)

    D: *jetzt hast du ganz bunte hände.*
            now have you very colorful hands
    Anna: **abwasch.**
            off-wash
    D: *ach, machen wir nachher,*
            allright, do we later
            brauchst du jetzt noch nicht.
            must you now not yet
    Anna: *doch,* **wasch** *ich* **ab**
            no, wash I off

(20) 'Verb fronting' in Anna (2;1–2;2)

    mami **ruft** *jetz* **an.** (2;1)
    mommy calls now up
    das krokodil **frisst** *dich* **auf.** (A 2;1)
    the crocodile swallows you up
    der **frisst** *dich* **auf.** (A 2;1)
    he swallows you up
    schmeißt *du den* **weg**? (A 2;2)
    throw you that away?
    die **frisst** *dich* **auf** xx. (A 2;2)
    she swallows you up

To conclude, language acquisition in Dutch and German children is a developmental process. It proceeds from an initial, lexical stage to the adult-like, functional stage. The essential move towards the functional stage concerns the acquisition of the linguistic means to express semantic finiteness and topicality. Both the verbal element carrying the semantic function of finiteness and the non-verbal element with topic function occur in the functional prefield of the utterance, i.e. in V2 and initial, topic position, respectively. They are elements of a functional projection (F). Semantic finiteness is a linguistic feature of information structure which indicates that the utterance is to be interpreted as an assertion, i.e. as a means to express that a particular situation is the case. Topicality is a linguistic feature of information structure that holds for elements that are used to *identify* the situation that the assertion applies to (i.e. the topic situation TS). Both semantic finiteness and topicality cooperate as far as their communicative function is concerned. This seems to warrant the conclusion that language development in Dutch and German children is geared towards the acquisition of the functional features of the target language as a linguistic means to establish contextual cohesion.

References

Bittner, Dagmar. 2003. The emergence of verb inflection in two German speaking children. In Dagmar Bittner, Wolfgang U. Dressler & Marianne Kilani-Schoch (eds.), *Development of verb inflection in first language acquisition*, 53–88. Berlin: De Gruyter.

Chomsky, Noam. 1995. *The Minimalist Program*. Cambridge, MA: MIT Press.

Clahsen, Harald. 1986. Verb inflections in German child language: Acquisition of agreement markings and the functions they encode. *Linguistics* 24, 79–121.

Clark, Eve V. 2003. *First language acquisition*. Cambridge: Cambridge University Press.

Corder, S. Pit. 1978. 'Simple codes' and the source of the second language learner's initial heuristic hypothesis. *Studies in Second Language Acquisition* 1, 1–10.

De Haan, Ger. 1987. A theory-bound approach to the acquisition of verb placement in Dutch. In Ger de Haan & Wim Zonneveld (eds.), *Formal parameters of generative grammar. Yearbook 1987*, 15–30. Dordrecht: ICG.

Dimroth, Christine, Petra Gretsch, Peter Jordens, Clive Perdue & Marianne Starren. 2003. Finiteness in Germanic languages. A stage-model for first and second language development. In Christine Dimroth & Marianne Starren (eds.), *Information structure and the dynamics of language acquisition*, 65–93. Amsterdam: John Benjamins.

Gillis, Steven. 2003. A case study of the early acquisition of verbs in Dutch. In Dagmar Bittner, Wolfgang U. Dressler & Marianne Kilani-Schoch (eds.), *Development of verb inflection in first language acquisition*, 171–203. Berlin: De Gruyter.

Hoekstra, Teun & Peter Jordens. 1994. From adjunct to head. In Teun Hoekstra & Bonnie D. Schwartz (eds.), *Language acquisition studies in generative grammar*, 119–149. Amsterdam: John Benjamins.

Ingram, David & William Thompson. 1996. Early syntactic acquisition in German: Evidence for the Modal Hypothesis. *Language* 72, 97–120.

Jolink, Anke. 2009. Finiteness in children with SLI. A functional approach. In Christine Dimroth & Peter Jordens (eds.), *Functional categories in learner language*, 235–259. Berlin/New York: De Gruyter.

Jordens, Peter. 1990. The acquisition of verb placement in Dutch and German. *Linguistics* 28, 1407–1448.

Jordens, Peter. 2012. *Language acquisition and the functional category system*. Berlin/New York: De Gruyter.

Klein, Wolfgang. 1997. Learner varieties are the *normal* case. *The Clarion. Magazine of the European Second Language Association* 3, 4–6.

Klein, Wolfgang. 1998. Assertion and finiteness. In Norbert Dittmar & Zvi Penner (eds.), *Issues in the theory of language acquisition*, 225–245. Bern: Peter Lang.

Klein, Wolfgang. 2008. The topic situation. In Bernt Ahrenholz, Ursula Bredel, Wolfgang Klein, Martina Rost-Roth & Romuald Skiba (eds.), *Empirische Forschung und Theoriebildung. Beiträge aus Soziolinguistik, Gesprochene Sprache- und Zweitspracherwerbsforschung. Festschrift für Norbert Dittmar zum 65. Geburtstag*, 287–305. Frankfurt am Main: Lang.

Klein, Wolfgang & Clive Perdue. 1997. The Basic Variety (Or: Couldn't languages be much simpler?). *Second Language Research* 13, 301–347.

Perdue, Clive. 2006. "Creating language anew": Some remarks on an idea of Bernard Comrie's. *Linguistics* 44, 853–871.

Poeppel, David & Kenneth Wexler. 1993. The Full Competence Hypothesis of clause structure in early German. *Language* 69, 1–33.

Selinker, Larry. 1972. Interlanguage. *International Review of Applied Linguistics* 10, 209–231.

Vainikka, Anne & Martha Young-Scholten. 2011. *The acquisition of German. Introducing Organic Grammar*. Berlin/Boston: Walter de Gruyter.

Verrips, Maaike. 1996. *Potatoes must peel. The acquisition of the Dutch passive*. Ph.D. dissertation: University of Amsterdam.

Peter Jordens
Developmental language disorder and the functional category system

Abstract: Developmental language disorder (DLD) in children learning their mother tongue concerns 'persisting linguistic difficulties' (Fletcher 1999) leading to 'a significant delay' (Leonard 2014) in language acquisition. Empirical investigations have shown that these linguistic difficulties can be characterized as due to a morpho-syntactic deficit. This leaves us with the question of the exact nature of this selective deficit. In a seminal study, Clahsen (1999) has put forward his 'missing agreement hypothesis'. It should account for the fact that German speaking children with DLD would have difficulty with the linguistic feature of control agreement playing a role in, for example, subject-verb agreement (*ich bleibe* vs. *du bleibst* vs. *er bleibt*.- I stay vs. you stay vs. he stays) and case marking (*sie vertraut* **ihm** vs. *sie mag ihn*. – she trusts him vs. she likes him), while they would not have a problem with linguistic features such as noun plurals (*Wiese* vs.*Wiesen* – meadow vs. meadows; *Buch* vs. *Bücher* – book vs. books) and past-participle inflection (*gesucht* vs. *gefunden* – searched vs. found) where control agreement does *not* play a role. For English speaking children with DLD, Leonard (2014) has categorized a range of grammatical elements that are associated with 'the notion of functional categories' such as articles (*a* and *the*), prenominal determiners (*this, that, these, those*), third singular -*s* (agreement), regular past -*ed* (tense), the use of the complementizers *that, if*, auxiliary inversion and *wh*-questions. The present study is concerned with DLD in children speaking Dutch and German. Focus of this study is the developmental characteristics of DLD in these languages. As a point of reference an overview is given of the developmental process of language acquisition in typically developing children. Language development in these children is a two-stage process in which at some point the initial, lexical system will be given up in favour of a targetlike, functional system. It is argued that the relevant developmental process in children with DLD is subject to delay. It is claimed that this accounts for the linguistic difficulties that these children are facing. However, this leaves us with the question of the cause of the delay. Our findings will be interpreted in terms of the computational demands of language processing at the functional stage, more specifically, the computational problem to establish contextual cohesion. It will be argued that this computational problem is due to an underdeveloped working memory.

Peter Jordens, Amsterdam VU University, The Netherlands; Max Planck Institute for Psycholinguistics, Nijmegen, The Netherlands; e-mail: jorde074@planet.nl

https://doi.org/10.1515/9783110712025-002

Keywords: developmental language disorder, Dutch and German, linguistic deficit, control agreement, functional category system, contextual cohesion, working memory

1 Introduction

Children with Developmental Language Disorder (DLD) are diagnosed as "children for whose non-typical language acquisition there is *no identifiable* physical or psychological basis." In other words, children with DLD "have normal hearing, intelligence within normal limits, an apparently intact neurological substrate, and no behavioural or emotional disorder. They nevertheless have persisting linguistic difficulties" (Fletcher 1999, 350) that are characterized as a 'significant delay' (Leonard 2014, 3).[1] The cause of this delay is commonly stated as 'unknown'. Hence, the manifestation of this defect is labelled as 'unexplained language problems' (Bishop 2014, 382).

The conclusion that there is *no identifiable* physical or psychological basis for DLD is appreciated among linguists as evidence that the development of grammar is "largely autonomous from developments in other cognitive domains" (Clahsen 1999, 700). Consequently, it is argued that DLD typically involves "selective deficits of the language faculty itself" (Clahsen 1999, 676).

2 DLD as a selective linguistic deficit

In the following, we will discuss a few proposals that have been shown relevant with respect to the idea that DLD should be caused by a selective deficit of the language faculty.

2.1 Morphological deficit

Given the idea of a DLD as a morphological deficit, there is the observation that children with DLD have a problem with the use of /s/ in *keeps* and not in *dance*. Leonard (1995) accounted for this by claiming that this particular problem is due

---

[1] Leonard (2014, 3): "A significant delay in language learning that cannot be attributed to hearing loss, low nonverbal intelligence or neurological damage."

to the fact that children with DLD have "a limitation in [their] processing capacity that is overburdened when the children are faced with grammatical morphemes of relatively short duration" (1273). Clahsen (1999), however, has argued against DLD as a general defect of inflectional morphology. He shows that independently of its duration inflectional morphology is sometimes impaired, sometimes it is not. That is, he found that, on the one hand, inflectional morphology is *impaired* with person and number agreement, the use of auxiliaries and modals, case and gender marking, while, on the other hand, it is *not impaired* with noun plurals and participle inflection. Examples are given in (1).

(1) Inflectional morphology in children with DLD (Clahsen 1999)

   impaired:
   - Person and number agreement as it becomes manifest with suffixes on finite verbs controlled by the subject (683f.), like in *ich bleibe* vs. *du bleibst* vs. *er bleibt* vs. *sie bleiben*. (I stay vs. you stay vs. he stays vs. they stay).
   - Auxiliaries and modals as they are controlled by the non-finite verb (684f.), like in *hat geschlafen* vs. *ist gefallen* vs. *kann schlafen* (has slept vs. is fallen vs. can sleep).
   - Case marking as it is controlled by the lexical verb (685f.), like in *mich friert* vs. *mir schwant Böses* (me freezes vs. me presumes evil) or *sie vertraut ihm* vs. *sie mag ihn* (she trusts him-DAT vs. she likes him-ACC).
   - Gender marking as it is controlled by the noun (686f.), like in *der schöne Garten, ein schöner Garten* (masc.) vs. *die schöne Wiese, eine schöne Wiese* (fem.) vs. *das schöne Schloss, ein schönes Schloss* (neuter) (the nice garden, a nice garden vs. the nice meadow, a nice meadow vs. the nice castle, a nice castle).

   not impaired:
   - Noun plurals, like in *Garten* vs. *Gärten* (garden vs. gardens), *Wiese* vs. *Wiesen* (meadow vs. meadows), *Schloss* vs. *Schlösser* (castle vs. castles) (687f.).
   - Participle inflection, like in *gesucht* vs. *gefunden* (searched vs. found) (691f.).

Given these observations, Clahsen concludes that "[DLD] children do not have a general deficit in inflectional morphology" (692). Instead, he puts forward the claim that DLD is due to a *grammatical agreement* deficit (see 2.4 below). This should explain why in children with DLD plural marking as for example in *many bikes* is generally correct, while person and number marking as in *he bikes* is not.

2.2 Morpho-syntactic deficit

In a study on the spontaneous production data of a typically developing German child, Poeppel and Wexler (1993) have claimed that the only difference between child and adult grammar was the use of the so called 'optional infinitive'. This means that typically developing German children would initially use an infinite verb form in final position as in (2a) instead of the correct finite verb form in second position as in (2b).

(2) *haben* (have-Inf) vs. *hab, hat* (have-1st Sg, has-3rd Sg)
    a. *du das **haben***. (Andreas 2;1)
        you that have [= get. Inf]
        *saft **habe***. (Simone 1;10,20)
        juice have [= get. Inf]
    b. *ich **hab** tein bürse*. (Andreas 2;1)
        I have [a] small brush
        ***hat** noch schinken drauf.* (Simone 2;1,18)
        has also ham it-on

With respect to children with DLD, Rice and Wexler (1996) argue for the hypothesis of the 'Extended optionality of infinitives'. This means that, while their grammar does not lack finiteness, young children with [DLD] typically demonstrate "a lower-than-expected use of finite forms over an extended period of time" (227).

2.3 Functional-grammatical deficit

Leonard (1995) argues that the problem that children with DLD are faced with is the acquisition of a range of grammatical elements that are associated with "the notion of functional categories". This holds, as far as the D-system is concerned, for the use of articles (*a* and *the*), prenominal determiners (*this, that, these, those*), pronominal possessives (*my pillow, his hammer*), genitive *'s* and non-thematic *of*. As far as the I-system is concerned, it holds for the use of third singular *-s* (agreement), regular past *-ed* (tense), copula *be*, auxiliary *be*, infinitival *to*, modal (+ negative), auxiliary *do* (+ negative) and nominative case. Finally, as far as the C-system is concerned, it holds for the use of the complementizers *that, if,* auxiliary inversion in *wh*-questions (*what can we do?*) and indirect questions (*so I can see what I need; I know where that go*). Leonard, however, notes that it is not the case that these functional elements are absent.[2] It is just that children with DLD "used the grammatical elements associated with these categories to a more limited degree than their MLU controls" (1279).

In a similar vein, Hamann, Lindner and Penner (2001) argue that for children with DLD "it seems [. . .] that the problems are located in the language module, more specifically in the syntactic component" (183). They use the term 'CP trouble', that is, "the syntactic production of German children with DLD points to a deficit in the Complementizer Phrase (CP)" (184). This should explain their "difficulty in anchoring utterances in discourse" (183) "especially their bad performance with respect to the interpretation of complex tenses" (184). In addition, they note, that there is "a similar difficulty for normally developing children up to their third birthday" (183).

2.4 Grammatical agreement deficit

Clahsen (1999) argues, as mentioned before, that DLD children have difficulty "in establishing grammatical agreement processes" (678). The particular nature of this morphological deficit leads him to propose the 'missing agreement hypothesis'. Agreement he defines as "an asymmetrical relation between two categories, where one is a functor and the other is an argument controlling the functor" (681). For example, with subject-verb agreement, the finite verb (functor) is controlled by the subject (argument) since it provides information about the subject. The idea is that the linguistic principle of control agreement is "not accessible to [DLD] children" (681). This should explain why DLD children have difficulty with the expression of morpho-syntactic features such as subject-verb agreement, co-occurrence of auxiliaries (*have/be*) with non-finite verb forms, morphological case marking and gender marking on determiners and adjectives (see 2.1 above).

2.5 Summary

Assuming that there is no identifiable physical or psychological basis for DLD there is a general feeling that DLD typically involves 'selective deficits of the language faculty itself'. In order to account for this idea different proposals have been put forward: a 'limitation in processing capacity with grammatical morphemes of rela-

---

2 ". . . none of the measures used in this study revealed evidence that suggested the absence of a functional category" (Leonard 1995, 1278).

tively short duration' (Leonard 1995); an 'extended optionality of infinitives' (Rice and Wexler 1996); a difficulty with the use of grammatical elements associated with the functional category system (Leonard 1995); a 'deficit in the complementizer phrase' (Hamann et al. 2001); and finally: a 'grammatical agreement deficit' (Clahsen 1999).

It should be noted however that, for the most part, these studies provide just an account of a set of empirical data, i.e. observations of the linguistic difficulties in children with DLD. Clahsen's study (1999) is an exception to the extent that he uses the available empirical data in order to test his 'missing agreement hypothesis'. Furthermore, as noted by Leonard (1995), the fact that children with DLD have difficulty with particular features of the linguistic system may not be a question of absence vs. presence of these features. Rather, it might be a question of less vs. more. That is, the relevant difficulties would occur in typically developing children (Hamann et al. 2001) only in the initial stages, while children with DLD should experience them over an extended period of time (Rice and Wexler 1996). Finally, a problem with the acquisition of a linguistic feature may be a problem of either formal or functional linguistic origin. Take, for example, the acquisition of 'verb second' (V2), i.e. the fact that the finite verb in Dutch and German occurs in second-constituent position. Is it the mechanism of 'verb movement', i.e. the relation between the non-finite verb in final position and the finite verb in second position that is difficult to acquire? Or is it the acquisition of 'semantic finiteness' (Klein 1998, 227), i.e. the acquisition of the linguistic means used to assert that something is the case, that causes the problem?

In the following, we will, first, present a discussion of some relevant data from empirical studies on DLD carried out earlier. Then, assuming that DLD is primarily a developmental delay, we will provide a hypothesis based on evidence of a stage-wise process of language acquisition in typically developing children. Our focus will be on children learning Dutch and German. Finally, our findings will be interpreted in terms of the ability of typically developing and DLD children to meet the computational demands using the functional linguistic means to establish contextual cohesion.

3 DLD data discussion

In the following we will discuss a range of empirical data from children with DLD. These data are taken from studies by Clahsen (1999) and Hansson and Nettelbladt (1991). Clahsen's study is an extensive overview of relevant data as they are presented in the literature on children with DLD learning German, English and Italian. Hansson and Nettelbladt investigated the spontaneous language production in children with DLD learning Swedish.

3.1 Control agreement Clahsen (1999)

Clahsen's study is basically a re-analysis of a collection of empirical investigations. It aims to provide an account of the relevant DLD data in terms of morpho-syntactic features that are either 'impaired' or 'not impaired'. With this study, Clahsen seeks to substantiate his claim of DLD being a deficit "in establishing grammatical agreement processes" (677) referred to as 'missing control agreement'. As stated before, control agreement is obtained if there is "an asymmetrical relation between two categories, where one is a functor and the other is an argument controlling the functor" (Clahsen 1999, 681). Clahsen distinguished between morpho-syntactic features that are subject to control agreement (such as subject-verb agreement) and morpho-syntactic features (such as noun plurals) that are not. His prediction is that children with DLD will typically show evidence of 'missing control agreement' such that morphological inflection that is subject to control agreement is impaired, while morphological inflection that is *not* subject to control agreement is not impaired. The relevant empirical data seem to confirm Clahsen's predictions. However, Clahsen notes that impaired morphological inflection does not only occur as the result of missing control agreement. It also occurs in unpredicted cases such as 'tense' where missing control agreement does not play a role.

In the following, we will give a summary of Clahsen's (1999) findings on the impairment of morpho-syntactic features mainly in German children with DLD.

3.1.1 Impaired inflection in children with DLD

(a) **'Predicted impairment': Evidence of a morpho-syntactic deficit due to missing control agreement**

Subject-verb agreement: 'considerably delayed' (684)
Several studies on German-speaking children with DLD show that overall subject-verb agreement emerged "considerably later than in normal children" (683f.), that is in many of these children not before they were 6 years of age. While typically developing children were able to use finite verb forms correctly inflected for person and number, DLD children typically used zero morphology or the infinitive form *-n* as a default form. Nevertheless, although DLD children generally do not use subject-verb agreement productively, they have "a small set of (stored)

finite verb forms, for example modals, a restricted class of verbs appearing with the suffix -*t* and a few auxiliaries" (699).³

Auxiliaries and copulas: 'much less frequent and often omitted' (685)
Clahsen notes that "[a]ll the children used modal verbs, but auxiliaries and copulas were rare and were omitted in most of the obligatory contexts" (685)⁴

Case marking: 'regular case affixation remains to be problematic' (686)
German-speaking DLD children "only have a binary case system with nominative forms and either accusatives or datives [while] in most cases, the genitive suffix was left out." Furthermore, "there were no instances of case agreement within NPs" (685).

Gender marking: '[no] gender oppositions being established' (687)
While in typically developing children gender oppositions are completed by age 3;0, most of the German-speaking DLD children "neutralized gender distinctions of adult German by using gender-neutral articles." These gender-neutral articles were used to express 'definiteness vs. indefiniteness'. That is, either *de* or *die* for definite and *ein* for indefinite noun phrases. "Other children, who had different gender-marked articles, produced many errors." It should be noted that 'definiteness' as it is used by DLD children depends on whether the NP occurs in initial (topic) position or in final (focus) position. Definiteness as a morpho-syntactic feature of the target language is used independently of the position of the NP to indicate whether its referent is identifiable or not.

(b) 'Unpredicted impairment': Cases of a morpho-syntactic deficit outside the range of missing control agreement

As Clahsen notes, outside the range of missing control agreement, DLD children have problems with verb second, tense marking and reversible passives. These problems are evidence of what he refers to as 'unpredicted impairment'.

---

3 As we will argue below, this is also the case in typically developing Dutch and German children at the initial, lexical stage. At the relevant stage, there is a small set of finite verb forms, usually referred to as 'light verbs', that has aspectual meaning and is used with the same function as modal verbs. Furthermore, the restricted class of verbs with the suffix -*t* pertains to the semantic category of state and change-of-state verbs. These verbs occur in the input systematically in second position and therefore, at the lexical stage, they are stored as 'finite-verb' forms, too (Jordens 2012, 124ff., Jordens and Bittner 2017, 377ff.).

4 It seems a distinction has to be made between *is* serving as the copula as in *Er ist groß* and *is* serving as a lexical state verb as in *Er ist zu hause*.

Verb second: 'no generalized V2'
In a study by Clahsen (1991) it was shown that "none of the 10 [DLD] children had generalized V2, that is, the syntactic rule of adult German that moves all finite verbs to the second structural position in main clauses" (692). Thus, these children did not systematically use, for example, both *jetzt ei* **essen** (now egg eat-Inf) vs. *papa* **isst** *ei* (daddy eats-3Sg egg) or *krokodil* **kommt** (crocodile comes-3Sg) vs. *du auch* **kommen** (you too come-Inf). Clahsen argues that the relevant syntactic phenomenon of verb movement is 'indirectly controlled' by the presence of subject-verb agreement. Thus, "if the grammar has a productive subject-verb agreement paradigm" (699), it should also have verb second. Hence, absence of subject-verb agreement would explain impairment of V2.[5]

Tense marking: 'difficulty with the regular past-tense rule'
According to Clahsen, tense marking as, for example, in *Er macht einen Spaziergang* vs. er *machte er einen Spaziergang,* is "directly marked on the verb rather than being controlled by some other sentential element" (699). Tense marking is therefore *not* a case of control agreement. This is in consonance with Booij (1996) who categorizes tense as an example of inherent inflection. Thus, when Clahsen notes that DLD children have problems with past-tense marking, he views the relevant data as cases of unpredicted impairment (699). Hence, "the nature of the DLD children's problems with TENSE is unclear" (700).

Reversible passives / Word order: 'for example, *John was killed by Bill*'
Word order variation causes problems for DLD children, too. More specifically, referring to Van der Ley and Harris (1990) among others, Clahsen notes that "English-speaking DLD children [were] unable to correctly comprehend reversible passive sentences with novel verbs" (699). So, for example, in an utterance such as *John was killed by Bill*, "*John* is identified as the external argument of the verb *kill*" (699). Reversible passives, however, have nothing to do with control agreement. Hence, DLD children's problems with this type of word order variation are, according to Clahsen, to be labelled as cases of unpredicted impairment, too.

---

[5] For Clahsen subject-verb agreement is a condition for the acquisition of V2. However, we would rather argue that V2 is a condition for the acquisition of subject-verb agreement. The acquisition of V2, in turn, depends on the availability of a structural position for a finite verb as is evident from the presence of an auxiliary or a modal verb in, for example, *Er hat einen Spaziergang* **gemacht** (He had a walk made) or *er* **will** *einen Spaziergang* **machen** (He wants a walk make) vs. *Er* **macht** *einen Spaziergang (He makes a walk).*

3.1.2 Not-impaired inflection in children with DLD: Evidence of correct inflection outside the range of control agreement

According to Clahsen, as noted before, "[DLD] children do not have a *general* deficit in inflectional morphology" (692). Inflectional morphology is impaired only in cases of grammatical control agreement. Thus, inflectional morphology that is grammatically independent, i.e. outside the range of control agreement, should be not impaired. This explains why plural marking with nouns, participle inflection, inflectional morphology with modals and some frequently used lexical verbs is generally correct.

Noun Plurals: 'not impaired in [DLD]'
Clahsen (1999) refers to several studies showing that in spontaneous speech "the acquisition of German noun plurals is not impaired in [DLD]" (689). Plural marking was generally correct for most of the DLD children while the error types were the same as with normal children.

Participle inflection: 'generally correct participle marking'
Clahsen and Rothweiler (1993) found that "the [DLD] children they have studied generally have correct participle marking and the same error types as normal children" (691). "Apart from occasional cases of zero suffixation, [i.e. unmarked present-tense stems], the only source of errors is that strong verbs in German are categorized by the children as regular verbs, and are suffixed with the default affix *-t* instead of the irregular affix *-n*, for example, *geheht instead of *gegangen* (gone) or *gebratet instead of *gebraten* (fried)" (691).

Modals: 'all the children used modal verbs'
"In several studies on German-speaking [DLD] children, it has been reported that these children have considerable difficulty with auxiliaries, but not with modals and lexical verbs." (685).

3.2 Missing verb second

As Clahsen argued above, due to the absence of verb movement children with DLD have no verb second. Absence of a structural verb second position also means that the current grammatical system does not have a structural position for a constituent with topic function utterance-initially. So, with this grammatical system it should be impossible for DLD children to use non-subjects, i.e. adverbs or objects, in initial, topic position, and consequently it should also be impossible to use the subject (S) after V2. In short, children with DLD will not be able to produce XVS word order. Evidence for this is shown in the data presented in Håkansson and Nettelbladt (1993). The relevant data in Table 1 show that typically developing Swedish children use XVS from relatively early on, whereas for children with DLD it takes a long time before they may use this option too.

Table 1: Sentences *without* V-2nd: XSV (Håkansson and Nettelbladt 1993).

L1				DLD			
Karin		Martin		Alfons		Beda	
age	%XSV	age	%XSV	age	%XSV	age	%XSV
1;11	0	2;8	0	5;11	26	5;07	35
2;07	0	2;11	1	7;01	20	6;07	13
3;01	0	3;01	0	8;03	0	8;04	0

Nevertheless, due to input pressure DLD children with no V2 may want to produce utterances with an element in initial position to establish a relation to a 'topic situation', i.e. a situation that the utterance applies to. This 'topic element' may be a non-subject like an object or an adverbial. However, given the fact that the grammatical system of children with DLD at the relevant stage has no V2 position, and therefore also no position for the subject after V2, these children are faced with the problem where to put the subject. In order to solve this problem, the children with DLD find two possible ways to accommodate for this. Either they use both the topicalized adverbial *and* the subject in initial position before the finite verb, or they simply omit the subject. As shown in (3), this is what happened in (3a) and (3b) and in (3c) and (3d), respectively.

(3) 'No V-2nd' and 'subject omission' in DLD Swedish (Hansson and Nettelbladt 1995)
    a. *nu jag **vill** lyssna.*
         now I will listen
    b. *sen jag **äta** sa manga ganger.*
         then I eat so many times
    c. *inte kann ha blommor i skorsten.*
         Not can have flowers in chimney
    d. *vann med bilen.*
         won with car-the

Thus, as shown in Clahsen (1999) for children with DLD learning German, the grammatical system of Swedish children with DLD has no targetlike V2 position, either.

3.3 Summary

Research on language impairment in children with DLD leads Clahsen to conclude that there is no *general* deficit in inflectional morphology. The deficit in inflectional morphology seems limited to agreement morphology when agreement is defined in terms of an asymmetrical relation between argument (controller) and functor (controllee). In other words, when children with DLD show a developmental delay in the acquisition of inflectional morphology, it seems to matter whether the inflectional morphology is a case of agreement morphology or not. However, considering the relevant data, Clahsen acknowledges that children with DLD have morpho-syntactic problems that his missing agreement hypothesis cannot account for. Table 2 provides an overview of Clahsen's account of the DLD the data as presented in the literature.

Table 2: Inflectional morphology in children with DLD: impaired vs. not impaired.

	impaired / morpho-syntactic deficit	not impaired / no morpho-syntactic deficit
predicted:	**missing control agreement** subj-verb agreement; auxiliaries and copulas; case marking; gender marking	**no control agreement** noun plurals; participle inflection; modals
not predicted:	**no missing control agreement** verb second; tense marking; reversible passives / word order	

In the following, in order to understand *why* DLD children have the morpho-syntactic and syntactic problems as outlined in Section 3.1 and 3.2, we will propose an alternative view of the relevant data. It aims to cover not only what Clahsen identified as evidence of a grammatical agreement deficit but also what appears as evidence of morpho-syntactic difficulty outside the range of missing agreement. That is, we will argue that the whole range of problems comprises precisely what typically developing children encounter when they proceed from a simple, lexical learner system to a fully-fledged, adult-like functional system.

4 Hypothesis

Spontaneous language learning in typically developing children shows that language development occurs stage-wise. A stage is defined as a period of time during which language production is based on a coherent system of linguistic principles and categories. Although language learning proceeds gradually, it seems possible to define stages of language development in terms of language systems with increasing degrees of complexity. Developmental progress is achieved when a system that is linguistically relatively simple is given up in favour of a system that is linguistically more complex.

As will be shown in Section 5, the early language system of children learning Dutch or German is a lexical system, i.e. a language system that is solely based on the lexical projection of types of verb-argument structure. This basic, learner system marks the beginning of a two-stage process of language development in which the initial, lexical system will be given up in favour of a targetlike, functional system. This functional system provides the linguistic means to produce utterances as entities of information structure. It implies that the speaker is able to meet the computational demands to achieve contextual cohesion.

In the following, it will be argued that the morpho-syntactic problems of Dutch and German children with DLD are due to the fact that these children tend to keep with their initial, lexical language system. More specifically, it will be claimed that the problem of DLD is in fact the problem of children having to deal with the linguistic demands of a functional language system, i.e. a language system with functional morphology (i.e. morphological finiteness, tense-, case- and gender marking), function words (i.e. auxiliary verbs, determiners, anaphora, question words) and word order variation (i.e. verb movement and 'topicalization'[6]).

5 Stage-model of language development in Dutch and German

Language development in Dutch and German is basically a two-stage process. At the initial, lexical stage, both typically developing children and children with DLD are going to acquire the kind of knowledge that can be categorized in terms of

---

[6] Topicalization is the syntactic mechanism that accounts for the placement of any constituent in sentence-initial position to establish a relation of the utterance with the topic situation (TS), i.e. the situation that the utterance applies to.

constituent structures: VP (verb phrase), NP (noun phrase), AP (attribute phrase) and PP (prepositional phrase). Examples are given in (4) – (8).

For examples of utterances with VP-constituents, i.e. lexical verbs (V) with or without a deontic modal (Mod) and verbal particles (Prt), see (4).

(4) VP-constituents in early child language
Dutch   German

*poes **bal hebbe**.* (J 1;11)   *du auch **malen**.* (A 1;11)
kitty ball get   you too draw
***kannie bal pakke**.* (J 1;9)   ***magnich nase putzen**.* (C 2;0)
can-not ball get   like-not nose clean
*ikke **glijbaan (ge)maakt**.* (J 2;1) *so, **noch eine macht**.* (A 2;0)
I slide [have] made   thus, [daddy has] another one made
*popje **valt** bijna.* (J 1;10)   *ente **fällt**.* (C 2;0)
doll falls nearly   duck falls
*g(r)ote paard **is** hier.* (A 2;1)   *die **is(t)** da.* (C 2;1)
big horse is here   that-one is there
*goene **aan**.* (A 1;11)   *mund **zu**.* (A 2;0)
shoes on   mouth closed

For examples of utterances with NP-constituents: nouns, proper names and deictic pronominal elements, see (5).

(5) NP-constituents in early child language
Dutch   German

***poes** bal hebbe.* (J 1;11)   ***du** auch malen.* (A1;11)
kitty ball get   you too draw
***Jaja** magwel hondje aaie.* (A 2;2) ***papa** nich(t) soll hier reinkomm(en).* (A 2;0)
J may-indeed doggie caress   daddy not must here it-in-come
***jij** g(l)ijbaan make.* (A 2;1)   ***ich** tür aufmachen.* (C 2;1)
you slide make   I door open-make
***Jaja** heef(t) koud.* (A 2;1)   ***eina** fehlt noch.* (C 2;1)
J has cold   one misses still

For examples of utterances with AP-constituents: adverbials and adjectives, see (6).

(6) AP-constituents in early child language
 Dutch German

*poes komt **niet**.* (J 1;11)   ***hier** kommt die mamma, **hier**.* (A 1;11)
kitty comes not   here comes mommy here
***da** zit mama.* (J 1;11)   *die is(t) **da**.* (C 2;1)
there sits mommy   that-one is there
*uil, **zo** komt.* (J 1;10)   *du **auch** malen.* (A 1;11)
owl, so comes   you too draw
*kan**wel** papa zitte.* (A 2;1) *tan-**schon** dis (r)eintun.* (C 2;1)
can-indeed [with] daddy sit-down can-indeed this in-do
*Jaja mag**wel** hondje aaie.* (A 2;2) *muss **aba** uhu anmalen.* (C 2;1)
J may-indeed doggie caress   must however owl on-paint
*mag-ikke **ook** gijbaan?* (A 2;0) *der teddy will **auch noch**.* (A 2;1)
may-I too slide?   the teddy wants also
*popje valt **bijna**.* (J 1;10) *passt **bald**.* (C 2;0)
doll falls nearly   fits soon
*Jaja heef(t) **koud**.* (A 2;1) *ist das **nass**.* (A 2;0)
J has cold   is that wet

For examples of utterances with PP-constituents: prepositional phrases, see (7).

(7) PP-constituents in early child language
 Dutch German

*pop da-**in**.* (J 1;10)   *ke(r)ze **drin**.* (A 2;0)
doll there in   candle in
*[popje] sit-ie **da-in**.* (J 1;10) *passt nicht **rein**.* (A 2;0)
doll sit-it there-in   fits not it-in
*da valt-ie **uit**.* (J 1;7)   *Jonas passt noch **rauf**.* (A 2;0)
there falls-it off   J fits also it-on
*magniet **oppe dak**.* (J 1;11) *ein (k)nopf (d)**ran**.* (A 1;11)
may-not on-the roof   a button it-on
*[paard] zit-ie **oppe dak**.* (J 1;11) *kein mütze **auf**.* (A 2;0)
horse sits-it on-the roof   no cap on
*kom es **inne huisje**.* (J 2;0) *da geht der **aus**.* (A 2;0)
come in-the house   there goes he out

VP-, NP-, AP- and PP-structures are the building blocks of a basic, lexical system. This learner system will at some point be given up in favour of a targetlike, functional system. At the initial stage this basic, learner system has available two types of lexical structure: agentive utterances (type A) and non-agentive utterances (type B).

The agentive utterances of type A may typically be used with a modal/aspectual element (Mod/Asp) in second-constituent position, while the utterances of type B may not. Elements of Mod/Asp serve as the head of a head-complement structure that is used to express the semantics of volition, ability, permission or obligation. In other words, they express the meaning of some kind of 'control'. So, presence or absence of control (CTL) explains why utterances of type A are agentive, while utterances of type B are not.

In utterances of type A, the modal/aspectual head has an agentive VP as its complement and an agent as its external argument, that may be left unexpressed as in Dutch **kannie bal pakke** ([I] can-not ball get) or German **magnich nase putzen** ([I] like-not nose clean). The head of the projection of CTL, i.e. a modal or aspectual element, may also be left unexpressed as, for example, in Dutch *poes bal* **hebbe** (kitty [want] ball get) or German *du auch* **malen** (you [may] too draw). Whether or not this is the case, type-A utterances are always used with a modal/aspectual meaning.[7]

The non-agentive utterances of type B are the projection of a non-agentive, verbal element (V) that refers to a state or a change of state. In utterances of type B, this verbal element serves as a predicate that has a theme as its external argument. Examples are Dutch *poes* **komt** *niet* (kitty comes not), *Jaja* **valt** *niet* (J falls not) and German *mama* **liegt** *da* (mommy lies there), *ente fällt* (duck falls). Utterances of type B are used to express that an object (the theme) is either in a particular state or undergoing a particular change of state.

At the lexical stage, word order is determined by the semantic principle 'Agent first'. Only in absence of an agent, the theme may occur in initial position. Furthermore, verb forms are used morphologically unanalyzed, i.e. as they occur in the input. Hence, in type-A utterances the agentive verb occurring in final position appears as 'infinite', while in type-B utterances the state- or change-of-state verb occurring in second position appears as 'finite'.

As shown in Figure 1, the utterances of type A and type B are structurally identical. As soon as children recognize that this is the case, they have discovered that, at the lexical stage, utterances are the linguistic expression of the projection of a lexical head V as represented in Figure 2.

---

[7] At the relevant stage, children may leave anything unexpressed except for the predicate. Unexpressed means: left to be inferred.

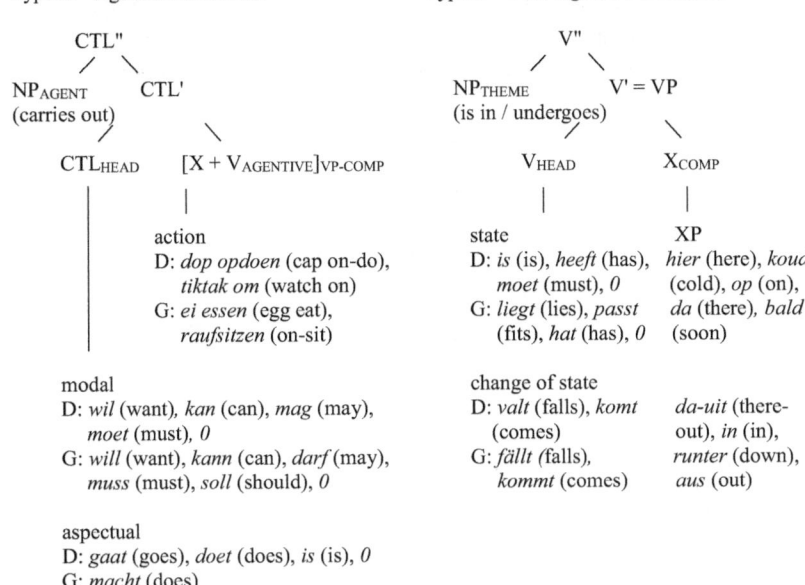

Figure 1: Utterance structure at the lexical stage.

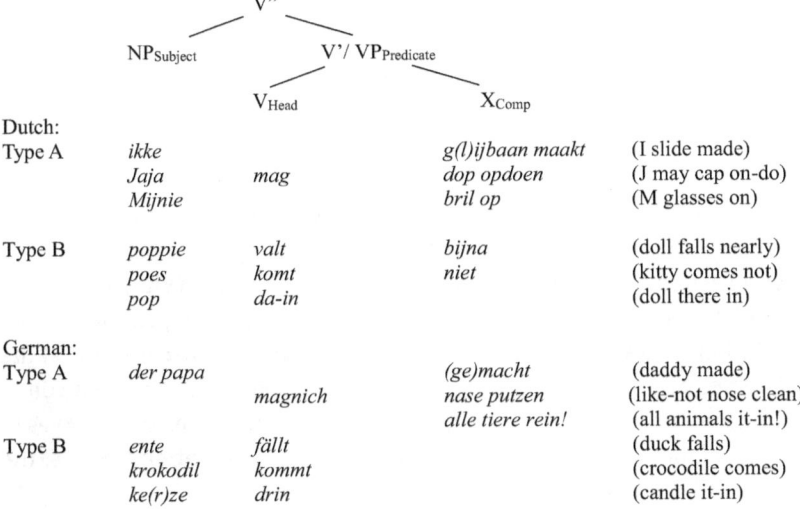

Figure 2: The full projection of the lexical head V.

In the target language, as shown in Jordens and Bittner (this volume), utterances are the expression of an underlying structure as represented in Figure 3, i.e. utterances are the expression of the projection of the functional head F.

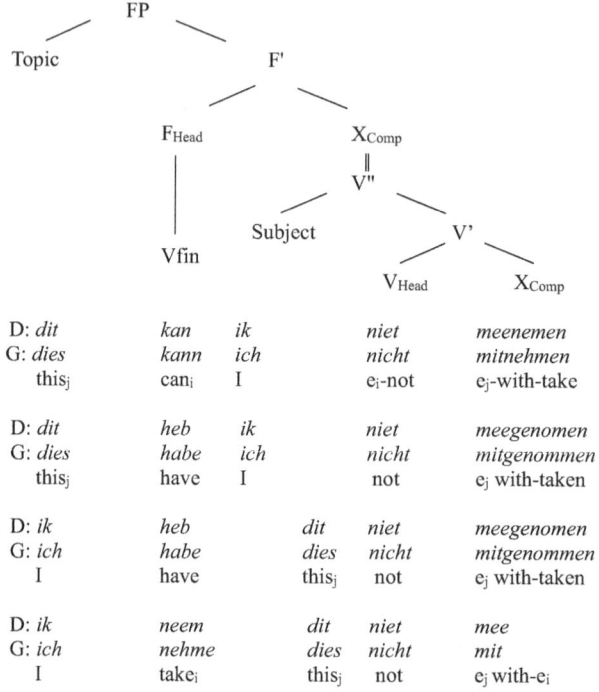

D: *dit*	*kan*	*ik*		*niet*	*meenemen*
G: *dies*	*kann*	*ich*		*nicht*	*mitnehmen*
this$_j$	can$_i$	I		e$_i$-not	e$_j$-with-take
D: *dit*	*heb*	*ik*		*niet*	*meegenomen*
G: *dies*	*habe*	*ich*		*nicht*	*mitgenommen*
this$_j$	have	I		not	e$_j$ with-taken
D: *ik*	*heb*		*dit*	*niet*	*meegenomen*
G: *ich*	*habe*		*dies*	*nicht*	*mitgenommen*
I	have		this$_j$	not	e$_j$ with-taken
D: *ik*	*neem*		*dit*	*niet*	*mee*
G: *ich*	*nehme*		*dies*	*nicht*	*mit*
I	take$_i$		this$_j$	not	e$_j$ with-e$_i$

Figure 3: The full projection of the functional head F.

The presence of a functional head F accounts for the fact that the target-language system has two structural positions in the so-called functional prefield of the utterance: a second-constituent position F for the finite verb (Vfin) to express semantic finiteness and an initial position for a constituent to express topicality. Semantic finiteness is a category of information structure used to express that the utterance serves as an assertion. It indicates that the speaker asserts that something is the case. Topicality is a category of information structure, too. It serves to establish the relation between the assertion and the topic situation (TS), i.e. the situation that the assertion applies to.

As argued in Jordens and Bittner (this volume), the acquisition of the functional head F seems to be the driving force of a developmental process as a result of which children are going to give up their current lexical system in favour of the adult-like functional system as represented in Figure 3.

In the following, we will argue that the morpho-syntactic problems of Dutch and German children with DLD are NOT due to just a linguistic deficit. Rather, these problems appear to be evidence of a developmental delay in the cognitive ability to meet the computational demands to express contextual cohesion. In fact, the linguistic features used to *create* contextual cohesion are linked to the functional linguistic mechanisms referred to as verb movement and topicalization. In order for these mechanisms to become in force, the grammatical system needs the instantiation of a structural, second position (F) for the finite verb and a structural initial position for a constituent functioning as the topic.

6 Predictions: DLD and the problem of contextual cohesion

As stated before, at the functional stage Dutch and German learners are going to create a language system with two structural positions utterance-initially to express contextual cohesion: the second-constituent position (F) for verb forms to express semantic finiteness and the initial-constituent position for elements to express topicality.

Semantic finiteness and topicality are expressed by particular morpho-syntactic features. So, semantic finiteness is carried by a verbal element. This verbal element can be either an auxiliary/modal verb or a lexical verb. If it is a lexical verb, it is placed in second position as the result of verb movement. The use of lexical verbs in second position is conditional for the acquisition of the morphological features of the finite verb, i.e. the morphological features of subject-verb agreement (person and number marking) and tense. Furthermore, identification of the subject as the argument controlling verb agreement is a prerequisite to the acquisition of case marking (nominative vs. non-nominative).

Topicality is exerted by a (pro)nominal or adverbial element in initial, topic position. Elements are placed in this position as the result of topicalization. In order for learners to acquire topicalization as a syntactic mechanism, they should know that any constituent no matter its semantic function can be placed in initial position to establish the relation between the assertion and the situation that the assertion applies to. Placement of an element in initial, topic position as the result of topicalization leads to the acquisition of the morphological features of the determiner to express definiteness (i.e. definite vs. indefinite) and the use of anaphora. That, in turn, is the condition for the acquisition of gender and nominal agreement. Finally, in addition to topicalization, elements can also be placed in initial position as the result of 'focalization'.[8] Focalization entails the acquisition of question words.

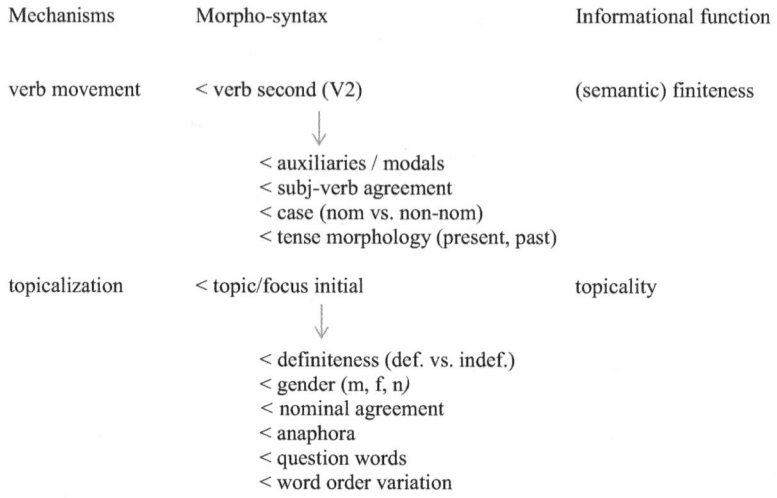

Figure 4: Morpho-syntactic features at the functional stage.

As summarized in Figure 4, at the functional stage, the possibility for Dutch and German children to establish contextual cohesion depends on the availability of a position for the expression of semantic finiteness and a position to express topicality. Both these positions are conditional for a number of morpho-syntactic features. The position for the expression of semantic finiteness is conditional for the acquisition of auxiliaries/modals, subject-verb agreement, case and the morphology of tense. The position to express topicality is conditional for the acquisition of definiteness vs. indefiniteness, gender, nominal agreement, anaphora and question words. Placement of elements in either of these positions is determined by the syntactic mechanisms of verb movement and topicalization (or focalization). Hence, verb movement and topicalization are the linguistic mechanisms defining the possibilities of word order variation.

In sum, in the target language Dutch and German, the presence of both a position for the expression of semantic finiteness and topicality provides the possibility to establish contextual cohesion. Assuming that for Dutch and German

---

[8] Focalization is the syntactic mechanism that accounts for the placement of any constituent in sentence-initial position *to ask for* a relation of the utterance with a topic situation (TS), i.e. the situation that the utterance *should* apply to.

children, DLD is due to the cognitive problem of how to meet the computational demands creating contextual cohesion, this should explain why these children are challenged to use the syntactic mechanisms of verb movement and topicalization.

7 Account of the empirical research data

Clahsen (1999) notes that children with DLD have no problem with the acquisition of noun plurals and participle marking, while with the acquisition of agreement, case and gender they do. He argues that this is because the language system of children with DLD is "missing control agreement". Clahsen's hypothesis covers a large amount of data, many from German speaking children with DLD. He concedes however, that this hypothesis fails to account for the absence of verb second, past tense and reversible passives, i.e. word order. These features are, according to Clahsen, "outside the range of missing agreement" and he therefore categorizes them as "unpredicted impairment".

In the following, we will argue that Clahsen's observation about inflectional morphology that is *not* impaired (as in noun plurals and participle marking) as opposed to inflectional morphology that *is* impaired (as in agreement, case, and gender), is fully in line with our hypothesis of a developmental delay in the acquisition of the linguistic means to establish contextual cohesion. That is, we claim that for children with DLD the problem is the developmental process from an initial system based on semantic categories to a targetlike system based on functional categories. This explains why DLD children have no problem with the acquisition of inherent (independent) inflectional morphology while with contextual (dependent) inflectional morphology they do. Inherent inflection contributes to the semantics of the noun or the verb, while contextual inflection depends on relevant external information. Furthermore, we will argue that our hypothesis of a developmental delay is also fit to account for what Clahsen labels as cases of 'unpredicted impairment', i.e. absence of verb second, past tense and reversible passives.

7.1 Inflectional morphology

Inherent inflectional morphology

As indicated before, Dutch and German children with DLD have no problem with some cases of inflectional morphology from early on. It concerns the inflectional morphology noun plurals and past-participle forms. Examples of noun plurals already occurring at the lexical stage are in Dutch: *brokjes* (kibbles), *blokketjes* (kibbles), *haartje(s)* (hair-Pl), *oge* (eyes), *plantjes* (plants), *beese* (animals), *sleutels* (keys), *vlokke* (flakes), *haare* (hair-Pl), *tanne* (teeth), *handjes* (little hands); and in German: *haare* (hair-Pl). Examples of past-participle forms also occurring at the lexical stage are in Dutch: *auvedaan* (ow-done), *omvald* (down-fallen), *wonne* (won), *afhaald* (away-taken), *knoeid* (messed), *scheurd* (torn), *opgete* (up-eaten), *afberope* (finished), *vonne* (found), *kege (gotten)*; and in German: *abwascht (up-washed)*, *abholt* (off-taken), *reingossen* (it-in-poured), *hinfallt* (down-fallen), *schafft* (made), *auskippt* (over-turned).

Why would this be so? Noun plurals and past participles are cases of so-called inherent inflectional morphology. That is, noun plurals and past-participles are lexical elements that are morphologically marked independently of other elements in the context. Therefore, lexical elements with this kind of morphology have a tendency to receive idiosyncratic meaning. That is, they may receive a meaning that holds for the lexical element as an unanalyzed whole. Thus, plural nouns as *haartjes* (Dutch) and *Haare* (German) (hair) refer to a concept such as a 'head of hair'.[9] The same is true for past participles. They are used to refer to a result state. For example *maakt* (Dutch) and *macht* (German) may refer to a concept such as 'fixed'. Typical examples are also child Dutch *afgelopen* (ended) and child German *aufgeschmissen* (desperate). As they are independent lexical elements, children do not use them with a finite or infinite form either.

Summarizing, inherent inflection is a linguistic feature of the lexical stage. Pluralization and past-participle formation are cases of inherent inflection. So, they are present at the lexical stage in children with DLD as is the case in typically developing children.

Contextual inflectional morphology

Inflectional morphology that depends on contextual information is a problem for children with DLD. Clahsen used the term 'control agreement' to indicate that this type of inflectional morphology depends on an external category that exerts control. Typical cases of contextual inflectional morphology are subject-verb agreement and case marking. So, with respect to subject-verb agreement Clahsen

---

9 Plural noun forms may also serve as input to processes of word formation as in Dutch *huizenmarkt* (housing market), *meisjesachtig* (girlish) and in German *Bücherregal* (bookcase), *kinderlos* (childless).

(1999) noted that typically developing children were able to use finite verb forms correctly inflected for person and number, while DLD children used zero morphology or the infinitive form -*n* as a default form. Furthermore, he also found that German-speaking DLD children "only have a binary case system with nominative forms and either accusatives or datives, [while] there were no instances of case agreement within NPs" (685).

Why would this be the case? In verb forms with subject-verb agreement as, for example, in Dutch *kookt* (cooks. 2/3Sg) or German kocht (cooks. 3Sg 2Pl), inflectional morphology is not part of the semantics of the verb. It is determined by contextual information regarding person and number of the subject. This means that the speaker needs to keep this kind of information in mind to be able to produce the correct verb form. Thus, as a linguistic feature of contextual cohesion, subject-verb agreement is typically acquired at the functional stage. For children with DLD however, keeping contextual information in mind makes subject-verb agreement computationally complex and therefore too demanding to produce.

Somewhat different is the situation with respect to the morphology of tense. For the use of a past-tense form as Dutch *kookte* (cooked. 1/2/3SgPast) or German *kochte* (cooked. 1/3SgPast) there is no particular linguistic category to serve as the controller. Therefore Clahsen argues that tense should not be problematic for children with DLD. However, Clahsen found that tense *is* a problem and, therefore, problems with tense should be categorized as cases of *unpredicted* impairment (Clahsen 1999, 699). Nevertheless, although it is certainly true that tense marking is not being controlled by some other sentential element, tense marking is yet under control. What controls the use of past-tense morphology is the particular time slot (the topic time: TT) that the assertion is about.[10] So, here too, inflection is determined by contextual information. As a linguistic feature of contextual cohesion, past-tense morphology is typically acquired at the functional stage. For children with DLD however, keeping contextual information in mind makes past-tense marking computationally complex and, thus, for children with DLD too demanding to produce.

Finally, case marking, i.e. the use of, for example, either the nominative or the accusative, depends on which participant has been selected to serve as the subject. This means that case marking is determined by contextual information, and, therefore, it should constitute a problem for children with DLD, too. However,

---

10 *Tense* is defined as in Klein (1994). It expresses the relation between the topic time (TT), i.e. "the time span to which the speaker's claim is confined" (6) and the time of utterance (TU), i.e. "the time at which the utterance is made" (3). Past tense is used to express that "TU is after TT" (124). The notion of the topic time as the time that the assertion is about presupposes a particular situation (topic situation TS) as a given.

this seems contrary to Clahsen (1999) who claimed that DLD children may "have a binary case system with nominative forms and either accusatives or datives" (685). Clahsen's observation can be explained, though, by the fact that at the lexical stage the relevant NPs are likely to refer to the *semantic function* of an external (nominative-marked) and an internal (accusative-marked) argument, respectively. In other words, at the lexical stage, case forms appear to be used as unanalyzed lexical elements. Evidence for this should be the fact that with German DLD children "most accusative and dative case markings occurred in personal pronouns" while there are "no instances of case agreement within NPs" (685).

Summarizing, contextual inflection is a linguistic feature of the functional stage. Subject-verb agreement, tense and case marking are cases of contextual inflection. They are acquired at the functional stage and therefore, while they are acquired by typically developing children, they are absent in children with DLD.

Unanalyzed contextual inflection

Strictly speaking the morphology of the finite verb form is a case of contextual inflection and should therefore be problematic for children with DLD. However, as Clahsen (1991) notes, the use of "a small set of (stored) finite verb forms, for example modals, a restricted class of verbs appearing with the suffix -*t* and a few auxiliaries" (699) is not impaired.[11]

The reason why inflectional morphology with modals and light verbs (auxiliaries) in children with DLD is not impaired lies in the special status of these verbal elements. At the lexical stage, as shown in Section 5, modals and light verbs are elements of a small set of modal and aspectual verbs that may serve as the lexical head of an agentive utterance. Modals are used to express the meaning of the willingness, ability, permission or obligation to perform an action.[12] Light verbs are the expression of the lexical-aspectual meaning of 'continuing' or 'going' to perform an activity. At the lexical stage, the verbal elements of this small set are frequently occurring verb forms. Hence, they are used unanalyzed which means that their inflectional morphology is irrelevant. It is therefore, that they are used by typically developing children as with children with DLD.

---

11 See note 5 above.
12 Modal verbs may be used with deontic meaning as in *Hij kan niet komen* (He is not able to come) or with epistemic meaning as in *Hij kan gevallen zijn* (He can be fallen). At the lexical stage, *kan* is used with deontic meaning only, while at the functional stage it may be used with epistemic meaning, too.

The same is true for "the restricted class of verbs appearing with the 'suffix-*t*'" that Clahsen (1999, 699) refers to. As noted in Section 5, the relevant verbs belong to the category of state or change-of-state verbs like Dutch *zit* (sits), *blijft* (stays), *vindt vies* (tastes bad), *valt* (falls), *komt* (comes) and German *geht nicht* (works not), *passt* (fits), *fehlt* (lacks), *kommt* (comes), *schläft* (sleeps), *läuft* (goes). As with modals and light verbs, these verb forms are used morphologically unanalyzed, too (see Figure 1, type B). Within the language system at the lexical stage, state and change-of-state verbs are used in opposition to causative-action verbs (see Figure 1, type A) like Dutch *maken* (make), *drinken* (drink), *afpakken* (away-take), *vasthouden* (on-hold) and German *bauen* (build), *essen* (eat), *abmachen* (off-make), *hinlegen* (down-put) and agentive-motion verbs like Dutch *klimmen* (klimb), *op(s)taan* (on-stand), *inzitten* (in-sit), *weglopen* (away-walk) and German *reiten* (ride), *hüpfen* (gambol), *runtergehen* (it-down-go), *absteigen* (dismount). This opposition concerning the semantics of non-agentive (state and change of state) vs. agentive (action) verbs correlates with their placement in either second- or final-constituent position. Evidence for this is the fact that at the lexical stage subject-verb agreement, i.e. agreement *regardless* of the semantics of the verb, systematically does *not* occur. Thus, at the relevant stage there is no systematic opposition between verb forms such as, for example, Dutch *blijft* vs. *blijven* (stays vs. stay-Inf) or German *fällt* vs. *fallen* (falls vs. fall-Inf) and Dutch *eet* vs. *eten* (eats vs. eat-Inf) or German *geht runter* vs. *runtergehen* (goes down vs. down-go-Inf). Consequently, state and change-of-state verbs are not going to be analyzed as verb forms with a suffix-*t*. It explains why state and change-of-state verbs are systematically used with unanalyzed 'finite' verb forms both in typically developing children and in children with DLD.

Verb forms such as Dutch *is, heb, heeft* (is, have, has) and German *ist, habe, hat* (is, have, has) can be used either as lexical verbs or as auxiliaries/copulas. As a lexical state verb *is, ist* is used in child Dutch *is beetje in* (is a-little in) and in child German *da ist die ente* (there is the duck), while as a copula it is used in child Dutch *dit is fles* (this is bottle) and child German *ist das nass* (is that wet). As expected, at the lexical stage, both typically developing children and children with DLD appear to use of *is, ist* as a state verb, while the use of *is, ist* as a copula is rare. A similar situation obtains with the use of the verb *heb, heeft* in Dutch and *hab, hat* in German. At the lexical stage, state verbs as in child Dutch *Tompoes heeft koffie* (T has coffee. J 1;11) and child German *die hat an* (that-one has [it] on. A 2;0) are used to express the meaning of possession both in typically developing children and in children with DLD, while the auxiliary verb as in child Dutch *ik heef afgespoeld* (I have off-washed. J 2;2) and child German *der hat auseschlafen* (he has outslept. A 2;1) is seldomly used. These differences in meaning may explain why for German-speaking DLD children, Clahsen (1999) notes: "All the children used modal verbs, but auxiliaries and copulas were rare . . ." (685). Similarly, for English speaking children with DLD, Leonard et al. (1992, 159, Table 2) found that in only 41% of obligatory contexts the copula was correctly supplied. It should be noted, however, as pointed out in Bittner and Jordens (this volume), that whenever the DLD child makes use of auxiliary verb forms there is reason to believe that these verb forms are in fact 'light verbs' used to express a particular lexical aspectual meaning. So, the German DLD child in the relevant study is using the auxiliary verb forms *habe*, *hat* and *ist* (have, has and is) to express the lexical aspectual meaning of 'result state'. This unanalyzed lexical use explains why the DLD child produces errors such as *hat* instead of *habe* and *hat* instead of *ist*. It is further evidence that DLD children may use contextual inflectional morphology provided the relevant verb form is used unanalysed.

A final case of unanalyzed contextual inflectional morphology is the use of *de* or *die* for 'definite' and *ein* for 'indefinite' noun phrases (see Section 3.1.1). Instead of serving as a feature of contextual inflection, these elements reflect the use of noun phrases occurring in either initial or final position due to their informational status of either topic or focus. Therefore, depending on their position, noun phrases may be used with unanalyzed *de/die* or *ein* by typically developing children as with children with DLD.

Summary

Inflectional morphology is used by children with DLD if it is 'inherent', i.e. if its use is *not* under external control and therefore may be learned *unanalyzed*. Inflectional morphology in children with DLD is not used if it is 'contextual', i.e. if it is under control of an external element and therefore learned *analyzed*.

7.2 Morpho-syntax

As stated above, our hypothesis of DLD as a developmental delay is also fit to account for what Clahsen labels as cases of 'unpredicted impairment', i.e. absence of verb second, past tense and reversible passives. As argued before, it is our hypothesis that DLD is not a matter of 'missing control agreement' but the manifestation of a developmental problem which affects the computational demands to achieve contextual cohesion at the functional stage. According to this hypothesis, children with DLD will be stuck with the initial, lexical stage. This means that the relevant language system has no structural position to express semantic finiteness and no structural position to express topicality either. Absence of a position for the expression of semantic finiteness means absence of the syntactic features of verb second and verb movement. Furthermore, as argued before, absence of the expression of semantic finiteness as such also means absence of the possibility to express of the relation between the assertion and the topic time (TT) that the assertion holds for. In other words, absence of semantic finiteness makes it impossible to express of (past) tense. Finally, absence of a position for the expression of topicality means absence of a position utterance-initially to express the relation between the utterance and the topic situation with any topicalized constituent. In other words, absence of the expression of topicality means absence of the possibility to vary word order including the possibility to produce reversible passives.

8 DLD: A linguistic deficit or a computational problem?

The data as given above are evidence to suggest that DLD is the problem of having to deal with the computational demands of language processing at the functional stage. More specifically, it seems these data are evidence of a developmental delay in children's ability to make use of the linguistic features to establish contextual cohesion. The question is, is this developmental delay due to the fact that these linguistic features are difficult to acquire? In other words, is DLD a structural linguistic deficit? Or is this developmental delay due to the fact that these linguistic features are difficult to process? In other words, is DLD the outcome of a computational problem?

Lebeaux (1988) argued that normally "during the developmental transition from an underlying grammar without functional categories to a grammar with functional categories, young children might use utterances generated by either." He points out that this occurs "when the computational demands of the adult version of the utterance are too great." However, according to Lebeaux, "the precise nature of such computational difficulty has not yet been defined" (cited by Leonard, 1995, 1280). The same could hold for children with DLD. They might not be able to use the grammatical features associated with the functional category system due to a computational difficulty.

Evidence for this hypothesis can be found in research by Kolk (1998). According to Kolk computational difficulty in language processing is due to an underdeveloped working memory. It affects the *speed* with which language is normally produced. As a consequence language production will be correct but too slow or, when it occurs with normal speed it becomes incorrect or grammatically less complex. As shown in Kolk (1998), this should explain variable behaviour and priming effects with speakers suffering from aphasia, dyslexia and stuttering.

In his presentation of a neurocognitive model of language impairment, as shown in Figure 5, Kolk (1998, 5) argues that cases of language disorder such as aphasia, dyslexia and stuttering are due to a slowdown of the speed with which language production normally occurs. The assumption is that the computational process underlying language production takes place in working memory (located in the ventromedial part of the prefrontal cortex). This computational process deals with the selection, placement and inflection of words. Furthermore, Kolk claims that under the influence of the 'focusing mechanism' (located in the frontal part of the gyrus anguli) speakers suffering from language impairment may choose one of two options. Either they choose to speak with normal speed or they choose to speak correctly. If they choose to speak with normal speed they can only do so to the detriment of grammatical correctness or complexity. On the other hand, if they choose to speak grammatically correctly, they can only do so, to the detriment of normal speed. The focusing mechanisms itself, as stated by Kolk, is controlled by feel (emotion), not by choice.

working memory / computation / minimal speed limit
(ventromedial part of prefrontal cortex)
↕
focusing mechanism ⟶ normal speed + errors / avoid complexity
(gyrus anguli) ⟶ correct + too slow

Figure 5: Neurocognitive model of language impairment.

Kolk's account of language impairment in speakers suffering from aphasia, dyslexia and stuttering might hold for children with DLD, too. Evidence comes from a study of narratives in children with DLD by Reilly et al. (2004a). In this study, it was found that "errors of omission and commission (. . .) were of the same categories as those found in the stories of *younger* typically developing children" (242). As a tentative conclusion, it is suggested "that it is the speed rather than the nature of the process that seems to differ across groups" (242). The notion of speed also plays a role in experimental settings studied by Johnston (1997). In one situation children were asked to make similarity judgments about rotated geometric forms, in another situation they had to choose the object that matched the original target. Johnston found that "[the DLD] children (. . .) needed more time to orient, more time between stimuli, or more time to respond" (170). She claimed that the computational difficulty that DLD children apparently had to deal with were due to a limitation in attentional resources. So, in case of language production in children with DLD, it seems that it is this particular disability of a limited attentional capacity that accounts for the fact that DLD children are not able to meet the speed with which the computational process of language production typically occurs.

Given the fact that children with DLD need more time to execute the computational processes underlying language production we should expect that under normal speed conditions of spontaneous speech these children have the following options. Either they find a means to avoid structures that are computationally complex or they make more errors. This is precisely what seems to happen when children with DLD intend to use structures that are considered syntactically complex. Evidence comes from a study by Duinmeijer (2013). As far as the production of complex structures such as relative clauses, passives or *wh*-questions is concerned, Duinmeijer notes that "[c]hildren with DLD either use them to a lesser extent than typically developing children, or they make more errors in these structures" (34). Duinmeijer also refers to a study of English and French adolescents with DLD who "tend to avoid complexity in their spontaneous speech by the use of coordination/juxtaposition (rather than subordination), by the omission of a complementizer and via direct speech" (34). Finally, Duinmeijer notes that Dutch adolescents with DLD "seem to use complex structures to the same extent as their typically developing peers, but find them more difficult since they make more errors", such as "omissions,[13] errors in inflectional features or syntactic errors like word order errors" (35).

In order to account for her observations, Duinmeijer (2013, 40) refers to Bishop (1994, 526) who claims "that children with [DLD] have knowledge of grammatical functions of morphological markers, but these markers are highly sensitive to loss if sentence processing puts a 'severe strain on a limited capacity system'." It explains the findings discussed in Duinmeijer (2013, 40f.) which show that Dutch adolescents with DLD who are able to acquire the relevant knowledge of the language, have problems with certain grammatical features particularly in situations in which the speech production system is stressed. "The fact that Dutch adolescents with DLD do not improve in the production of article assignment compared to younger children, but improve in judgement indicates that knowledge can develop while performance keeps falling short. Also the fact that adolescents with DLD obtain high accuracy rates on the judgement and produc-

---

[13] One may wonder if 'errors' such as omissions may not be instances of avoidance of complexity too. When DLD children choose zero marking instead of regular past tense formation or third person singular inflection, they choose a structure that is morphologically less complex. The fact that a *syntactic* structure that is less complex happens to be correct, while a *morphological* structure that is less complex happens to be incorrect may be relevant from the normative point of view of the target language, it should be irrelevant from the point of view of the DLD child.

tion of past tense marking and subject-verb agreement, but still make a significant amount of errors seems to indicate that rule knowledge is there, but is not implemented in performance. And, finally, the fact that a difference was found between error rates on the same grammatical construct in different linguistic contexts, seems to indicate that the processing load caused by the context plays a role" (40/41). Thus, as Kolk (1998) argued with respect to adult speakers suffering from aphasia, dyslexia and stuttering, it seems that "differences between rule knowledge and rule implementation are expected in the whole range of grammatical aspects that are problematic in DLD when processing load is increased" (Duinmeijer 2013, 42). However, as far as the kinds of problems are concerned, Duinmeijer points out that "the theory does not specify which aspects of processing are impaired in DLD" (42).[14] Therefore, why is it that some grammatical features are computationally difficult, while others are not?

9 Why is it that some grammatical features are computationally difficult?

As research in Section 2 and 3 has shown, computational difficulty is linked to certain grammatical features. Bishop (1994) uses the term 'vulnerable markers' to refer to 'problems in inflection, assigning gender, using complex syntax'. However, 'vulnerable markers' is just a cover term for a diverse set of observations. So, similarly to the morpho-syntactic problems discussed in Section 2 and 3, Reilly et al. (2004b) found, on the one hand, "omission errors in tense and number agreement for verbs (*he growl*) and agreement for pronouns" and, on the other hand, underrepresentation of complex sentences such as adverbial clauses (45). Furthermore, in a study on the use of tag questions in atypical populations, Weckerly et al. (2004) found that children with DLD (like children with early focal lesions) appeared to have problems with the use of the correct tag question after a prime sentence as,

---

[14] Duinmeijer (2013), who is mainly concerned with DLD in adolescents, notes that "[i]n childhood, problems in rule learning and rule implementation cannot easily be separated because rule knowledge is still developing" (42). This would mean that for children it might be difficult to decide if DLD is a representational problem, i.e. a problem of lacking rule knowledge, or a processing problem, i.e. a problem of rule implementation. Whether one or the other is the case is an empirical problem. As mentioned before, evidence provided by Leonard (1995) indicates that in children with DLD it is indeed a matter of processing. This is confirmed by Reilly et al. (2004b) who note that "the difference [between typically developing children and children with DLD] is in quantity, but not in quality of errors" (45).

for example, in *He takes the morning train. Doesn't he?* Errors occurred in the use of agreement (**don't he?*), the auxiliary (**isn't he?*), the subject (**doesn't she?*) and polarity (**does he?*). So, using the term 'vulnerable markers' to refer to these diverse problems typically found in children with DLD does not have explanatory value. In order to explain why it is that some grammatical features may put a severe strain on the attentional capacity while others may not, we need a theoretical underpinning.

As we argued before, language acquisition in children occurs stage-wise, meaning that an early simple lexical system develops into a functional system that is linguistically more complex. Given this view on language development, our argument is that DLD becomes evident in children who, compared to typically developing children, have problems meeting the computational demands of language production at the functional stage. The grammatical features that are involved are specified in Figure 4. They are all connected with grammatical features linked to either verb movement or topicalization.

Considering the observations by Reilly et al. (2004b) and Weckerly et al. (2004), we may add to these grammatical features of the functional category system the structural configuration of complex sentences (Duinmeijer 2013) and tag questions (Reilly et al. 2004b). Why are these features computationally difficult, i.e. why do they put a strain on the computational processes in working memory or the attentional capacity? As is the case with verb movement and topicalization, the structural configuration of complex sentences and tag questions is used to establish contextual cohesion. As Reilly et al. (2004b) note, they serve as mechanisms "to tie episodes of the story together" (45). So, this is evidence once more that for children with DLD the grammatical features of the functional category system are difficult to handle because they make heavy demands on the computational demands of language processing to establish contextual cohesion.

10 Summary

Current opinion has it that language impairment in children with DLD has no identifiable physical or psychological basis (Fletcher 1999, Bishop 2014). The fact that it typically involves particular morpho-syntactic features of the target-language system, is appreciated as evidence that the grammatical system develops independently of other cognitive domains. In order to come to grips with the characteristics of this linguistic deficit a number of proposals has been put forward. Clahsen (1991, 1999), for example, interpreted the relevant data as evidence of a problem to establish the morpho-syntactic features of grammatical agreement, while Leonard (1995) understood them as evidence of a problem to use the linguistic features of the functional category system. Take, for example, the grammatical feature of verb second in Dutch and German. The question is, is this particular feature difficult to acquire because it depends on the acquisition of subject-verb agreement as a case of control agreement as Clahsen (1991, 1999) has claimed, or is it difficult to use due to the fact that it is a functional feature of the C-system as stated by Leonard (1995)?

We argued that DLD is in its origin neither a morpho-syntactic deficit nor a deficit in the acquisition of the grammatical features of the functional category system. Rather, the problems of children with DLD are claimed to be evidence of a developmental delay in the ability to express contextual cohesion. Furthermore, we argued that in order to create contextual cohesion learners need to be able to *handle* the functional linguistic mechanisms of verb movement and topicalization. With the acquisition of verb movement the language system has a position of verb second to express semantic finiteness, meaning that given a particular situation the speaker asserts that something is the case. This position serves as prerequisite for the acquisition of auxiliaries and lexical verbs carrying the morphological features of subject-verb agreement (as a prerequisite to case) and tense. With the acquisition of topicalization the language system has an initial, topic position for elements to establish a relation between the assertion and the topic situation (TS). These elements are typically definite NPs (requiring gender), question words or anaphora.

Finally, establishing contextual cohesion is a computational process that takes place in working memory. DLD has been argued to be due to a computational difficulty in language processing which is caused by an *underdeveloped* working memory. So, whether or not children with DLD are able to process the linguistic features relevant to establish contextual cohesion depends on the computational demands of the particular communicative situation. More specifically, it depends on the strain that is put on the attentional capacity. This explains as noted by Leonard (1995, 1279) why children with DLD used the linguistic features associated with the functional category system just to 'a *more limited* degree' than their MLU controls.

References

Bishop, Dorothy V.M. 1994. Grammatical errors in specific language impairment: Competence or performance limitations? *Applied Psycholinguistics* 15. 507–550.

Bishop, Dorothy V.M. 2014. Ten questions about terminology for children with unexplained language problems. *International Journal of Language & Communication Disorders* 49(4). 381–415.

Booij, Geert. 1996. Inherent versus contextual inflection and the split morphology hypothesis. In Geert E. Booij & Jaap van Marle (eds.), *Yearbook of morphology 1995*, 1–16. Dordrecht: Kluwer.

Clahsen, Harald. 1991. *Child language and developmental dysphasia. Linguistic studies of the acquisition of German*. Amsterdam: Benjamins.

Clahsen, Harald. 1999. Linguistic perspectives on specific language impairment. In W.C. Ritchie & T.K. Bhatia (eds.), *Handbook of child language acquisition*, 675–706. San Diego: Academic Press.

Clahsen, Harald & Monika Rothweiler. 1993. Inflectional rules in children's grammars. In G. Booij & J. van Marle (eds.), *Yearbook of morphology 1992*, 255–288. Dordrecht: Foris.

Duinmeijer, Iris. 2013. Persistent problems in SLI: which grammatical problems remain when children grow older? *Linguistics in Amsterdam* 6. 28–48.

Fletcher, Paul. 1999. Specific language impairment. In Martyn D. Barrett (ed.), *The development of language*, 349–37. Hove: Psychology Press.

Hansson, Kristina & Ulrika Nettelbladt. 1995. Grammatical characteristics of Swedish children with SLI. *Journal of Speech and Hearing Research* 38 (3). 589–598.

Håkansson, Gisela & Ulrika Nettelbladt. 1993. Developmental sequences in L1(normal and impaired) and L2 acquisition of Swedish. *International Journal of Applied Linguistics* 3. 131–157.

Hamann, Cornelia, Katrin Lindner & Zvi Penner. 2001. Tense, reference time, and language impairment in German children. In Caroline Féry & Wolfgang Sternefeld (eds.), *Auditur vox sapientiae. Festschrift für Arnim von Stechow*. Studia Grammatica 52. 182–213. Berlin: Akademie Verlag.

Johnston, Judith. 1997. Specific language impairment, cognition and the biological basis of language. In Myrna Gopnik (ed.), *The inheritance and innateness of grammars*. Vancouver Studies in Cognitive Science 6. 161–180. New York/Oxford: Oxford University Press.

Jordens, Peter. 2012. *Language acquisition and the functional category system*. Berlin/Boston: Walter de Gruyter.

Jordens, Peter & Dagmar Bittner. 2017. Developing interlanguage: Driving forces in children learning Dutch and German. *International Review of Applied Linguistics in Language Teaching (IRAL)* 55 (4). 365–392.

Klein, Wolfgang. 1994. *Time in language*. London/New york: Routledge.

Kolk, Herman. 1998. *Compenseren voor een taalstoornis. Een neurocognitief model*. Radboud Universiteit: Nijmegen.

Lebeaux, David. 1988. *Language acquisition and the form of grammar*. PhD Diss. Univ. of Mass.: Amherst.

Leonard, Laurence B. (1995), Functional categories in the grammars of children with specific language impairment. *Journal of Speech and Hearing Research* 38. 1270–1283.

Leonard, Laurence B. (2014), *Children with specific language impairment. Second edition*. Cambridge, Mass.: The MIT Press.

Leonard, Laurence B., Umberta Bortolini, M. Cristina Cadelli, Karla K. McGregor & Letizia Sabbadini. 1992. Morphological deficits in children with specific language impairment: The status of features in the underlying grammar. *Language Acquisition* 2. 151–179.

Poeppel, David & Kenneth Wexler. 1993. The Full Competence Hypothesis of clause structure in early German. *Language* 69. 1–33.

Reilly, Judy, Molly Losh, Ursula Bellugi & Beverly Wulfeck. 2004a. „Frog, where are you?" Narratives in children with specific language impairment, early focal brain injury, and Williams syndrome. *Brain and Language* 88. 229–247.

Reilly, Judy, Jill Weckerly & Beverly Wulfeck. 2004b. Neuroplasticity and development: The acquisition of morphosyntax in children with early focal lesions and children with specific language impairment. In Ludo Verhoeven & Hans van Balkom (eds.), *Classification of developmental language disorders. Theoretical issues and clinical implications*, 39–59. Mahwah NJ: Erlbaum.

Rice, Mabel L. & Kenneth Wexler. 1996. A phenotype of specific language impairment: Extended optional infinitives. In Mabel L. Rice (ed.), *Toward a genetics of language*, 215–238. Mahwah N.J.: Erlbaum.

Van der Ley & Harris. 1990. Comprehension of reversible sentences in specifically language-impaired children. *Journal of Speech & Hearing Disorder* 55(1). 101–117.

Weckerly, Jill, Beverly Wulfeck & Judy Reilly. 2004. The development of morphosyntactic ability in atypical populations: The acquisition of tag questions in children with early focal lesions and children with specific-language impairment. *Brain and Language* 88. 190–201.

Dagmar Bittner and Peter Jordens
Language acquisition in a German DLD child

Abstract: As shown in Jordens (this volume), Developmental Language Disorder (DLD) in children learning their mother tongue leads to 'a significant delay' (Leonard 2014) in language acquisition. The present study is a case study of Bastian, a DLD child learning German as his mother tongue. As with typically developing (TD) children, language development with Bastian is a two-stage process. At the initial, lexical stage, Bastian's language system is based on two types of utterance structure, i.e. utterances with an agent in initial position referring to situations that are under control and utterances with a theme in initial position referring to situations that happen to occur. As with TD children, at some point Bastian is going to give up this initial, lexical system in favour of a targetlike, functional system. However, compared to TD children, language development with Bastian is subject to a delay of about 2 years. Given that language disorder in Bastian is not a particular linguistic deficit, it seems that Bastian has problems with the use of the linguistic features that serve to establish contextual cohesion. It is argued that this is caused by an underdeveloped working memory which prevents him from dealing with the relevant computational demands. Nevertheless, Bastian is cognitively more mature than younger TD children who have reached the same level of language development. So, it is claimed that it is this cognitive ability that allows Bastian, while he is still at the lexical stage, to accommodate the linguistic features of the target language such that they meet the constraints of a limited working memory.

Keywords: developmental language disorder, typical development, finiteness, topicalization, contextual cohesion, working memory

1 Introduction

As indicated by Jordens (this volume), language production seems to proceed along the same developmental path in children suffering from developmental language disorder (DLD) as in typically developing (TD) children. The present Chapter aims at testing this claim by the analysis of the spontaneously produced utterances

Dagmar Bittner, Leibniz-Zentrum Allgemeine Sprachwissenschaft, Berlin, Germany, e-mail: bittner@leibniz-zas.de
Peter Jordens, Amsterdam VU University, Netherlands; Max Planck Institute for Psycholinguistics Nijmegen, The Netherlands; e-mail: jorde074@planet.nl

https://doi.org/10.1515/9783110712025-003

of the DLD child Bastian who learned German as his mother tongue. The relevant data were collected from his first word at 9 months up to age 7;4. The present study concerns the age range from 3;5 to 4;1. As late as at age 3;5, Bastian's utterances provide evidence of the productive use of the same lexical language system as is the case with TD children at age 1;10–2;1. This means that Bastian's initial language system has two types of utterance structure: on the one hand, agentive utterances which occur with a predicate referring to an action and the agent as the external argument that is placed in initial position and, on the other hand, non-agentive utterances which appear with a predicate referring to a state or a change of state and the theme as the external argument in initial position.

In the following we will show that despite the late onset and the slow progress of the acquisition process in the DLD child, there is no qualitative difference between the developmental path of this child vs. TD children. This leaves us with the question of what it is that makes language development of this DLD child, and other DLD children too, so slow-going. On that point, we will provide evidence suggesting that DLD children may typically suffer from a deficit in language processing by an underdeveloped working memory.

2 The DLD child Bastian

The boy Bastian was born in 1998. Bastian's early language development was followed by his mother in a diary. Recordings were made from age 1;8 on, when Bastian came to produce reasonable amounts of utterances within a limited time span. Recordings were made for 60 to 90 minutes a week up to age 7;4. The sessions took place at Bastian's home in situations of playing together with his mother and sometimes his younger sister or during everyday family routines like having breakfast or dinner. Most recordings were transcribed in CHAT format (MacWhinney 2000) by Bastian's mother. A smaller number of recordings was transcribed in the same format by student assistants.

Bastian produced his first word, *Mama*, with 9 months. Further word learning proceeded comparatively slowly and a high amount of Bastian's productions are unintelligible words. The recordings from age 1;8 to 2;0 document 15% (1728) intelligible words, while 85% is unintelligable words or syllables (Siegmüller and Bittner 2005). Up to age 2;0, the early diary data and the recordings document 61 different words and a few two-word combinations (e.g. *Papa alle* meaning 'Papa has finished'). 38 of these words are listed in the ELFRA-2 (Grimm and Doil 2000) which is a German version of the MacArthur Communicative Developmental Inventory (CDI; Fenson et al. 1993). As discussed in detail by Siegmüller and

Bittner (2005), it can be assumed that Bastian matched the criteria for being in the normal range of language development at age 2;0. These criteria are the productive use of at least 50 different words including some verbs and production of first word combinations up to the second birthday (see Fenson et al. 1993). Given that the recordings cover only a small portion of Bastian's language production from age 1;8 to 2;0 it is very likely that Bastian has command of 50 words entailed in the CDI. Nevertheless, Bastian's language development at age 2;0 is well below the average and continues to slow down in the following years. Until age 3;2 the data contain 823 different words. This amounts to 50 new words on average per month between age 2;0 and 3;2. About 10% of the words appear only ones in the data up to age 4;11. The 400 word mark – assumed to be a threshold for the acquisition of function words (Bates et al. 1994) – is reached by Bastian at about age 2;9. However, except for some quantifiers (*alle* 'all', *mehr* 'more', *viel(e)* 'many/much', *kein(e)* 'none'), deictic pronouns (*ich* 'I', *du* 'you', *wir* 'we', *die* 'the-fem/these', *das* 'the-ntr'), possessive pronouns (*mein* 'my/mine', *dein* 'your/yours') and the connector *und* 'and' (appearing after 3;0), function words are missing until age 3;3. They remain rare until age 3;11 (Bittner and Siegmüller 2013). MLU-word exceeds 2.0 at age 3;6 and approaches 2.5 at age 3;11. Two-constituent utterances are produced as frequently as one-constituent utterances from age 3;6 on. Three-constituent utterances become as frequent as one- and two-constituent utterances at age 3;11. In terms of MLU-word 2.0, i.e. at age 3;6, Bastian is about 18 months behind the two German TD children studied in Bittner and Siegmüller (2013). Bastian's DLD was clinically diagnosed at age 4;6. At that time, he showed reduced hearing performance and productive and receptive delays in lexical semantics and in morpho-syntax. After clinical treatment of his hearing problems (removal of polyps), language therapy started at age 4;10 and continued until age 7.

3 Bastian's utterance structure at the lexical stage (3;5–3;11)

3.1 Predicate-argument structure

At age 3;5–3;11, Bastian's utterances can be categorized in terms of either of two types that are used in complementary distribution on the basis of the semantics of the predicate. Type-A utterances with agentive predicates (actions), such as *ausmachen* (out-put), typically occur with the agent in initial, external argument position, while the predicate has an infinite verb form (Vinf) in final-constituent position. Type-B utterances with non-agentive predicates (states and changes of state), such as *schläft* (sleeps) and *fällt runter* (falls down), typically occur with the theme in initial, external argument position, while the predicate has a finite verb form (Vfin) in second-constituent position. Agentive utterances are used to express that the agent – which often remains implicit – has control over the action, while non-agentive utterances are used to express that the theme is 'in' a state or 'undergoes' a change of state. Finally, in agentive utterances control may or may not be explicitly espressed with either modal or aspectual verb forms such as *will* (want), *kann* (can), *darf* (may) or *macht* (does). Examples of type-A and type-B utterances with Bastian at 3;5 and 3;6 are given in (1) and (2).

(1) Utterance structure with Bastian (3;5)

Type A	Type B
Agentive predicates with Vinf	Non-agentive predicates with Vfin
auto fahr(e)n, de(r) wauwau.	*mehr raucht [eisenbahn].*
car drive, the dog	more steams [train]
auge küsschen geben.	*sonne scheint.*
(on) eye kiss give	sun shines
noch piepiep [= vogel] weggehen.	*Mama, Evi fällt runter.*
also bird away-go	Mommy, Evi falls down
bimbaum [= glocke] muss schlafen.	*hier schläft.*
bell must sleep	here sleeps
Oma puzzle bielen [= spielen], ja?	*sonne xx sieht komisch aus, wa ?*
Grandma puzzle play, yes?	sun xx looks weird out, doesn't- it?
kann nicht hochhoppsen.	*baby (hat) angst (vor) rauch.*
cannot up-jump	baby (has) fear (for) smoke.
maus auskippen [farbe].	*dunkel, scheint sonne nicht.*
mouse out-dump [paint]	dark, shines sun not
Mama, bettrolle haben, bitte.	*Mama b(r)aucht lampen.*
Mommy, bedroll have, please	Mommy needs lamps
rutschen geh(e)n, nicht.	*auto dläft [= schläft].*
slide go, not	car sleeps
oben dlafen [= schlafen].	*wasser reg(n)et.*
above sleep	water rains
maus angucken.	*da deht [= steht] Mama(s) bett.*
mouse at-look	there stands Mommy's bed
maus turm bau(e)n.	*passt auf [maus].*

mouse tower build
sonne geht (sch)lafen.
sun goes (to) sleep
ich ausmachen [kamera].
I off-turn [camera]
kindergarten (an) ohren halten [kuscheltier].
kindergarden (on) ears hold [cuddly toy]
(für) Evi auch mal(e)n haus.
for Evi too paint house
hier mugik [= musik] machen.
here music make
wolf hauen.
wolf hit
(s)chuhe anzieh(e)n.
shoes on-put
nicht kaputtmachen.
not kaput-make

watches on [mouse]
wasser geht an.
water goes on
mein dift [= stift] malt.
my pen paints
wasser kommt wolf raus.
water comes wolf out-of-it
hab oben puzzle.
(I) have up(stairs) puzzle
Bas(t)i [= Bastian] deht [= steht] hier.
Bastian stands here
sonne (s)cheint nicht dunkel.
sun shines not dark
hier passt nicht.
here fits not
brennt an.
burns on

(2) Utterance structure with Bastian (3;6)

Type A

Agentive predicates with Vinf

draussen (sch)lafen.
outside sleep
hier kann laufen.
here can walk
maus anmachen.
mouse on-make
frosch (sch)wimm(en).
frog swim
ziege ranmachen.
goat it-on-make
muss dleiten [= schneiden] krokotier.
must cut crocodile
Bastian gucken haus.
Bastian look (at) house
muss gucken.
must look
muss brötchen abdleiden.

Type B

Non-agentive predicates with Vfin

wiese esst [= isst] hier.
meadow eats here
hier liegt bett.
here lays (in) bed
kommt mädchen bett.
comes girl(s) bed
haus deht da.
house stands there
xx geht nicht raus, fahren auto.
xx goes not out, drive car
essen, (sch)meckt gut [schnecke].
food, tastes good [slug]
schläft sonne xx.
sleeps sun xx
macht lieb.
makes nice
gehen [pl] nicht runter.

must buns off-cut
abbeissen menschen.
off-bite people
brötchen zieh(e)n.
buns pull
Basti(an) aufessen.
Basti(an) up-eat
(s)chiff hinsetzen.
ship down-sit
haus teddy haben.
house teddy (want) get
mach(e) auto fahren.
make car drive
muss haus abreissen.
must house down-tear
muss auch (s)choenes xx haben.
must also (something) nice xx get
könn(en) nicht (sch)lafen.
(they) cannot sleep
mach(e) alles abreissen.
make all off-tear
hier heute nicht seifenblasen.
here today not soap-bubble

(they) go not down
macht xx kaputt.
makes xx kaput
hier xx brennt.
here xx burns
feuer kommt.
fire comes
katze hat angst.
cat has fear
hier macht (s)chick sauber, ja?
here makes nice clean, yes?
ist lieb?
is nice?
guck durch xx.
look through xx
hier hinten sitzt papa.
here back sits Dad
kann nicht ran.
cannot it-on
hier kommt xx katze.
here comes xx cat
kaffee. deht oben kaffee
coffee, stands above coffee

Both types of utterance structure as exemplified in (1) and (2) are representative of Bastian's language system at 3;5–3;11. With nearly no exception the utterances of type A (agentive) and type B (non-agentive) account for what we refer to as the initial, lexical stage of language acquisition. Due to the position in which the lexical verb occurs in the input, they appear as either morphologically infinite or morphologically finite.

Thus, observational evidence indicates that at the relevant stage verb forms are complementary distributed. That is, on the one hand, action verbs are expected *not* to occur as Vfin in second-constituent position, while, on the other hand, state and change-of-state verbs should *not* occur as (Mod +)Vinf in final position. Given that this observation is correct, we are in the position to make some specific predictions about some distributional features present in our data.

First, simple verb forms with the *same lemma* occurring in both final and second-constituent position should differ semantically. The relevant data show that this prediction appears to hold for the opposition between verb forms such as in (3a). Here the same lemma may refer to either an action when it is used transitively in final position or to a state when it is used intransitively in second-constituent position.

(3a)   transitive action   intransitive state

    *(für) Evi auch **mal(e)n**, haus.* (3;5)   *mein dift (= stift) **malt**.* (3;5)
    (for) Evi too draw house   my pencil draws
    *(sch)necke **malen** xx.* (3;5)
    spider draw
    *and(e)re seite **mal(e)n**.* (3;5)
    (on) other side draw
    ***malen**. bild auch.* (3;6)
    draw. (this) picture too.

Furthermore, it also holds for the opposition between intransitive verb forms as in (3b), referring to either an intransitive, agentive movement or an intransitive state

(3b)   intransitive movement   intransitive state

    *hier noch **schlafen**, katze.* (3;5)   *sonne scheint, mond **schläft**.* (3;5)
    here too sleep, cat   sun shines, moon sleeps
    [the cat should go to sleep here too]   [B describes a situation in book][1]
    *bimbaum [=! glocke] **muss schlafen**.*(3;5)
    bell must sleep
    [the bell should go to sleep]
    *ich **will** da **s(ch)lafen**.* (3;9)   *das **schläft** auch weiter.* (3;11)
    I want there (go to) sleep   it sleeps too further
    *frosch **(sch)wimm(en)**.* (3;6)   *frosch **(sch)wimmt**.* (3;6)
    frog (wants to go) swim   frog floats

Finally, it holds for the opposition between transitively used verb forms such as in (3c) referring to either a transitive action or a transitive state.

(3c)   transitive action   transitive state

    *haus teddy **haben**.* (3;6)   ***hab** oben puzzle.* (3;5)
    house teddy (want/must) have   (I) have got upstairs puzzle
    *foto **haben**.* (3;6)   *katze **hat** angst.* (3;6)

---

[1] B uses the inflected form although his mother repeatedly used the infinitive before.

picture have	cat has fear
*ich **muss** sehen.* (3;9)	*ich **seh** dich nicht.* (3;9)
I must (that) see	I see you not

In all these cases the semantic difference between the use of the relevant verb forms as either an action verb or a (change-of-)state verb co-occurs with the use of the external argument as either agent or theme. Furthermore, our data show that at the relevant stage, the utterances with an action verb may or may not be used with a modal verb form, while the utterances with a (change-of-)state verb may not.

Second, in the target language, complex particle verbs may occur without or with the separation of the particle from the verb. If the particle has not been separated as, for example, in *kaputtmachen* (kaput-make), the particle verb appears as Vinf in final position. If the particle has been separated as, for example, in *macht kaputt* (makes-kaput) the verb form occurs as Vfin in second-constituent position, while the particle stays in final position. Given the lexical system at the relevant stage, the prediction is similar as with simple verbs. That is, particle verbs with the *same lemma* occurring in both final and second-constituent position should differ semantically. The relevant data show that this prediction appears to hold for the opposition between verb forms such as in (4a). Here the *same lemma* may refer to either an action when it is used transitively in final position or to a state when it is used intransitively in second-constituent position.

(4a) transitive action   intransitive change of state

*alle **tumachen** (= zumachen) xx.* (3;5)   *ubahn **macht zu**.* (4;1)
everything closed-make   makes closed

It also holds for the opposition between intransitive verb forms as in (4b), referring to either an intransitive, agentive movement or an intransitive change of state.

(4b) intransitive movement   intransitive change of state

***durch**gucken.* (3;6)   *guck **durch** xx.* (3;6)
through-look   look through xx
*kann nicht **rausgucken** (mädchen).* (3;11)   *guck **raus** (tiere).* (3;11)
cannot out-look   look out [animals]
*nicht **weglaufen**.* (3;8)   *schnecke **läuft weg** nicht.* (3;8)
not away-run   slug runs away not
***weggeh(e)n**, hat angst.* (3;8)   *geht katze **weg**.* (3;9)
away-go, has fear   goes cat away

*Eve **hochgehen**.* (3;6)
Eve upstairs-go
*das **rauslaufen**.* (3;11)
that out-run [animals]
***rausgehen**?*
out-go?
*hier kommt er, **hochklettern**.* (3;8)
here comes he, up-climb

*miekekatze **geht** stuhl **hoch**.* (3;9)
kitty goes chair up
***läuft** nicht **raus**.* (3;11)
runs not out [animals]
*xx geht nicht **raus**, fahren auto.* (3;6)
xx goes not out, drive car
***klettert hoch** (löwe).* (3;11)
climbs up [lion]

Finally, it holds for the opposition between transitively used verb forms such as in (4c) referring to either a transitive action or a transitive state.

(4c)   transitive action   transitive state

*maus **angucken**.*(3;5)
mouse at-look
***muss** ein flugzeug **angucken**.* (3;7)
must an airplane at-look
*bücher **angucken**.* (3;6)
books at-look
xx grossen (*grosses) buch
***angucken**.* (3;5)
big book at-look
***muss** mädchen **angucken**.* (3;9)
must girl at-look
*mama **angucken**.* (3;6)
mommy at-look
*nein, Bas(t)ian **muss festhalten**.* (3;7)
no, B must tight-hold

*flugzeug **guck** ich **an**.* (3;8)
airplane look I on

*ich **guck** noch **an**.* (3;9)
I look once-more at

*Opa xx **hält fest**.* (3:9)
opa xx holds tight

In all cases the semantic difference between the use of these particle verb forms as either an action verb or a state/change-of-state verb co-occurs with the use of the external argument as either agent or theme. Finally, as with the simple verbs given above, our data show that with particle verbs referring to an action, the utterance may be used with a modal verb, while with particle verbs referring to a (change of) state this may not.

However, the fact that verb forms with the agentive verb *machen* (make) such as *abmachen* (off-make), *musik machen* (music make), *zumachen* (closed-make), *kaputtmachen* (kaput-make), *anmachen* (on-make), *reinmachen* (it-in-make), *ausmachen* (out-make), *saubermachen* (clean-make), *ranmachen* (it-on-make) are used in *both* final and second position, too, seems to be due just to the frequency with which these verb forms occur in the input.

The opposition between utterances of type A and type B as in (1) and (2) also determines utterance structure at the initial, lexical stage of TD children learning Dutch and German. This is shown in Figure 1, see also Jordens (this volume). This means that at the relevant stage, the initial language system of Bastian at 3;5–3;11 appears to be the same as is with TD children at age 1;10–2;1. The only difference is the fact that language development in Bastian is delayed with about 2 years.

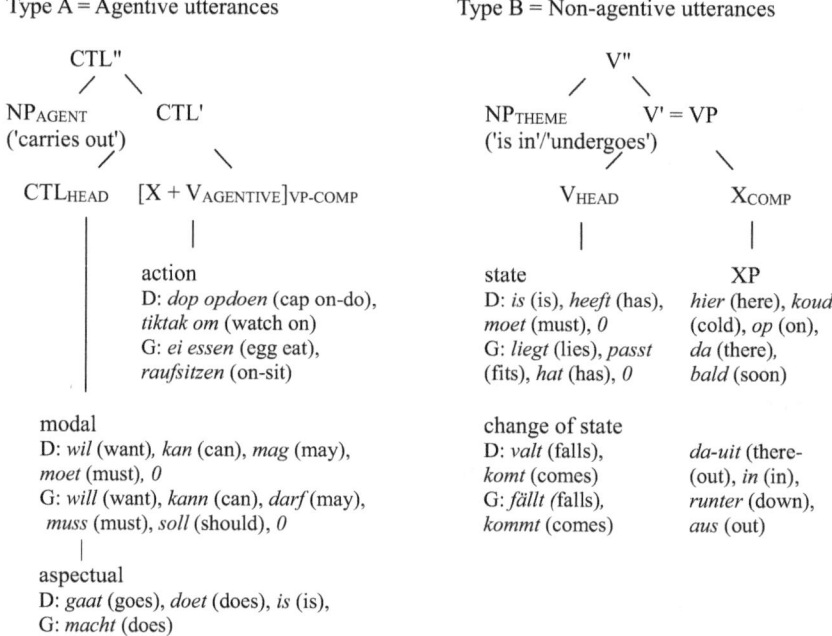

Figure 1: Utterance structure in Dutch and German TD children at the lexical stage (1;10–2;1).

3.2 Word order at the lexical stage

In TD children, word order at the lexical stage appears to be determined by the semantic principle 'Agent first'. This principle states that if there is an agent, it has to occur in initial position. Hence, in agentive utterances objects or adverbs may occur in initial position only if there is no agent. This accounts for the fact that, at the lexical stage, utterances with a topicalized object or adverbial in initial position and a postverbal agent are 'ungrammatical'. That is, at the relevant stage, they do not occur. However, topicalization does occur in the input. Thus, in order to accommodate both topicalization and 'Agent first', TD children may produce utterances with topicalized objects or adverbials in initial position, while they leave the agent unexpressed. This is a suitable way to solve the problem as the agent is implied by the modal or aspectual verbal element that is used to express control. Evidence is given in Jordens and Bittner (this volume). Some examples are Dutch **disse** *hoeniet meeneme* (this must$_{AG}$-not with-take, A 2;1); **da** *kanwel opzitte* (there can$_{AG}$-indeed on-sit, J 2;0) and German **hase** *wollte gucke?* (hare$_{OBJ}$ wanted$_{AG}$ look, C 2;3); **hier** *auch hingehen, opa* (here O$_{AG}$.also to-go, grandpa, A 2;0).

'Agent first' is a typical feature of the lexical system, which appears to hold for both the TD children and Bastian alike. It explains why, at the relevant stage, Bastian is going to produce not only, non-targetlike utterances such as in (5), but also utterances with a left-dislocated adverbial, object or predicate as in (6).

(5) NP$_{Obj}$/Adv in initial position with agent implied

    3;6: *hier kann laufen.*
         here can walk
    3;7: *das muss bau(e)n.*
         this must build
    3;8: *licht (= gesicht) muss malen.*
         face must draw
         fliege muss angucken xx.
         fly must at-look xx
    3;11: *das muss aufmach(en).*
         this (I) must open
         da kann nicht ausschütten.
         now (juice) cannot out-pour
         jetzt geht enten holen.
         now (girl) goes fetch ducks

(6) Adv/ NP$_{Obj}$ left-dislocated

    3;7: *hier, papa muss laufen.*
         here, Dad must walk
    3;9: *fenster, ich will haben.*
         window, I want have
         darf pusten, ich leise?
         may blow, I quietly?

In some cases, as shown in (7), it seems that at the relevant stage topicalization does occur while the agent is placed postverbally. However, here the agent is a pronominal element which may occur postverbally due to its low degree of 'informativeness'. This particularly holds for *man* (one). Pronouns are less informative than Ns or NPs and may therefore be produced as an integrated part of the modal element which explains why they do not need a structural position.

(7) NP$_{Obj}$/Adv in initial position with the pronominal agent as part of the modal element

    3;7: *0 muss-**ich** flugzeug an(gucken).*
          0 must-I airplane on-look
    3;9: *da muss-**xx** abmachen.*
          there must-xx off-take
          *0 kann-**man** essen.*
          0 can-one eat
    3;11: *da kann-**man** zumachen.*
          there can-one closed-make
          *da kann-**man** machen.*
          there can-one make
          *da kann-**man** da rein.*
          there can-one there it-in

3.3 Presentatives

At the relevant stage, as is the case with TD children, Bastian not only uses utterances of either type A (agentive) or type B (non-agentive). That is, he not only uses utterances that are fit to express the presence or absence of control. He also uses types of utterance that are called 'presentatives'. Presentatives typically have no external argument. They are used to attribute focus function. That is, they introduce or reintroduce out of a set of alternatives a new referent or state of affairs which is going to be linked to the 'here and now'. Therefore, presentatives frequently occur with non-agentive verb forms such as *geht* (goes), *kommt* (comes), *ist* (is) as in *jetzt geht tür zu* (now goes door closed), *hier kommt da(s) loch raus* (here comes that hole out), *hier ist dis, auto, fahren* (here is, this, car, drive). Examples from Bastian (3;5–3;6) are given in (8).

(8) Presentatives

    3;5: *hier andere seite hagel.*
          here other side hail
          da alles sauber.
          there all clean
          sonne scheint.
          sun shines
    3;6: *hier deht couch.*
          here stands couch
          hier kommt mädchen bett.
          here comes girl bed
          schläft sonne xx.
          sleeps sun xx
          hier passt.
          here (it) fits
          feuer kommt.
          fire comes
          ende. ist ende.
          end. is end
          hier reicht.
          here (is) enough
          hier hinten sitzt papa.
          here in-the-back sits dad
          ist heiss.
          is hot
          hier kommt katze.
          here comes cat

At the lexical stage, focus is mainly marked by word order. The relevant constraint is: 'Focus expression last' as, for example, in *kommt feuer* (comes fire). In the marked case, when the focus expression is first, this is indicated with contrastive stress as in *sonne scheint* (sun shines), *feuer kommt* (fire comes).

3.4 Summary

The relevant data show that Bastian's basic grammatical system is like that of TD children at the lexical stage. Utterances can be categorized in terms of a complementary distribution based on the semantics of the predicate, which is either agentive (actions) or non-agentive (states and changes of state). Word order is determined by the semantic principle 'Agent-first'. Topicalization occurs only in a non-targetlike way. Utterances referred to as 'presentatives' are used to introduce an entity or a state of affairs.

In Bastian's basic, lexical system functional features are typically absent and so is the so-called 'functional prefield', that includes both the V2 position and the initial, topic position. In the target language, however, the relevant linguistic categories are used to express the functional features of finiteness in V2 position and topicality in initial, topic position. More specifically, in absence of a V2 position there is:
- no category of auxiliary verbs (hence, no scrambling, i.e. placement of an element between V2 and the negation),
- no verb movement,
- no inflectional morphology (hence, no agreement and no tense).

Furthermore, in absence of a topic position there is:
- no topicalization (i.e. no 'subject-verb inversion'),
- no focalization (i.e. no *wh*-questions),
- no *yes/no*-questions (i.e. questions with a postverbal subject position[2]),
- no determiners (i.e. no elements marking definite vs. indefinite),
- no pronominal anaphora.

It should be noted, that at the lexical stage the use of finite vs. infinite verb forms is not to be seen as evidence of the presence of inflectional morphology. At the relevant stage, these verb forms are complementarily distributed based on the semantics of the verb. That is: agentive predicates occur in final-constituent position and therefore, as is the case in the input, they are used with an infinite verb form of the lexical verb (Vinf); non-agentive predicates occur in second-constituent position and therefore, as is the case in the input, they are used with a finite verb form of the lexical verb (Vfin).

Finally, as opposed to the TD children we studied in Jordens and Bittner (this volume), Bastian seems to use the auxiliary verbs *hat* (has-3rdsg) and *hab* (have-1stsg) in utterances such as *mama **hat** desucht* (mommy has looked-for. 3;5) and *ich **hab** gefunden* (I have found. 3;9) already at 3;5–3;11, i.e., while he is still at his lexical stage. In the next Section, we will show however, that at the relevant stage Bastian's use of *hat* and *hab* is premature in the sense that these verbal elements do not function as auxiliary verbs, yet.

---

[2] The term (grammatical) subject is used for the syntactic function of the external argument (agent or theme) at the functional stage.

3.5 *haben* + Vpp at the lexical stage

As far as constituent structure is concerned, the main development at the functional stage is the acquisition of the functional prefield which provides an initial, topic position to express topicality and a verb-second position to express finiteness. Both positions are functional in the sense that they are not linked to a particular lexical category. Therefore, the topic position may host any constituent not just the external argument (agent or theme) to express topicality. This explains the phenomenon referred to as '(subject-verb) inversion'. The second position may host any verbal element to express finiteness. This explains the acquisition of functional verbs such as auxiliary verbs and the phenomenon of verb movement, i.e. the use of any lexical verb in V2 position.

In Bastian, at his lexical stage (3;5–3;11), there is no evidence of a functional prefield. At this stage, according to the semantic principle 'Agent first', the initial position is regularly taken by the external argument, i.e. the constituent with the semantic function of either agent or theme. Neither agent nor theme may occur postverbally. Furthermore, non-agentive verbs are systematically used in second position, while agentive verbs are not. Thus, at the relevant stage, this second position is not yet fit for the expression of finiteness. Nevertheless, it appears that, at this lexical stage, Bastian produces a substantial number of utterances with *hat* or *hab* + Vpp (past-participle verb). Examples are given in (9). Given the amount of variation, this type of utterance is used fairly productively from age 3;6 on. See **Appendix** for an overview of all the relevant data in Bastian 3;3–3;11.

(9) Utterances with **hat** + Vpp or **hab** + Vpp

	Type A: NP$_{AGENT}$ + hat/hab + Vpp$_{[RES. STATE of ACTION]}$	Type B: NP$_{THEME}$ + hat/hab/(ist)+ Vpp$_{[RES. STATE of CHANGE-of-STATE]}$
3;3	**hab** xx demacht. (I) have xx made	
3;4	**hat** baby xx hier gehabt. has baby xx here had	
3;5	mama **hat** desucht. mommy has looked-for	**hat** depasst. (it) has fitted
3;6	**hat** kaputtgemacht. has kaput-made **hab** aufgegessen. have up-eaten	so, aufgeräumt **ist**. so, up-cleaned is bus **hat** [/] gemalt.*/** bus has / painted

3;7	Dennis **hat** kopf gehaut. Dennis has (on) head hit **hat** rausdemacht. has it-out-made ich **hat** fingern aua gemacht.* I has fingers ouch made ich **hat** kaffee nemacht.* I has coffee made	uni **hat** es geregnet. (at) university has it rained **hat** gewachsen. has washed
3;8:	**hat** kein haus gebaut. has no house built Bas(t)ian **hat** den bagger gekauft. Bastian has the excavator bought ich **hat** (s)tulle aufgegessen.* I has sandwich up-eaten da, ich **hab** &kiku gemalt. there, I have kiku painted **hat**, osterhase nicht angst haben. has, Easter bunny not fear had	hier **hat** hänger abedüzt.** here has car down-fallen (s)chiff **hat** kaputdegang.** ship has kaput-gone **hat** weggefahrt.** has away-driven u-bahn **hat** an(g)ehalten. tube has at-stopped **hat** wegdeflog(en).** has away-flown
3;9:	ich **hat** tür nemacht.* I has door made ich **hab** viel reingemacht. I have much it-in-put	**hat** dedossen (= gestossen). has bumped ich **hab** gefunden, muh. I have found, cow
3;10:	mama **hat** nicht weggebringt. Mommy has not away-taken ich **hat** nicht an(g)efasst.* I has not touched	ein boot **hat** rüber(ge)fahr(e)n.** a boat has over-passed ich **hat** gestinken. I has smelled
3;11	ich **hab** schick gemacht. I have fancy made ich **hab** da rangemacht. I have there it-on-made	das haus weggeflogen **hat**. ** the house away-flown **hatte** nicht geklebt. had not stuck

*hat = hab(e); **hat = ist*

In the target language, utterances with the auxiliary verbs *hat* and *hab* are evidence of a structural V2 position and, hence, of a functional prefield. In TD children, they typically appear at the functional stage. However, given that Bastian's grammatical system at 3;5–3;11 has no further evidence of a functional prefield, the question is, how to account for Bastian's use of the utterances with *hat* or *hab* + Vpp as shown above, in (9).

At the lexical stage, as shown in Jordens and Bittner (this volume), Dutch and German TD children use Dutch *heeft* (has) and German *hat* (has) as a lexical verb to express 'possession' of either an object as in Dutch *heeft plak op* (has glue on) and German *hat hut auf* (has hat on) or a physical or mental state as in Dutch *heeft koud* (has cold) and German *hat angst* (has fear). So, at this stage, TD children do not use the functional element *heeft* or *hat* with a past participle, yet. As shown in (9), Bastian however, the DLD child, does. In order to account for this observation, we claim that Bastian uses *hat, hab* + Vpp similar to TD children, who use *gaat* (goes) + Vinf in Dutch to express perfect aspect lexically or *doet, is* (does, is) + Vinf in Dutch and *macht* (makes) + Vinf in German to express progressive aspect lexically. That is, we assume that Bastian uses *hat, hab* + Vpp to express the lexical aspectual meaning of 'result state'. More specifically, as also shown in the data given in (9), with predicates referring to an action, *hat, hab* + Vpp is assumed to express the lexical aspectual meaning 'result state of an action', while with predicates referring to a change of state *hat, hab* + Vpp is assumed to express the lexical aspectual meaning 'result state of a change of state'.

Thus, Bastian's utterances with *hat, hab* + Vpp perfectly fit into the lexical system that is based on the complementary distribution of utterances with either agentive or non-agentive predicates. More specifically, when in agentive utterances as in type A, *hat, hab* + Vpp is used to refer to the result state of an action, it means 'has succeeded', while in non-agentive utterances as in type B, when *hat, hab* + Vpp is used to refer to the result state of a change of state, it means 'has happened'. The relevant system can be represented with Figure 2. It is essentially the same system as shown for TD children in Figure 1.

As argued above, Bastian's utterances with *hat, hab* + Vpp at age 3;5–3;11 adhere to the grammatical system at the lexical stage. Evidence for this claim is provided by word order. As shown in Jordens and Bittner (this volume), at the lexical stage, word order is determined by the semantic principle 'Agent first'. This principle implies that if there is an agent, as in utterances of type A, it occurs in initial position. Consequently, in utterances of type B in which a theme occurs in initial position, this is only possible because there is no agent present. The relevant semantic principle also accounts for word order in Bastian's utterances with *hat, hab* + Vpp as in (9). It explains why in his data an object or an adverbial in initial position and an agent postverbally do not occur. So, the presence of the semantic principle 'Agent first' is evidence that Bastian's utterances with *hat, hab* + Vpp are part of his grammatical system at the lexical stage.

Given the semantic principle 'Agent first', interesting cases are utterances with an adverbial as in **uni** *hat es geregnet* (university has it rained. 3;7); **hier** *hat gebaut* (here has build. 3;8); **hier** *ist drauf(ge)macht* (here is on-made. 3;10). In absence of an external argument, i.e. agent or theme, these utterances may have the adverbial in initial

Type A = Agentive utterances

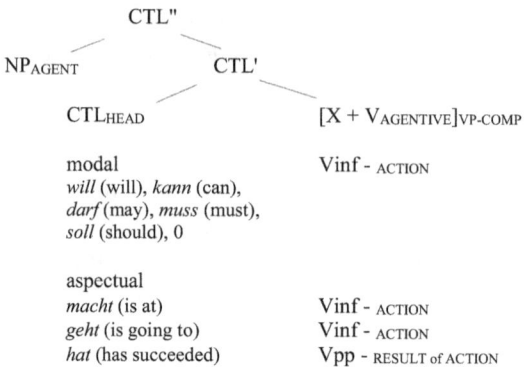

Type B = Non-Agentive utterances

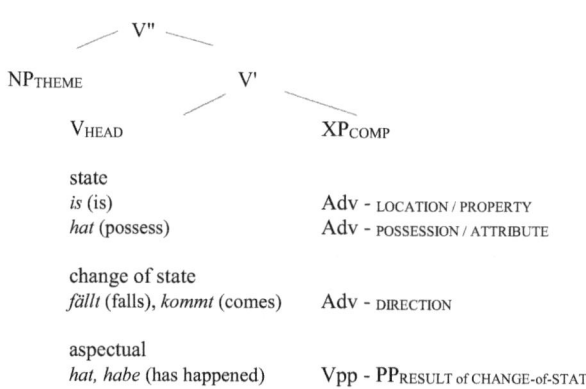

Figure 2: Utterance structure at the lexical stage in the German DLD child Bastian.

position. A similar case is the utterance *frosch,* **hier** *hat depasst* (frog, here has fitted. 3;6). As in the earlier examples, the structural position of the theme has been taken by the adverb *hier*, too, while the theme *frosch* is expressed in left-dislocated position.[3]

Examples of another type of utterance in which the semantic principle 'Agent first' plays a role are **bus** *hat gemalt* (bus has drawn. 3;6) and **das** *hat dreckig (ge)mach(t)* (this has dirty made. 3;11). Here, it is the object that occurs in initial position, while the agent is left unexpressed. Finally, under the same conditions both object and adverb are used in **das, hier** *hat gross gebaut* (that, here has big

---

3 In **hier** *hat hänger abedüzt* (here has trailer plummeted. 3;8) the initial position has been taken by *hier*. Furthermore, the lexical verb *hat*, meaning like 'hat es' or 'gibt es' (there is), is the head of an OV structure with *hänger* (trailer) serving as the object of V.

built. 3;8). Here, in absence of the agent, the adverbial may occur in initial position, while at the same time the object *das* (that) appears left-dislocated.

Further evidence that in Bastian's language system at the relevant stage *hat* and *hab* do not serve as an auxiliary verb is the fact that at age 3;5 through 3;10 both *hat* and *hab* are used unanalyzed. That is, *hat* is used irrespective of whether it is used with a 1stsg or 3rdsg subject as in *ich **hat** kaffee nemacht* (I has coffee made. 3;7) and *mama **hat** eingekauft* (Mama has bought. 3;7), while with a subject-1stsg both *hat* and *hab* are used as in *ich **hat** kaffee nemacht* and *ich **hab** aufgegessen* (I have up-eaten. 3;7). Furthermore as, for example, in *(s)chiff **hat** kaputtdegang* (ship has broken down. 3;8) and ***hat** wegdeflog(en)* (has away-flew. 3;8), *hat* is systematically used instead of targetlike *ist*. So, apparently, agreement does not play a role. It serves as evidence that at the relevant stage *hat* is not used in verb-second position (where it should receive finite morphology) and therefore it is not used as an auxiliary verb, yet.

3.6 Conclusion

To summarize, in the acquisition of Dutch and German by TD children, utterance structure is initially, i.e. at the lexical stage, based on semantic principles. They determine the production of two types of utterance structure, i.e. agentive (type A) vs. non-agentive (type B). Furthermore, they also determine word order in accordance with the semantic principle 'Agent first'. Functional features such as 'Topic first' and 'finite verb in V2 position' are absent. So, utterances with so-called 'inversion', i.e. with an object or an adverbial element in initial, topic position and the agent occurring postverbally, do not occur. As with TD children, the examples given earlier, in (7), show that Bastian has become aware of inversed structures in the input, too. Moreover, like TD children, he also shows no evidence of a functional V2 position that would allow the subject to occur in postverbal position as the result of a productive mechanism.

As far as the DLD child Bastian is concerned, language disorder seems to be essentially a matter of delay. At age 3;11, Bastian is still at the lexical stage. So, for Bastian the way to deal with the input is to accommodate the relevant utterances in terms of his current lexical system. For his seemingly targetlike utterances with the auxiliary verb *hab, hat* this means that he uses *hab* and *hat* as a lexical verb with the aspectual meaning of 'result state', i.e. either 'result state of an action' or 'result state of a change of state', while at the same time he adapts the restrictions on word order variation based on the semantic principle 'Agent first'.

At the lexical stage, it is remarkable that Bastian produces only a few examples as in (10) with the verb form *hat* that seem *not* to adhere to the semantic principle 'Agent first'.

(10) *hab, hast, hat, hab(e)n* (have-1stSg, have-2ndSg, has-3rdSg, have-1stPl) + postverbal pronoun[4]

    3;6:   *weg, deckt [= versteckt]* **hat xx** *[= babypuppe] gemacht.*
           gone, hidden has xx (babydoll) made
    3;8:   **hab(e)n wa** *desucht.*
           have we looked-for
    3;10: *das* **hab ich** *gebaut.*
           that have I built
           das **hat xx** *wieder gespielt.*
           this has xx again played
    3;11: **hast du** *alles weggenommen?*
           have you all away-taken?

This very small number shows that the grammatical system at the lexical stage is fairly stable. Utterances with a pronoun in postverbal position seem to be tolerated because due to the low degree of informativeness of the pronoun, it does not necessarily need a structural position. So, as with TD children, these data seem to be evidence for the fact that different combinations of *hat, hast* + pronoun may be learnt as unanalysed structural entities first before they eventually become evidence of the acquisition of a targetlike functional system.

4 Emergence of the grammatical system at the functional stage. Bastian 4;0–4;1

4.1 The functional prefield

As pointed out before, the grammatical system of adult German has available two structural positions utterance-initially establishing the so-called 'functional prefield'. These two positions, i.e. an initial, topic position and a V2 position, are typically *not* linked to a particular syntactic function. So, the topic position may host constituents functioning as the grammatical subject, an object or an adverbial, while the V2 position is available for verbal elements such as an auxil-

---

[4] There are only two examples with a nominal subject in postverbal position. One of them, **hat** *papa derdeckt* (has daddy hidden. 3;8), might have been produced also as an unanalyzed entity, the other one, **hat** *puppe fitzt* (has puppet tangled 3;6) has been produced according to the model provided by the mother.

iary verb, a modal verb or a lexical verb. The function of the constituent in topic position is to establish 'topicality', which means that it creates a relation between the utterance and the topic situation as the situation that the utterance applies to. The function of the verbal element in second position is to serve as carrier of 'finiteness', which means that the speaker asserts that his utterance holds for the situation that his/her utterance applies to. In other words, 'finiteness' is the means by which the speaker asserts that what (s)he says is really the case.

The expression of both topicality and finiteness entails a number of grammatical features. Topicality is expressed with the constituent that occurs in initial position. If this topic constituent is either an object or an adverbial, the subject must be placed in postverbal position. This operation is referred to as 'subject-verb inversion'. Furthermore, the topic position is also used for the expression of *wh*-questions and, if it stays empty, for *yes/no*-questions, too. Finally, the topic position fits the use of anaphoric pronouns and the expression of definiteness. The verbal element in V2 position serves as carrier of finiteness. In the default case, i.e. in its non-finite form, the lexical verb occurs in final position. The relation between the lexical verb in V2 position relative to its default final position is referred to as 'verb movement'. The V2 position is the position where the 'subject-verb agreement' rule determines the morphology of the verb, whether it is an auxiliary verb, a modal verb, a copula or a lexical verb. These grammatical features used to express topicality and finiteness are summarized in Table 1.

Table 1: The functional prefield. Grammatical features to express topicality and finiteness.

	Functional prefield	
Position:	Topic	Verb second (V2)
Function:	Topicality	Finiteness
Grammatical features:	Subject; object; adverbial *Wh*-form; *yes/no*-question Anaphoric pronouns Definiteness	Modal verb; Copula Auxiliary verb Verb movement Subject-verb agreement

4.2 The acquisition of a functional V2 position

At the functional stage, the V2 position serves as a structural position for verbal elements used to carry the functional properties of finiteness. That is, it may take any verbal element to express that the utterance is meant to serve as an assertion. Thus, this position may be taken *not* only by state and change-of-state verbs, but also by auxiliary and action verbs.

In the following, evidence will show that Bastian's grammatical system at age 4;0–4;1 has established a functional, V2 position that suits the productive use of any verbal element to serve as a carrier of both semantic finiteness and subject-verb agreement (morphological finiteness).

4.2.1 Auxiliary verbs in V2 position

Evidence of the productive use of auxiliary verbs shows that Bastian (4;0–4;1) is able to use the whole range of finite verb forms of both the auxiliary verbs *haben* and *sein* as given in the target language. That is, Bastian uses not only *haben* vs. *sein* as is required by the predicate, like in *hab gegessen* (have-1^{st}sg eaten) vs. *bin gefahren* (am-1^{st}sg driven), but also the finite verb morphology according to the agreement rules of the target system as in *hab* (1^{st}sg) vs. *hat* (3^{rd}sg) vs. *habn* (1^{st}pl) and *bin* (1^{st}sg) vs. *ist* (3^{rd}sg) vs. *sind* (1st,3^{rd}pl). Examples are given in (11)

(11) Auxiliary verb in V2 position

    4;0:   ich **hab** viel gegessen.
            I have much eaten
            mädchen **hat** oben geschlafen.
            girl has upstairs slept
            Opa **hat** nicht oben geschlafen.
            grandfather has not upstairs slept
            ich **bin** hochgefahr(e)n.
            I am up-driven
            xx **sind** mal gerennt.
            xx are once ran
            das **ist** zu fest-geworden.
            that is to tight-become
    4;1:   ich *****hat** (= habe) tür zugemacht.
            I has door closed-made
            ich **habe** nicht eingekauft.
            I have not in-bought
            ubahn **hat** aufgemacht wieder.
            tube has open-made again
            neue unser haus **ist** hochgegangen.
            (in) new our house is (x) upstairs-gone

This productive use of the morphological paradigm of the auxiliary verb is evidence that, at age 4;0–4;1, Bastian has established the functional position of V2 as a structural position for the finite verb. Given this to be the case, Bastian's grammatical system at the relevant stage should also be expected to provide the possibility for action verbs to be used in V2 position, too.

4.2.2 Action verbs in V2 position

At the functional stage, action verbs such as *trinken* (drink) not only occur in final position as is the case at the lexical stage in, for example, *milch **trinken*** (milk drink 3;5), but also in V2 position as in *ich **trink** alles aus* (I drink all out 4;0). This is true for both simple verbs such as *trinken* (drink) and complex, particle verbs such as *vorlesen* (out read). Thus, while at the lexical stage particle verbs such as *vorlesen* (out-read) may only occur in final position as in *mama hier all xx **vorlesen*** (mommy here all out-read 3;6), at the functional stage, they may also be used as in *ich **lese** vor* (I read out 4;0). So, in the default case, i.e. as far as the underlying grammatical system is concerned, agentive lexical verbs appear morphologically infinite in final position. As the result of what is referred to as 'verb movement', they are used in V2 position, too.

As shown in Section 3.1, state and change-of-state verbs typically occur in second-constituent position from early on. Thus, it is not surprising that at the functional stage, when the second-constituent position has become a structural V2 position, most of the utterances with V2 appear with state or change-of-state verbs. This holds for both simple verb forms such as: *ist* (is), *bist* (you) are, *bin* (am), *war* (was), *hat* (has), *kommt* (comes), *fliegt* (flies), *geht* (goes), *stört* (= *stürmt*) (storms), *guckt* (looks), *sieht* (sees), *hab(e)* (have), *ist drin* (is it-in), *wird* (becomes), *weiß(t)* (know-s), *fehlt* (is missing), *reicht* (is enough), *dreht* (turns), *bleibt* (stays), *sitzt* (sits), *weint* (cries), *lacht* (laughs), *heult* (cries), *schläft* (sleeps), *ruft* (calls), *steckt* (is), *fährt* (drives), *passt* (fits), *möchte* (wished), *darf* (may), *muss* (must), *will* (will) (4;0); *brauche* (need), *finde* (find), *wohnt* (lives), *gehe* (I-go), *fällt* (falls), *mag* (may), *steckt* (is), *war da* (were there) (4;1), and complex verb forms such as: *komme wieder* (come back), *kommt raus* (comes it-out), *fliegt weg* (flies away), *geht dran* (goes it-on), *geht weg* (goes away), *geht raus* (goes it-out), *geht auf* (goes up), *geht zu hause* (goes home), *kommt raus* (comes it-out), *kommt rein* (comes it-in), *komme rein* (come it-in), *wach(t) auf* (wake-s up), *passt rein* (fits it-in), *guckt raus* (looks it-out) (4;0); *gehe rein* (go it-in), *komm(e) rein* (come it-in), *hör auf* (stop), *hält fest* (hold tight), *mach(t) zu* (make-s closed), *läuft weg* (walks away), *fährt mit* (drives with), *passt auf* (is careful), *fällt um* (falls down), *fällt runter* (falls down) (4;1).

Evidence of the establishment of a functional V2 position is the fact that action verbs that were used only as Vinf in final position at the lexical stage, come to be used as both Vinf in final position and as Vfin in V2 position. Examples from Bastian (4;0–4;1) are given in (12).

(12) Action verbs used in both final and V2 position

4;0: *ich möchte milch **trinken**.*   *ich **trink** alles **aus**.*
I want milk drink   I drink all out
*ich möchte nicht **essen**.*   *Julie **iss** xx.*
I want not eat   Julie eats xx
*xx nicht xx **vorlesen**.*   *ich **lese vor**.*
xx not xx read out   I read out
*das hier **abbeissen**.*   *ich **beisse**.*
that here off-bite   I bite
*ich möchte was **gucken**.*   ***gucke** auch ja; **guckt** Opa.*
I want something look   look too yes; looks grandfather
*lass mal **killern**.*   *das **killert**.*
let now tickle   this tickles
*mehr **reinmachen**.*   *ich **mach rein**.*
more it-in-make   I make it-in
*ich möchte das **ranmachen**.*   ***machst** du das **dran**.*
I want this it-on-make   make you this it-on
*apfelsaft ich **machen**,*   *ich **machs** nicht richtig,*
*muss alle **machen**.*   *laut **macht** da, der papa.*
apple-juice I make,   I make-it not right,
must empty make   loud makes there, the daddy
   *du **machst** die ohr(e)n, ja, **machst** du.*
   you make the ears, yes, make you

4;1: *nein, nicht **rausmachen**.*   *Evi **macht** da alles **raus**.*
no, not it-out-make   Evi makes there all it-out
*guck mal, so **machen**.*   *ich **mach** das alleine.*
look, like-this make   I make this alone
*kannst du **schwimmen**?*   *der **schwimmt** da.*
can you swim?   he swims there
*ich kann **tauch(en)**.*   *ich **tauche** schiff.*
I can dive   I dive ship
***spielen** kann.*   *du **spielst** da ein monster.*
play can   you play there a monster
*alles **zumachen**.*   *ich **mach zu**.*

all closed-make	I make closed
schreiben.	*hier **schreib** ich.*
write	here write I
*da chethup **draufmachen**.*	*ich **mache** wurst **drauf**.*
there ketchup it-on-make	I make sausage it-on
***ausmalen**.*	*ich **mal aus** blume.*
in-color	I color in flower
***sauber machen**.*	***macht sauber**.*
clean-make	makes clean

With regard to the establishment of a functional V2 position, it seems interesting to note that in Bastian (4;0–4;1) there are a few examples of action verbs that occur both as Vinf in final position and as Vfin in V2 position within the same context (13).

(13) Verb movement within the same context. [M = mother]

4;0: *Mama, ich hab das. / ich moechte das **ranmachen**. / **machst** du das ran? /* [M: *was soll ich ranmachen?*] */ das hier. / das hänger.*
Mommy, I have that. / I want that it-on-fix. / make you that on? / [M: what shall I it-on-make?] / this here / the trailer.

*mir glas, ich **trink** da **aus**, ja? / . . . / ich **trink** da **aus**, ja? /* [M: *das ist aber mama's trinken.*] */ nicht alles **austrinken**.] /* [M: *doch.*] */ nein, ich **trink** alles **aus**. / . . . / dein glas alles **austrinken**.*
to-me glass, I drink it out, yes? / . . . / I drink it out, yes? / [M: that is just Mommy's drink.] / not all out-drink. / [M: though.] / no, I drink all out. / . . . / your glas all out-drink.

ab. [M: *was abbeissen?*] */ das hier **abbeissen**. / **bissen**. / . . . / ich **beisse**.*
off. [M: what off-bite?] / that here off-bite. / bit. / . . . / I bite.

***kaputtmachen** / **kaputtgemacht** / ich hat de haus **kaputtgemacht** / ich **mach** alles **kaputt**.*
kaput-make / kaput-made / I has the house kaput-made. /I make all kaput.

4;1: *zettel xx **schreiben, schreiben**. hier **schreib** ich. **schreiben**, schreiben, schreiben.*
note xx write-inf, write-inf. Here write I. write-inf, write-inf, write-inf

*ich **pass**, ich nicht **aufpassen** kann.*
I pay attention, I not attention-pay can

At the lexical stage, state and change-of-state verbs typically occur in second-constituent position. Thus, as pointed out before, it is not surprising that at the functional stage, they also occur as Vfin in V2 position as carrier of finiteness. Furthermore, at the lexical stage, state and change-of-state verbs were also used as Vpp in final position as, for example, in *geschlafen, umgefallen* to express a result state. So, at the functional stage, these Vpp forms come to be used preceded by the auxiliary verb *hab, ist* in final position, too. Thus, with Bastian (4;0–4;1), state and change-of-state verbs occur both as Vfin and with **hab, hast, hat, ist** as Vpp, as in (14).

(14) State and change-of-state verbs in both V2 and in final, Vpp position

	Vfin in V2	hab, hast, hat, ist + Vpp-final
4;0:	*schläft klein haus, bett.* sleeps (in) small house, bed	*mädchen hat oben geschlafen.* girl has above slept
	das stört [= stürmt]. it storms	*draussen hat das gestört [= gestürmt].* outside has it stormed
	jetzt wird sauber. now (it) becomes clean	*das ist zu fest geworden.* that is too tight become
4;1:	*ich finde gar nicht bausteine.* I find no-at-all bricks	*hast du nicht defund(en).* have you not found
	du sehen nicht, nein. you see not, no.	*ich hab nicht gesehen.* I have not seen
	ubahn macht zu. tube make closed	*ubahn, jetzt hat ubahn zugemacht.* tube, now has tube closed-made
	das, da passt auf holz. that, that fits on wood	*ich hab aufgepasst.* I have attention-payed

With the acquisition of the auxiliary verbs *hat, habe* and *ist, bin* in V2 position, any lexical verb may occur as Vpp. Thus, with Bastian (4;0–4;1), action verbs also occur both as Vfin and Vpp as in (15).

(15) Action verbs in both V2 and in final, Vpp position

    4;0:   *Julie **isst** xx.*   *ich hab viel **gegessen**.*
           Julie eats xx   I have much eaten
          *ich **macht** da loch.*   *alle hat **gemacht**.*
           I makes there hole   empty has made
          *ich **mach** alles **kaputt**.* *ich hat de haus **kaputtgemacht**.*
           I make all kaput   I has the house kaput-made
          ***guckt** Opa ?*   *urlaub habn auch **aneguckt**.*
           (does) looks Grandpa?   holiday have also on-looked [pictures]
          ***steckt** mund nicht.*   *ich hab nur schlafen **reinesteckt**, ja?*
           puts (in) mouth not   I have only sleeping it-in-put, yes?
    4;1:   *ich **mach zu**.*   *ich hat tür **zugemacht**.*
           I closed-make   I has door closed-made
          *ich **fähr** ubahn.*   *ich hat dreirad **fahrn**.*
           I drive tube   I has tricycle driven
          *guck xx, ich **klopfe** da.* *jetzt habe ich **detlopft**.*
           look xx, I knock there   now have I knocked

At the relevant stage, the relation between Vfin and Vpp as in (14) and (15) has become productive. This explains why at this stage there are a few cases where Bastian (4;1) uses an intransitive change-of-state verb incorrectly (*) as a transitive action verb with the auxiliary *hast, habe* in final, Vpp position (16).

(16) Change-of-state verbs incorrectly as action verbs in final, Vpp position

    4;1:   *da **fällt** da nicht **runter**.*   **hast du mein löffel hier **runtergefallen**?*
           there falls there not   have you my spoon here it-down-
           it-down   fallen?
          *hier **komm(e)** ich **rein**.*   **alles habe ich nicht xx / nicht xx*
           here come I in   ***reingekommt**.*
                                            all have I not xx / not xx it-in-come

Summarizing, at the functional stage, i.e. with the acquisition of a functional V2 position, Bastian is able to use any lexical verb, i.e. state, change of state or action verb, both as Vfin in V2 position and as Vpp in final position.

4.2.3 Subject-verb agreement and verb movement

At the relevant stage, the V2 position ist most frequently taken by a state or change-of-state verb. Utterances with these verbs are used with a theme as the external argument which refers quite often to the speaker (*ich*) and less frequently to someone or something else. A few examples are given in (17).

(17) Subject-verb agreement with state and change-of-state verbs

    4,0: *ich war nicht wasser.*
            I was not (in) water
            das schmeckt gar nicht.
            it tasts absolutely not
            weihnachtsmann kommt.
            Santa Claus comes
            ich bin kaputt.
            I am broken
    4;1: *ich finde nichts.*
            I find nothing
            ubahn ist kaputt.
            tube is broken
            Evi fährt ubahn.
            Evi drives tube
            ich hält fest.
            I hold tight

Reference to more than one person or object seldom occurs. Furthermore, in most cases there is only one verb form to be learnt together with either *ich* or someone / something else. Hence, these verb forms are likely to be learnt morphologically unanalysed. Moreover, in utterances with a modal or an auxiliary verb, morphological variation can also be learnt unanalyzed since it is most frequently linked to either the subject *ich* or *das* as in: *ich möchte* (I wanted*)*, *ich muss* (I must), *ich kann nicht* (I cannot), *kann ich* (can I), *kann man* (can one), *ich hab* (I have), *hab ich* (have I), *hast du* (have you), *ich hat* (I has), *haben wa* (have we), *das ist* (that is). Thus, as far as the morphology of subject-verb agreement is concerned, it seems that it is irrelevant as a driving force in the acquisition of the grammatical system at the functional stage. In other words, subject-verb agreement is not the cause of verb movement, as has often been argued, but its consequence.

4.3 The acquisition of a functional topic position

4.3.1 Topicalization with subject in postverbal position

As shown in Jordens and Bittner (this volume, Section 7.2), the use of auxiliary verbs in V2 position is evidence of a functional V2 position. With the instantiation of this V2 position, being the head position of the functional prefield, an initial, specifier position for constituents with topic function becomes available, too. Examples as in (18) from Bastian (4;0–4;1) show that this is indeed the case. This initial position is present not only for the subject (be it agent or theme), but also for an object (18a) or an adverbial (Adv) (18b). This indicates that, as is the case in the target system, the initial position has become a functional position that serves to express the functional feature of topicality.

(18) Topicalized objects and adverbials in utterances with Aux + Vpp

(a) Object + Aux + Vpp

4;0: *segel hat sich runtergeklappt.*
 sail has (itself) down-folded
 segel hat xx runtergemacht.
 sail has xx down-made
 [adv] hast du eisenbahn xx.
 0 have you train xx
 xx hab ich aufgegessen.
 xx have I up-eaten
 das hab ich aufgegessen.
 that have I up-eaten
 alle *hat (= ist) gemacht.
 all has-been made

4;1: *mein eimer hab ich gegessen (= vergessen).*
 my bucket have I forgotten
 alles habe ich nicht xx.
 all have I not xx
 [obj] hast du nicht defund(en)
 0 have you not found

(b) Adv + Aux + Vpp

4;0:   *[adv] hat opa zwei geträgt.*
       0 has Grandpa two carried
       draussen hat das gestört [= gestürmt].
       outside has it stormed
       kindergarten *hat [xx]⁵ gelb gegessen.
       kindergarden has 0 yellow eaten
       urlaub *habn [xx] auch aneguckt.
       holiday have (we) also on-looked
       draussen xxx kindergarten gespielt.
       outside xxx kindergarden played

4;1:   *ubahn, jetzt hat ubahn zugemacht.*
       tube, now has tube closed-made
       jetzt habe ich detlopft.
       now have I knocked
       [adv] ist alles rausgelaufen.
       0 is all out-ran

In (18), the initial position is taken by elements functioning as either object or adverbial. At this stage, the object is the element that refers to an entity that serves as the conceptual object. Thus, the object in topic position may be either the object of what in the target system is a transitive verb as in *(das) hab ich aufgegessen* (that have I up-eaten), a 'middle verb'⁶ as in *segel hat sich runtergeklappt* (sail has [itself] down-folded) or a passive verb as in *alle hat gemacht* (all has-been made). As shown in (19), Bastian (4;0–4;1) uses state and change-of-state verbs in V2 position with an object or an adverbial in topic position, too.

(19)   Vfin with object or adverbial in topic position

       (a) Obj + Vfin

4;0:   *0 hab ich.*
       0 have I
       das haben wa (=wir) schon, wasser.
       that have we already, water

---

5 [+] = a (pro)noun is missing.
6 A middle verb refers to an action whereby the participant performs an action upon itself.

4;1: *elefant möchte ich.*
elefant want I
xx chetchup mag ich.
xx ketchup love I

(b) Adv + Vfin

4;0: *drinne hab [xx] schon.*
inside have 0 already
4;1: *hier kann ich rein.*
here can-I it-in
da fällt der um.
there falls it over
unten läuft alles weg.
below runs everything away

Thus, the examples as in (18) and (19) show that with the acquisition of a V2 position a topic position has been created for an object or an adverbial to occur utterance-initially. Furthermore, these examples show that at the same time a subject position has been instantiated postverbally. It should be noted, however, that at the relevant stage this position is informationally less prominent and therefore mostly taken by a pronoun or may even remain empty. NP-subjects, on the other hand, are informationally prominent and are therefore typically used in the more prominent initial position.[7]

At age 4;0, topicalization in agentive utterances, i.e. utterances with a modal verb and an infinitive is not used productively, yet. This might be due to the fact that at the lexical stage, these utterances adhere to the semantic principle 'Agent first'. Thus, it might take some time before this principle will be given up. In the meantime, however, as a temporary solution, an object or an adverb may be used in initial position while the agent, as it is implied with the modal verb, apparently does not have to be present explicitely. This explains why the few instances of topicalization with either an object or an adverb occur with modal elements such as *kann-man, kann-ich, kann-nicht*. Examples from Bastian (4;0–4;1) are given in (20).

---

[7] The term 'NP-subject' is used to refer to an external argument that may serve as either agent or theme. NPs in presentatives do not serve as an external argument, hence they are not termed 'NP-subject'.

(20) Mod + Vinf with object or adverbial in topic position

    4;0: *elefant kann-nicht reinstecken.*
           elefant cannot in-put
    4;1: *kissen soll mitnehmen.*
           pillow shall with-taken
           da kann-man reinstecken.
           there can-one it-in-put
           hier kann-man ziehen.
           here can-one pull
           hier kann-ich aufpassen.
           here can-I attention-pay

In *yes/no*-questions, the topic position is structurally left empty. Nevertheless, questions are used with reference to a topic situation. Therefore, as shown in (21), Bastian (4;0) explicitly refers to it with an object and/or an adverbial in left-dislocated position.

(21) Mod + Vinf as *yes/no*-question

    4;0: *das hier, kann-man das essen?*
           that$_i$ here, can-one that$_i$ eat?
           das dunkelgelb / da, kann-man das essen?
           that dark-yellow$_i$ / there can-one that$_i$ eat?

At age 4;0–4;1, Bastian has only a few *yes/no*-questions with a Vfin as in: *weisst du?* (know you?), *stoert das?* (bothers that?), *kommt da ganz viel?* (comes there very much?) (4;0). Furthermore, attempts to produce a *wh*-question as in *steckt mama?* ([where] is Mama?) (4;0), *wo bist du?* (where are you?), *wo is(t) dein fenster?* (where is your window?) (4;1) are rare.

4.4 Summary

At age 4;0–4;1, Bastian's grammatical system has established the V2-position that fits the productive use of both auxiliary verbs and lexical verbs, e.g., *mädchen **hat** oben geschlafen* (girl has above slept), *ich **mach** das alleine* (I do it allone). These verb forms serve to carry the functional properties of finiteness. At the same time, the initial, topic position has become available, too. Placement of the subject postverbally only occurs with pronouns, e.g., *das hab **ich** aufgegessen* (this have I up-eaten). NP-subjects are informationally prominent, and therefore, it is not to be expected that they are placed in this position, too. Furthermore, while topicalization appears to occur productively in utterances with an auxiliary verb, this seems not to be the case in utterances with a modal verb and an infinitive as *kissen soll mitnehmen* (pillow shall with-taken). This is likely due to the fact that at the relevant stage, utterances with a modal verb and an infinitive may still be subject to the semantic principle 'Agent first'.[8]

4.5 Presentatives

As argued before, presentatives are used to introduce or reintroduce out of a set of alternatives a new referent or state of affairs that is going to be linked to the 'here and now'. While presentatives typically have no subject, they are linked to the relevant context with some frequently used deictic adverbials and pronouns such as *hier* (here), *da* (there), *jetzt* (now), *das* (that). With Bastian at age 4;0–4;1 this also occurs with adverbials such as *draussen* (outside), *(bei) uns* ([with] us), *Kindergarten* (kindergarten) that are less frequently used. The predicate of a presentative commonly refers to a state or a change of state. Examples from Bastian at (4;0) and (4;1) are given in (22).

(22) Presentatives

    4;0: *draussen **war** zu kalt.*
         outside was too cold
         *hier **ist** apfelsaft.*
         here is apple-juice
         *da **bleibt** offen.*
         there remains open
         *so **ist** verkehrt.*
         this-way is wrong
         *jetzt **ist** nichts da.*
         now is nothing there
         *das **fliegt** da haus **weg**.*
         that flies there house away
    4;1: *da **kommt** ja wenig.*
         there comes indeed few
         *da **lauft** alles **weg**.*
         there goes all away

---

8 The semantic principle 'Agent first' seems relevant here, because these utterances refer to situations that are mostly under control of an agent.

At the relevant stage, as shown in (23), the predicate nominal has often a determiner.

(23)   Presentatives with a determiner in the predicate nominal

    4;0: *hier ist weihnachtsmann.*
           here is Santa Claus
           hier ist (trom)pete.
           here is trumpet
           *das ist **ein** weihnachtsmann.*
           this is a Santa Claus
           *hier kommt **de** wasser raus.*
           here comes the water out
           *hier ist **eine** schnecke.*
           here is a slug
           *hier guckt **da** schwanz raus.*
           here looks the(re) tail out
    4;1: *hier ist ubahn.*
           here is tube
           das ist katze.
           this is cat
           *hier ist **ein** monster.*
           here is a monster
           *das ist **mein** essen.*
           this is my food
           *hier ist **dein** essen.*
           this is your food
           *hier ist **ein** geld.*
           here is a money
           *da lacht **der** sonne.*
           there laughs the sun
           *da kommt **der** rauch.*
           there comes the smoke
           *das ist **ein** kreis.*
           this is a circle

The use of determiners that are either definite or indefinite shows that at the functional stage Bastian is able to take into account the supposed knowledge state of the addressee.

4.6 Anaphoric pronouns

There is no evidence of Bastian (4;0–4;1) using the anaphoric third person personal or possessive pronoun *er* (he), *sie* (she), *ihn* (him), *sein* (his), *ihr* (her) etc. First and second person singular pronouns such as *ich* and *du*, however, occur allover and even possessive pronouns such as *mein* (my) and *dein* (your) are used. The reason for why this is the case, is the fact that first- and second-person pronouns are relevant with respect to immediate situational context, whereas anaphoric pronouns are relevant with respect to the *linguistic* context. The relevance of the immediate context also explains the frequent use of deictic pronouns and adverbials such as *hier* (here), *da* (there), *das* (that), *die* (that), *so* (so), *draussen* (outside), *drinne* (inside).

4.7 Conclusion

As far as the acquisition of his grammatical system is concerned, Bastian's developmental process is the same as in TD children. The major difference, however, is a delay of roughly two years for Bastian in order to come to grips with the use of the basic language system and its further development towards a targetlike functional language system in particular. This developmental delay seems to be due to the fact that Bastian has a hard time to make use of the linguistic features of the target system that are geared to establish contextual cohesion. It raises the question of whether this is due to a linguistic deficit or to the fact that the relevant linguistic features are difficult to process. In the following we will argue that it is not so much a linguistic deficit that causes the developmental delay but the computational demands to apply the relevant linguistic features as a function of contextual cohesion.

5 Developmental language disorder as a computational problem

As shown in Section 3.1, there seems to be no qualitative difference between Bastian compared to TD children as far as their course of language development is concerned. Both the DLD child and TD children are initially going to establish a basic lexical system which during the developmental process becomes reorganized into the fully-fledged, functional system of the target language. The basic language system of the lexical stage represents a cognitive state that is rather simple. It is linked to the 'here and now' and reflects the difference between states of affair that can and cannot be controlled. Grammatically, it accounts for a semantic system determined by types of predicate-argument structure that allow children to produce utterances with either an agent as the external argument or a theme. As shown in Jordens and Bittner (this volume), reorganization of this basic language system into the fully-fledged system of the adult language entails the establishment of a V2 position for a verbal element to express the functional properties of 'finiteness' and an initial, topic position for any constituent to express the functional properties of 'topicality'. As argued in Jordens and Bittner (this volume) both these positions constitute the so-called 'functional prefield' that is equipped to create contextual cohesion. Elements in V2 position are used to establish contextual cohesion in the sense that they are used to express that the utterance is meant to serve as an assertion, i.e. that the situation described by the utterance is indeed the case. Which situation this applies to, is indicated by the element in topic position. It establishes contextual cohesion in that it allows the speaker to link his/her utterance to a particular topic situation that is part of the relevant situational context.

The grammatical features that are involved in the acquisition of the structural positions of the functional prefield are specified in Figure 3. They are connected, on the one hand, with the placement of a verbal element in V2 position, referred to as 'verb movement' and, on the other hand, with the positioning of a nominal or adverbial constituent in initial position, referred to as 'topicalization'.

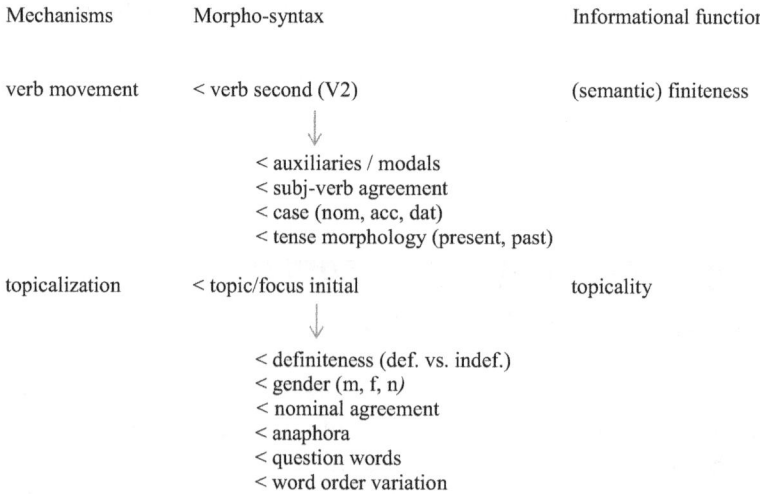

Figure 3: Morpho-syntactic features at the functional stage.

As we argued before, language acquisition in children develops from an early basic, lexical system into an adult-like, functional system that is linguistically much more complex. Given this view on language development, we showed that DLD becomes evident in children who, compared to TD children, have problems with the linguistic mechanisms that are appropriate to express both finiteness and topicality. In Jordens (this volume), we argued, along with Kolk (1998) and Duinmeijer (2013), that this is due to the fact that the application of these mechanisms imposes major computational demands. Thus, if DLD is not a linguistic deficit but rather a matter of processing, the question is: what is it that makes language production at the functional stage computationally more demanding.

In spontaneous language production, especially at an advanced level of language processing, working memory plays an important role. Working memory is a cognitive system with a limited capacity that can hold information for a short period of time such that mental operations can be performed on this information. In language production, these mental operations pertain to the linguistic mechanisms geared towards the representation of information in terms of the relevant utterance structure. In order for this to become accomplished, the speaker has to decide, first, on what (s)he wants to express, i.e. whether (s)he wants to make an assertion, ask a question or a give an order. In case of an assertion, it has to be expressed that the utterance holds true for a particular situation, i.e. that a particular state of affairs is indeed the case. This information is carried by the verbal element in second-constituent position. Furthermore, the relation between the assertion and the specific situation that it applies to has to be specified as well. This is taken care of by the element in initial, topic position. Both these linguistic functions serve to establish contextual cohesion. Due to the mental operations that are required, the activation of the relevant structures is a demanding computational undertaking.

As argued in Jordens (this volume), for DLD children these computational demands might be too onerous due to a poor working memory. The consequence of this is that language production is going to be either correct but too slow or, when produced with normal speed, incorrect or grammatically less complex. It seems that for children with DLD the latter is the case. This would explain why, in normal situations of language processing, DLD children are going to rely on their basic, lexical language system that is typically linked to the here and now, while it discriminates only between types of utterance that are either agentive or non-agentive. In other words, those features of the target language that syntactically account for the relation between the utterance and its contextual embedding are going to be avoided because they are grammatically too complex to process. This disposition explains Bastian's delay in the establishment of a basic language system and accordingly its further development towards a targetlike functional language system.

Thus, our claim is that DLD children have difficulty with the acquisition of the functional system of the target language due to the computational demands inherent to the application of the structural mechanisms used to establish contextual cohesion. As a consequence DLD children rather stay with their simple, lexical system. This does not mean, however, that this basic language system is fully identical with the lexical system of TD children. After all, despite their limited working memory, DLD children are cognitively more mature than the younger TD children with a similar level of language development. And so, it is this cognitive ability that seems to allow Bastian at age 3;5–3;11, while he is still at the lexical stage, to adapt some features of the target language that are relevant for the relation between the utterance and its situational context. These features typically concern the use of lexical aspect for the expression of finiteness and both left- and right-dislocation for the expression of topicalization and focalization, respectively.

5.1 Lexical aspect

A typical feature of adult German is the use of the auxiliary verbs *haben* (have) and *sein* (be) in structural V2 position which serves the expression of finiteness. As pointed out before in Section 3.5, Bastian at age 3;5–3;6 adapts this feature in terms of his basic language system. In doing so he manages to account for the target language input, on the one hand, while adhering to the limitation of his working memory, on the other. As shown in (24), this explains Bastian's use at (3;6) of *hab* and *hat* not as an auxiliary but as an element to express aspect lexically. More specifically, *hab* and *hat* are used to express perfect aspect, i.e. the result of either an action or a change of state as in (24a), while at the same time *mach(e), macht* (make, makes) are used to express progressive aspect, i.e. an ongoing action as in (24b), and *geht* (goes) is used to express inchoative aspect, i.e. an action that is at the point of going to take place as in (24c).

(24) The expression of lexical aspect [M = mother]

(a) perfective aspect: *hat, hab(e), hatte, haben, ist* (has-3^{rd}sg, have-1^{st}sg, had-1^{st}sg.past, have-1^{st}pl, is-3^{rd}sg)

*aufgeräumt **ist**.* [M: genau, mach das puzzle fertig]
up-cleaned is [M: right. make the puzzle complete]
*(ka)puttgemacht / auweia / **hat** kaputtgemacht / kaputtgemacht / ganz machen / hier*
*da **hat** / **hat** matten (z)wei.* [B points at a picture]
(ka)put-made / oh-oh / has kaput-made / kaput-made / complete make / here there has / has mats two

*guck durch xx. / . . . / **hatte** durchgeguckt, ja. / . . . / **hab**(e)durchgeguckt.*
[B has the camera]
look through xx / . . . / had through-looked, yes / . . . / have through-looked
*(f)rosch weg. **hat** aufgegessen.*
frog gone. has up-eaten
*Evi **hat** abgegibt.* [B does as though he has given his sister a smartie]
(to) Evi has over-given (= shared)
*er **hat** gegebt xx viele.*
he has given xx many
*xx gucken / . . . / xx **haben** gucken.*
xx see / . . . / xx have see

(b) progressive aspect: *mach(e), macht* (make-1stsg, makes-3rdsg)

***mach(t)** (d)rache pieken, ja.*
does dragon poke, yes
***mach(e)** auto fahr(e)n.*
does car drive
*hier kaputtmachen. **mach(e)** alles abreissen.*
here kaput-make. does all off-torn

(c) inchoative aspect: *geht* (goes-3rdsg)

*hier baby. **geht nicht** fahr(e)n.*
here baby, goes not drive
*xx **geht nicht** raus, fahren auto. **geht** fahr(e)n auto.*
xx goes not it-out, drive car. goes drive car
*hart, **geht nicht** dleiten [= schneiden].* [M: schmeckt nicht. das ist ganz hart]
hard, goes not cut [M: tastes not. that is very hard.]

5.2 Topicalization / focalization

Another typical feature of adult German is the positioning of a syntactic constituent in initial position to express topicality. Thus, in adult German the initial position may be taken not only by the grammatical subject but also by an object or an adverbial. These elements in initial position serve to establish the relation between the utterance and the topic situation, i.e. the situation that the utterance applies to. Placement of a constituent in initial position is the result of the functional mechanism of topicalization. If topicalization occurs with an object or an adverbial, the subject has to be placed in postverbal position.

At the lexical stage, only the external argument may occur with topic function. This means that in agentive utterances the agent occurs in initial, topic position, while in non-agentive utterances, it is the theme. Unlike children who are at the lexical stage, Bastian appears to adapt the functional feature of topicalization to his current basic language system, such that he is able to account for both the target language input and the limitations of his working memory. This becomes evident when he wants to specify the spatial-temporal setting of his utterance, while at the same time he holds on to the simple lexical system. This causes him to choose either of two strategies, both of them being non-targetlike. Examples from Bastian at (3;6) are given in (25). Thus, as in (25a), he may use the relevant adverbial *hier* (here) or *da* (there) in initial utterance position, while at the same time the external argument occurs in first position of its predicate argument structure. Alternatively, he may simply drop reference to the external argument as in (25b). At no time, however, would he place the external argument in postverbal position.

(25) Left-dislocated adverbial

(a) Adv with external argument

hier *baby. geht nicht fahren.*
here baby. goes not drive
hier*, Bas(t)ian vorlesen.*
here, Bastian out-read
hier*, eisenbahn wegfahr(e)n.*
here, train away-drive

(b) Adv without external argument

mama, ***hier****, alle xx vorlesen.*
Mommy, here, all xx out-read
da*, wurst haben.*
there, sausage (want) get
hier*, auch kaputtmachen.*
here, also kaput-make
hier*, vorlesen.*
here, out-read
hier*,* ***draussen****, schlafen.*
here, outside, sleep
hier*,* ***heute****, nicht seifenblasen.*
here, today, not soap-bubble

For the same reasons as with (25a) and (25b), Bastian (3;6) may also use the object in initial utterance position, while, as shown in (26), it occurs either before the external argument or with the external argument dropped.

(26) Left-dislocated object

> **viele brötchen,** *papa eingekauft.*
> many rolls, dad in-bought
> **da, Charly** *teddy. (sch)mutzigmachen.*
> there, Charly teddy, dirty-made
> **haus,** *teddy haben.*
> house, teddy (want) have
> **oma,** *gucken haus.*
> Grandma, look house
> **oma,** *xx gucken.*
> Grandma, xx look

The examples in (25) and (26) show that instead of the functional feature of topicalization, Bastian uses the simple strategy of left-dislocation. Again, it serves the DLD child as a means to accommodate the adult input to the restrictions given by his limited working memory.

As far as the placement of elements in final position is concerned, the basic language system adheres to the pragmatic constraint 'Focus expression last'. Usually, the focus element is a part of the predicate which is marked by intonation, i.e. sentence stress. The function of focusing, i.e. 'focalization', is used to express that from a set of alternatives one of those is claimed to hold. Examples from Bastian (3;6) are given in (27).

(27) Focalization

> *hier kann* **láufen.**
> here can walk
> *können nicht* **(sch)láfen.**
> can not sleep
> *muss* **gúcken.**
> must look
> **éisenbahn** *gefahren.*
> train driven
> *muss* **háus** *abreissen.*
> must house down-break
> *mach(e)* **álles** *abreissen.*

> make all down-break
> *hier eisenbahn **wég**fahren.*
> here train away-drive
> *hier **kapútt**machen.*
> here kaput-make
> *hier heute nicht **séifen**blasen.*
> here today not soapbubble
> *muss **áuch** (s)chönes xx haben.*
> must also nice xx have
> *mama **áuch** eisenbahn haben.*
> Mommy also train (want) have
> *ich **áuch** (ra)siert igel.*
> I also shaven hedgehog

As with topicalization, focalization is used to establish contextual cohesion, too. It serves to express that the speaker assumes that the relevant information is new to the hearer.

As it occurs with the topic element, dislocation may also take place with the element that is in focus. This explains, as shown in (28), why Bastian (3;6) may move the stressed element from its original position to a position to the right of the sentence. At the relevant stage, Bastian appears to apply the strategy of right-dislocation to the object, the verbal particle, contrastive *auch*, the subject or an adverb.

(28) Right-dislocation

> *aua machen, **háse**.*
> ouch make, rabbit
> *haben, **éisenbahn**.*
> have, train
> *muss dleiden, **brötchen**.*
> musst cut, rolls
> *iche wég. omi fahren, **wég**.*
> I away, (to) Grandma drive, away
> *fahrn, **lós**.*
> drive, go
> *geh(e)n, **háuse**.*
> go, (at) home
> *dleiden, Evi **áuch**?*
> cut, Evi too?

ich rasiert, áuch.
I shaven, too
malen, bild áuch.
draw, picture too
nicht hochgehen, dráchen.
not up-go, kite
viel vorlesen, Bás(t)ian.
much out-read, Bastian
hier xx dlafen, frósch.
here xx sleep, frog
rase, essen. essen, (d)ráussen.
meadow, eat. eat, outside
einkaufen haus, híer.
in-buy house, here

The examples in (28) show that, as with left-dislocation, this strategy of right-dislocation provides the DLD child with a means to accommodate the adult input to the restrictions given by a limited working memory

To summarize, the strategies of left- and right-dislocation may serve to alleviate the strain on language processing. It allows the DLD child, whose working memory is rather limited, to reduce the grammatical complexity that is inherent to the realization of the functional feature of both topicalization and focalization.

5.3 Summary

Evidence at 3;6 shows that the DLD child Bastian adapts the structural features of the target language geared to achieve contextual cohesion, such that they fit with his basic, lexical system. This holds for some verbal elements that are particularly used to express finiteness and for some non-verbal elements used to express topicality. Thus, verbal elements such as *hab(e)* and *hat* (have, has) that are used as auxiliary verbs at the functional stage, are adapted as verb forms used to express lexical aspect. Furthermore, the use of constituents in initial position to establish the relation between the utterance and the situation that it applies to, is going to be adapted with a left-dislocated position not only for adverbials such as *hier* and *da* but also for objects. This allows the external argument to stay in initial position as is typically a structural feature of the lexical stage. Finally, the use of intonation or stress to indicate which element is in focus, is adapted with a right-dislocated position for any such element be it the object, a verbal particle, the scope particle *auch*, the external argument or an adverb. These phenomena are evidence of how input processing of the functional features of finiteness and topicalization or focalization takes place in Bastian at the lexical stage.

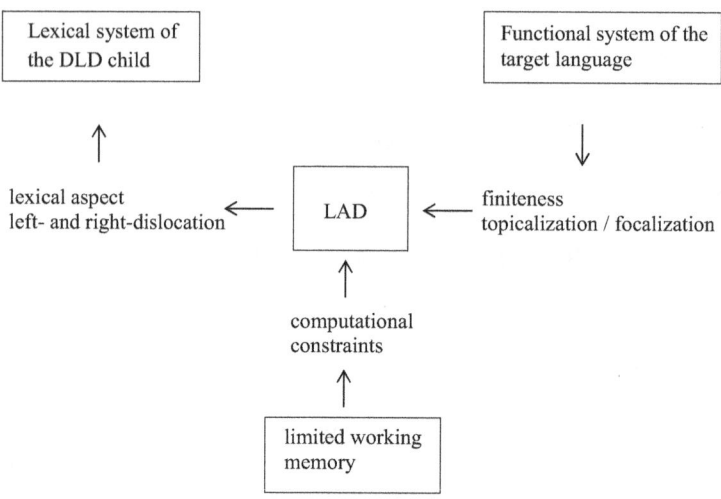

Figure 4: Adaptation of the functional features of the target system to express contextual cohesion in the DLD child Bastian.

This process, as represented in Figure 4, implies that Bastian is equipped with a language acquisition device (LAD) which accommodates the information-structural features of the functional system of the target language such that they meet the constraints of a limited working memory. The relevant phenomena of the auxiliary used to express lexical aspect and of both left- and right-dislocation to reduce the grammatical complexity of the target system confirm our claim that it is the computational limitations of the working memory that cause the delay in language development from a basic lexical system towards a complex targetlike functional system.

Appendix

Utterances with *hat* + Vpp and *hab* + Vpp

	Type A: NP$_{\text{AGENT}}$ + *hat/hab* + Vpp$_{\text{[RES. STATE of ACTION]}}$	Type B: NP$_{\text{THEME}}$ + *hat/hab* + Vpp$_{\text{[RES. STATE of CHANGE-of-STATE]}}$
3;3:	***hab** xx demacht.* (I) have xx made	
3;4:	***hat** baby xx hier gehabt.* has baby xx here had	
3;5:	*mama **hat** desucht.* mommy has looked-for	*hat depasst.* (it) has fitted
3;6:	***hat** kaputtgemacht.* has kaput-made	*so, aufgeräumt **ist**.* so, up-cleaned is
	*hier da **hat** / **hat** matten (z)wei.* here there has / has mats two	*bus **hat** [/] gemalt.*/*** bus has / painted
	***hab** aufgegessen.* have up-eaten	*frosch, hier, **hat** depasst.* frog, here, has fitted
	*ja, **hat** aufgegessen [vogel].* Ja, has up-eaten [bird]	
	*Evi **hat** abgegibt.** Evi has away-given	
	***hat** gepiekt / piek gemacht, der vogel.* has pricked / prick made, the bird	
	***hatte** durchgeguckt, ja / **hab**(e) durchgeguckt.* had through-looked, yes / have through-looked	
	*weg, deckt **hat** xx gemacht [babypuppe].* away, hidden has xx made [baby doll]	
	***hat** puppe fitzt.* has doll tickled	
	*er **hat** gegebt xx viele.* he has given xx many	
	*Timmy **hat** xx mitdebracht möwe.* Timmy has xx with-brought seagull	
	*Sandmännchen nicht /../ xx **haben** gucken.* Sandman not / xx have[-we] watched	

3;7:	*Dennis **hat** kopf gehaut.* Dennis has (on) head hit ***hat** rausdemacht.* has it-out-made *opa **hat** gemalt.* Grandpa has drawn *ich **hat** fingern aua gemacht.** I has fingers ouch made *mama **hat** eingekauft.* Mommy has bought *ich **hat** kaffee nemacht.** I has coffee made *ich **hab** aufgegessen.* I have up-eaten *Bas(t)ian **hat** den bagger gekauft.* Bastian has excavator bought *ich **hat** stulle aufgegessen.** I has bread up-eaten *ich **hab** gagor macht.* I have tractor made ***hat** (s)chon and(e)re eingelegt.* has already another in-put	*uni **hat** es geregnet.* (at) university has it rained ***hat** gewachsen.* has washed
3;8:	***hat** kein haus gebaut.* has no house built *Bas(t)ian **hat** den bagger gekauft.* Bastian has the excavator bought *ich **hat** (s)tulle aufgegessen.** I has sandwich up-eaten *da, ich **hab** &kiku gemalt.* there, I have kiku painted there, I have kiku painted has, Easter bunny not fear had *ich **hat** dedossen.** I has (myself) hit ***hat** ausgeruht.* has fully-rested	*hier **hat** hänger abedüzt.*** here has car down-fallen *(s)chiff **hat** kaputdegang.*** ship has kaput-gone ***hat** weggefahrt.*** has away-driven *u-bahn **hat** an(g)ehalten.* tube has at-stopped ***hat** wegdeflog(en).*** has away-flown ***hat** weggeflog.*** has away-flown *das hier **hat** gross gebaut.*** that here has big built *hier **hat** gebaut.*** here has built

3;9:	ich **hat** tür nemacht.*	**hat** dedossen (= gestossen).
	I has door made	has bumped
	ich **hab** viel reingemacht.	ich **hab** gefunden, muh.
	I have much it-in-put	I have found, cow
	ich **hat** kindergarten arbeitet.*	
	I has (in) kindergarden worked	
	Mama **hat** nicht alle esst [= gegessen].	
	Mommy has not all eaten	
3;10:	mama **hat** nicht weggebringt.	ein boot **hat** rüber(ge)fahr(e)n.**
	Mommy has not away-taken	a boat has over-passed
	ich **hat** nicht an(g)efasst.*	ich **hat** gestinken.
	I has not touched	I has smelled
	ich **hat** schlell [= schnell] (g)efahr(e)n.*	
	I has fast drove	
	ich **hat** geholt, teddy.*	
	I has taken, teddy	
3;11:	ich **hab** schick gemacht.	das haus weggeflogen **hat**. **
	I have fancy made	the house away-flown
	ich **hab** da rangemacht.	**hatte** nicht geklebt.
	I have there it-on-made	had not stuck
	ich **hab** das rein(g)efahr(e)n.	das **hat** dreckig (ge)mach(t).
	I have that it-in-driven	that has dirty made
	ich **hab** alles kaputtgemacht.	
	I have everything kaput-made	
	xx **hat** eine weggeschmissen.	
	xx **has** one away-thrown	

*hat = hab(e); **hat = ist

References

Bates, Elizabeth A. & Virginia Marchman, Donna J. Thal, Larry Fenson, Philip S. Dale, J. Steven Reznick, Judy Reilly & Jeff Hartung. 1994. Developmental and stylistic variation in the composition of early vocabulary. *Journal of Child Language*, 21, 85–123.

Duinmeijer, Iris. 2013. Persistent problems in SLI: which grammatical problems remain when children grow older? *Linguistics in Amsterdam* 6, 28–48.

Bittner, Dagmar & Julia Siegmüller. 2013. Function words and the bootstrapping of grammar in normally developing and impaired L1-acquisition of German. In Dagmar Bittner & Nadia Ruhlig (Eds.), *Lexical bootstrapping. The role of Lexis and Semantics in Child Language Development*, 187–216. Berlin, Boston: De Gruyter Mouton.

Fenson, Larry & Philip S. Dale, J. Steven Reznick, Donna Thal, Elizabeth Bates, Jeff Hartung, Steve Pethick, Judy Reilly. 1993. *MacArthur Communicative Development Inventories: User's guide and technical manual.* San Diego, CA: Singular Publishing.

Grimm, Hannelore & Hildegard Doil, 2000. *Elternfragebögen für die Früherkennung von Risikokindern ELFRA.* Göttingen: Hogrefe.

Kolk, Herman. 1998. *Compenseren voor een taalstoornis. Een neurocognitief model.* Radboud Universiteit: Nijmegen.

Leonard, Laurence B. 2014, *Children with specific language impairment. Second edition.* Cambridge, Mass.: The MIT Press.

MacWhinney, Brian. 2000. *The CHILDES Project: Tools for Analyzing Talk (third edition): Volume I: Transcription format and programs, Volume II: The database.* Mahwah, NJ: Lawrence Erlbaum Associates.

Siegmüller, Julia & Dagmar Bittner. 2005. Langzeitanalyse der frühen lexikalischen Entwicklung eines späteren SES-Kindes: wann gab es welche Warnzeichen? *Forum Logopädie* 19, 21–27.

Charleen List
Testing the extended optional infinitive hypothesis in a German child with DLD

Abstract: In this chapter, we analyse data from a German-speaking child with Developmental Language Disorder (DLD) and a typically developing language-matched control in order to investigate how they come to realize inflected verbs in second position in German. One theory that describes this process in typically developing children is the Optional Infinitive (OI) hypothesis (Poeppel & Wexler, 1993, Wexler, 1994; 1998). Rice, Wexler and Cleave (1995) also argue for an (Extended) Optional Infinitive ((E)OI) analysis of DLD, and Rice, Noll and Grimm (1997) extend this analysis to DLD in German. According to the (E)OI hypothesis, children's verb-marking reflects a stage in which their grammars allow infinitives (e.g. *er Turm bauen – he tower build-INF*) when finite forms (e.g., *er baut den Turm – he builds-3sg present the tower*) are required by the adult grammar. This stage extends further up the MLU range in children with DLD, such that children with DLD produce Optional infinitives (OI's)[1] at higher rates than both age-matched and language-matched controls. Rice et al. (1997) claim that, since children with DLD have early knowledge of word order and inflection, they do not make verb-placement or subject-verb agreement errors. In this chapter, we test these claims on rich corpus data from a German-speaking child with DLD (Bastian) and a typically developing German-speaking child (Leo), and compare them with the predictions of an alternative input-driven account: the Dual-Factor model (Freudenthal, Pine & Gobet, 2010; Freudenthal, Pine, Jones & Gobet, 2015a). Our analyses focus on the rate of OI's that Bastian and Leo produce at equivalent MLUs, the extent to which their use of finite forms and infinitives is sensitive to position, and the extent to which they make subject-verb-agreement errors in their speech. In a final analysis, we investigate the relation between the rate at which the children produce OI's with particular verbs and the rate at which those verbs appear as infinitive versus finite forms in the input.

---

[1] In this chapter we will use the term Optional infinitive (OI) in line with Wexler's theory of OI's (Wexler, 1994). By this term we mean verbs that are not inflected for tense or agreement in verb-second position but appear as bare infinitives in utterance-final position. Note that infinitives can also appear in utterance-final position in periphrastic constructions in the target language.

Charleen List, University of Liverpool, Charleen.List@gmx.de

Keywords: Optional Infinitive (OI)-Stage, Developmental Language Disorder, Dual-Factor Model, input

1 Introduction

The aim of this chapter is to use rich corpus data from a German-speaking child with Developmental Language Disorder (DLD) and a typically developing language-matched control to compare different models of the verb-marking deficit in DLD. Tomblin, Records, Buckwalter, Zhang, Smith and O'Brien (1997) report that approximately 7% of the preschool-aged population exhibits a significant deficit in language ability without showing other weaknesses that would lead to a diagnosis such as hearing impairment, intellectual disability, neurological impairment, or autism spectrum disorder. Children with this developmental profile are often referred to in the research literature as children with Specific Language Impairment (SLI). However, in recent years, the term Specific Language Impairment has becoming increasingly controversial (Ebbels, 2014), and a new consensus has emerged that Developmental Language Disorder (DLD) is a more appropriate term to describe these children's problems (Bishop, Snowling, Thompson, Greenhalgh & the CATALISE-2 consortium, 2017). Developmental Language Disorder is therefore the term that we will use in the present chapter. Children with DLD constitute a heterogeneous population (Leonard, 2014). They may show a delayed start in language learning, slow language development and deficits in a variety of language domains, including phonology, word learning, morpho-syntax and pragmatics (Kauschke, 2012). In this chapter, we will focus on morpho-syntax, and, in particular, on the deficit that children with DLD show in the acquisition of inflectional verb morphology.

Difficulties in verb-marking are a characteristic feature of young children's early multi-word speech. For example, between the ages of 2;0 and 3;0 years, English-speaking children often produce zero-marked verb forms in contexts that require a third person singular present tense form, see examples (1) to (3) produced by Anne from the Manchester corpus (Theakston, Lieven, Pine & Rowland, 2001).

(1) *Anne like strawberries.

(2) *That one go there.

(3) *Dolly go sleep.

Children with DLD show a particular deficit in this area. They produce bare forms for a much more protracted period of development. For example, Rice, Wexler and Hershberger (1998) report significantly higher rates of infinitives in English-speaking children with DLD than both age-matched and MLU-matched controls, with the children with DLD still failing to produce 3sg present tense –s in 90% of obligatory contexts as late as seven years of age.

Early analyses of these kinds of utterances assumed that they reflect incomplete knowledge of the target inflectional system (e.g. Brown, 1973), or that they were a matter of dropping the relevant inflection due to production limitations (Bloom, 1990; Valian, 1991). However, in languages other than English, the equivalents of these utterances often include verb forms marked with a particular infinitival morpheme, and hence cannot be explained in terms of inflection drop. In the following examples (4) to (6) below, the verb is marked with the infinitival morphemes –*ir* (French: Pierce, 1992), -*en* (German: Poeppel & Wexler,1993) and –*a* (Swedish: Josefsson, 2002).

(4) *Pas la poupée dormir.*
    Not the dolly sleep-INF
    'The dolly not sleep'

(5) *Thorsten Ball haben.*
    Thorsten ball have-INF
    'Thorsten have ball'

(6) *Pappa bära den.*
    Daddy carry-INF it
    'Daddy carry it'

These utterances clearly reflect the use of an infinitive when a finite verb form would be expected. This has led to the view that problems in verb marking across languages (including the incorrect use of zero-marked forms in English) reflect the use of non-finite forms when a finite form would be required by the adult grammar.[2] Since these utterances tend to occur during a stage in which the child is also producing correct finite forms, they are often referred to in the literature as Optional Infinitives (OI's) (Wexler, 1994).

---

[2] In this chapter the terms finite and non-finite will be used in the traditional way to refer to morphological finiteness (see also footnote 1 in Jordens' chapter: Developing language. Driving forces in children learning Dutch and German).

A number of theories have been proposed to account for the occurrence of OI's in children's speech (e.g. Rizzi, 1994, Hyams, 1996; Hoekstra & Hyams, 1998). The most influential is Wexler's Optional Infinitive (OI) hypothesis (Poeppel & Wexler, 1993, Wexler, 1994; 1998). According to this hypothesis, by the time children begin to produce multi-word speech, they have already set all the inflectional and phrase structure parameters of their language. However, their grammars allow the optional use of non-finite forms in utterances in which a finite form would be required by the adult grammar. The theory also explains why children's use of finite and non-finite forms is correct with respect to target-like clause structure.

In German, for example, finite forms are inflected for person, number and tense. They are also subject to the so-called verb-second rule, which means that, in declarative sentences, the <u>finite verb</u> must appear in second position (see examples (7) to (9)). Finite verbs in German typically occur after the subject and before the object (7). However, German has relatively flexible word order and also allows adverbials (8) and objects (9) to take first position. In such cases, the finite verb still takes second position, immediately following the adverbial or object, with the subject usually placed behind.

(7) *Die Mutter <u>kauft</u> das Brot.*
 'The mother buys the bread.'

(8) *Am Dienstag <u>kauft</u> die Mutter das Brot.*
 On Tuesday buys the mother the bread
 'On Tuesday, the mother buys the bread.'

(9) *Das Brot <u>kauft</u> die Mutter.*
 The bread buys the mother
 'The mother buys the bread.'

Non-finite forms, on the other hand, take utterance-final position, with the modal (10) or auxiliary (11) taking second position and other constituents intervening between the modal or auxiliary and the non-finite lexical verb.

(10) *Die Mutter <u>kann</u> das Brot <u>kaufen</u>.*
 The mother can the bread buy
 'The mother can buy the bread.'

(11) *Die Mutter <u>hat</u> das Brot <u>gekauft</u>.*
 The mother has the bread bought
 'The mother has bought the bread.'

When German-speaking children produce finite verb forms, they tend to mark them correctly for person, number and tense, while respecting the verb-second rule. However, when producing OI's, they tend to place the non-finite form in utterance-final position. This pattern is in line with the view that children in the OI stage distinguish between finite and non-finite forms in their input. It is taken by proponents of the OI hypothesis as evidence that children have already set all the inflectional and phrase structure parameters of their language.

In addition to providing a unified account of the cross-linguistic data, a key strength of the OI hypothesis is that it can also explain the pattern of verb-marking in children with DLD. Thus, Rice et al. (1995) argue for an Extended Optional Infinitive (EOI) Stage in English-speaking children with DLD. Furthermore, Rice et al. (1997) provide an EOI analysis of the verb-marking deficit in a group of German-speaking children with DLD. They analysed spontaneous language samples from 8 children with DLD and 8 typically developing language-matched controls at two measurement points spaced roughly 12 months apart. The DLD group had an age range of 3;9 to 4;8 and a range of MLU in words of 2.00 to 3.66 at Time 1; the typically developing group had an age range of 2;1 to 2;7 and a range of MLU in words of 2.13 to 3.77. Rice et al. (1997) found that the DLD group produced significantly more OI's than the control group at Time 1 (though not at Time 2), and that both groups made very few agreement or verb-placement errors, producing finite verbs in second position and non-finite verbs in utterance-final position. They therefore conclude that their results are consistent with an EOI account of the verb-marking deficit in DLD.

However, there are two potential problems with this conclusion. The first problem is that, in contrast to the MLU-matching effect Rice et al. (1995) found in English-speaking children with DLD, the MLU-matching effect found for German-speaking children (Rice et al., 1997) appears to be relatively short-lived, with both the DLD group and the MLU-matched controls producing very few OI's at the later MLU point. These data suggest that German-speaking children may only produce large numbers of OI's at low MLUs, and hence that there may be a difference in the rate at which English- and German-speaking children with DLD produce OI's at high MLUs that the EOI hypothesis cannot explain.

The second is that, although Rice et al. (1997) report very few agreement and verb-placement errors in their study, other studies of German-speaking children with DLD have reported different results. For example, Clahsen, Bartke and Göllner (1997) report both agreement and placement errors in their data and argue that children with DLD may have a particular problem with agreement marking.

In a more recent study, Rothweiler, Chilla and Clahsen (2012) compare German-speaking children with DLD and Turkish-German bilingual children. Rothweiler et al. (2012) report similar abilities in the two groups in their use of tense marking and complex syntactic structures such as wh-questions and embedded clauses. However, they also report that both groups struggled with the production of correctly agreeing verb forms. These findings count directly against Rice et al.'s (1997) conclusions. Rothweiler et al. (2012) note that one possible reason for this discrepancy is that Rice et al. restricted their agreement analysis to just two affixes, -t and -st and thereby "reduced the chances of finding agreement errors" (Rothweiler et al., 2012: 52).

The EOI hypothesis can be contrasted with accounts of verb-marking in children that attribute a much larger role to the child's input. These accounts take as their starting point the observation that, rather than occurring in free variation, finite verb forms and infinitives tend to occur in complementary distribution, with so-called OI's occurring in modal contexts, in which eventive verbs like 'play' or 'buy' are used to express desired or intended actions, while finite forms occur in non-modal contexts in which stative verbs such as 'want' or resultative verbs such as 'fall' are used to refer to states or changes of state. This pattern has been reported in a number of 'OI languages', including Dutch (Jordens, 1990; Wijnen, 1998); French (Ferdinand, 1996); German (Ingram & Thompson, 1996) and Swedish (Josefsson, 2002), and has led many researchers to question the claim that young children have adult-like knowledge of inflection. For example, Jordens (2012) argues for an initial lexical stage of development in which children do not have productive knowledge of verb movement or finiteness marking, while the form and position of the verb in the child's speech reflects the form and position in which it occurs in the input. This initial stage is followed by a functional stage in which children show the systematic use of topicalization and start to reorganize their grammar in a way that allows them to encode contextual information in their utterances. Evidence for the functional stage is the use of auxiliaries in second position. With the use of a functional verb in second position the child has discovered, that this position is used for verbal elements to express the pragmatic function of assertion (see also Jordens, chapter 1 in this volume). Jordens argues that "the contingency in the input between the position of the verb and its morphology makes it possible for the learner to discover the regularities of the variation in verbal morphology and thus to acquire the morphological properties of finiteness" (Jordens, 2012: 266).

Other input-driven models have sought to explain how the cross-linguistic pattern of verb-marking errors can be explained in terms of the interaction between the distributional properties of the language that the child is learning and the way the child processes this input. For example, in a series of studies, Freudenthal and his colleagues have shown that it is possible to simulate quantitative differences in the rate of utterances with OI's across a number of different languages as an outcome of the interaction between an utterance-final (and later edge-based[3]) bias in learning and the distributional properties of the input language (Freudenthal, Pine & Gobet, 2006, 2010, Freudenthal, Pine, Aguado-Orea & Gobet, 2007; Freudenthal, Pine, Jones & Gobet, 2015a; 2015b). Freudenthal and colleagues' Model of Syntax Acquisition in Children (MOSAIC) learns OI's from modal and other complex constructions in the input. Its utterance-final bias results in high rates of OI's in languages like Dutch and German, in which infinitives are tied to utterance-final position, and very low rates of OI's in Spanish in which utterance-final infinitives are much less common.

The model is also able to simulate the tendency for OI's in German and Dutch to have modal semantics and to be restricted to eventive verbs (Freudenthal, Pine & Gobet, 2009). However, as Freudenthal et al. (2010) point out, it substantially underestimates the rate of OI's in English. Freudenthal et al. (2010) therefore argue for a Dual-Factor model of verb-marking error in which some errors reflect the learning of OI's from modal structures and others reflect the tendency of the child to default to the most frequent form of the verb – which in English is the bare stem, and therefore results in defaulting errors that are indistinguishable from OI's.

The Dual-Factor model can explain both the very high rate of OI's in English and the tendency of children learning more highly inflected languages to use the most frequent form of the verb in inappropriate contexts. For example, Freudenthal et al. (2015a) show that a version of MOSAIC that combines the model's utterance-final bias in learning with a frequency-based defaulting mechanism can not only simulate the very high rate of OI's in English, but also the tendency of Spanish-speaking children to produce third person singular (3sg) forms in non-3sg contexts (Aguado-Orea & Pine, 2015; Radford & Ploenning-Pacheco, 1995). However, the model also predicts that, in German, children will default to the infinitive at low MLUs and to the third person singular present tense form at higher MLUs – and will hence produce at least some verb-placement and agreement errors when they substitute the default form into inappropriate contexts.

MOSAIC and the Dual-Factor model have so far only been used to simulate data on typically developing children, but the ideas implemented in MOSAIC have been incorporated into Leonard and his colleagues' Competing Sources of Input account of the pattern of verb-marking deficit in children with DLD (Leonard, 2014; Fey, Leonard, Bredin-Oja & Deevy, 2017). According to this view, OI's in children with DLD reflect the inappropriate extraction of non-finite structures from more complex structures in the input, when they compete with finite constructions. This is due to a weakness in their ability to process the finite verb

---

[3] Based on the beginning (left edge) or the end (right edge) of an utterance

forms earlier in the sentence (e.g. *Does the girl run fast? He helped Mom do the dishes*). Leonard and his colleagues provide support for this view using a variety of different experimental paradigms (e.g., Leonard & Deevy, 2011; Leonard, Fey, Deevy & Bredin-Oja, 2015; Purdy, Leonard, Weber-Fox & Kaganovich, 2014). They also provide evidence that at least some OI's in English-speaking children with DLD reflect defaulting to the bare stem. Thus, Kueser, Leonard and Deevy (2017) replicate a study by Räsänen, Pine and Ambridge (2014), which shows that English-speaking children's tendency to produce bare forms in 3sg elicitation contexts is significantly correlated with the relative frequency with which particular verbs occur as bare rather than 3sg forms in English child-directed speech. The Kueser et al. (2017) study shows the same effect in a group of children with DLD and a group of language-matched controls, with the children with DLD also producing significantly more bare forms in 3sg contexts than the typically developing children. The implication is that the Dual-Factor model can also account for the pattern of verb-marking error in English-speaking children with DLD – though it is less obvious whether it provides a plausible account of the pattern of verb-marking error in German-speaking children with DLD.

2 The present study

It is evident that the EOI hypothesis and the Dual-Factor model make different predictions about the pattern of verb-marking error in German-speaking children with DLD. With respect to OI's, the EOI hypothesis predicts that German-speaking children with DLD will produce OI's at higher rates than both age-matched and language-matched controls. Moreover, if it is to provide a unified account of the cross-linguistic pattern of verb-marking error in DLD, it should also predict an MLU-matching effect in German at high MLUs. The Dual-Factor model, on the other hand, predicts that OI's in German will only occur at low MLUs, and hence that children with DLD will show a deficit relative to age-matched, but not language-matched controls. With respect to verb-placement and subject-verb agreement errors, the EOI hypothesis predicts the absence of these kinds of errors, whereas the Dual-Factor model predicts some verb-placement errors and subject-agreement errors – and in particular the use of 3sg finite forms in non-3sg contexts. Finally, since, according to the EOI hypothesis, the occurrence of OI's reflects a difference between the child and the adult's underlying grammar, the EOI hypothesis predicts that correct finite forms and OI's will occur in free variation. However, the Dual-Factor model predicts that correct finite forms and OI's in German will occur in complementary distribution, with verbs that occur as correct finite forms in the child's speech tending to occur as finite forms in the input and verbs that occur as OI's tending to occur as infinitives. In the present study we use rich corpus data from a German-speaking child with DLD and a typically developing language-matched control to test these predictions.

2.1 Method

Corpora

In this study we compare data from two German corpora: the Bastian corpus and the Leo corpus. The Bastian corpus was made available by the Leibniz-Centre for General Linguistics in Berlin (Bittner, 2010). This corpus was originally meant to provide data on a monolingual typically developing German-speaking child, and consists of diary data for 9 months from the point when Bastian spoke his first words, followed by weekly 60- to 90-minute recordings from 1;8 to 7;4. These recordings were made in Bastian's home environment in everyday situations when he was interacting with his parents or his younger sister and are transcribed in CHAT format (MacWhinney, 2000). At the age of 4;6, Bastian was diagnosed with Developmental Language Disorder and began to receive therapy. His corpus thus provides detailed data on the early language development of a German-speaking child with DLD. The transcripts used in this study cover the age range from 3;0 to 4;6. They consist of 104 recordings and include 19,061 child utterances.

The Leo corpus was collected by the Max Planck Institute for Evolutionary Anthropology in Leipzig (Behrens, 2006). Leo's speech was recorded and transcribed for three years from the age of 1;11 to 4;11. In Leo's third year, five 60-minute recordings were made per week. Over the following years (until 4;11), five 60-minute recordings were made per month. These recordings were made in Leo's home environment in everyday situations when he was interacting with his parents or the researcher, and are also transcribed in CHAT format. The whole corpus consists of 383 recordings and includes 158,336 child utterances. Since the corpus is so extensive, Behrens (2006) is able to provide a very detailed description of Leo's language development. However, in the present study, we only analyse data from the period when Leo's age ranged from 2;2 to 2;7.

Procedure

In order to compare Bastian's data with data from Leo matched for MLU, the MLU for Leo and Bastian was calculated for each transcript. In line with Rice et al.'s

(1997) analysis, MLU in words was used to control for differences in the morphological complexity of the children's speech. Bastian's transcripts were then merged into monthly datasets, and transcripts were selected from Leo's corpus to provide a corresponding dataset with the same MLU in words based on a similar number of utterances (see Figure 1 for an example of this procedure).

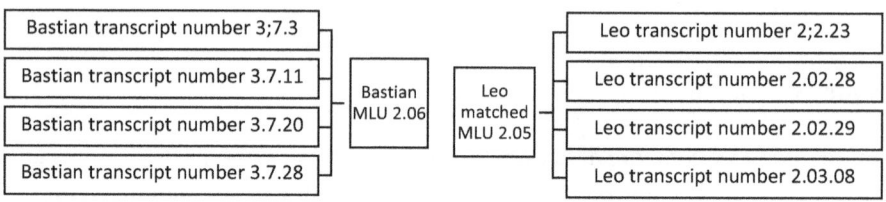

Figure 1: Example of MLU-matching procedure for one monthly dataset for Bastian and Leo.

This procedure resulted in 8 matched datasets covering the period from 3;4 to 4;0 for Bastian. One of these datasets collapsed across the ages 3;10 and 3;11, because, for these months there were fewer data points. For Leo the matched datasets cover an age range from 2;2 to 2;7. These data are used for analyses 1 and 2.

Once matching was complete, we followed the same exclusion criteria as Rice et al. (1997). First, we excluded all of the following utterance types: false starts and immediate imitations and self-repetitions; recitations of songs or stories; motor or play noises (e.g., *brumm brumm*); and utterances containing the child's idiosyncratic words or phrases. Second, we excluded all imperatives and questions. Third, we excluded all utterances that did not include an overt subject. Finally, we excluded all utterances that consisted of less than 3 constituents. Note that the use of this final criterion (in which we also follow Rice et al.) is designed to focus the analysis of OI rates on declarative utterances in which the verb can be unambiguously classified as a finite or non-finite form and in which verb-placement and agreement errors can therefore be clearly identified. However, it is worth noting that it does result in a large number of utterances being excluded from the analysis. For example, Bastian's 3;7 dataset consisted of 1039 utterances, 293 of which included a verb, but only 61 of which included an overt subject and at least 3 constituents.

These criteria were implemented by using the kwal program in CLAN to extract all fully intelligible utterances with three or more words that included a finite lexical verb, an infinitive or a modal from each child's data on the basis of the %mor tier in the transcripts. This tier contains an utterance-by-utterance morpho-syntactic coding of the child's (and the adult's) speech. The resulting output files were then checked by hand against the criteria and used to perform the following analyses for each of the two children. The kwal program was also used to extract all of the adult utterances that included finite and infinitive forms of the verbs used by the children. These output files were also checked by hand and any instances where infinitives had been incorrectly coded as plural verb forms were corrected.

Coding and analysis

Rate of OI's

The rate of OI's at each data point was established by identifying the number of utterances with 3 or more constituents including an overt subject and calculating the percentage of these utterances that were OI's as opposed to correct finite forms. In line with Rice et al. (1997), periphrastic structures such as modal + infinitive constructions were not included in this analysis. The percentages of OI's at each MLU point were then compared using Chi square or Fisher's Exact tests.

Rates of verb-placement errors

Rates of verb-placement errors were established by distinguishing between infinitives that occurred in utterance-final position and infinitives that occurred in second position and calculating the percentage of the utterances in which the infinitive occurred in second position; and by distinguishing between finite verbs that occurred in second position and finite verbs that occurred in utterance-final position and calculating the percentage of these utterances in which the verb occurred in utterance-final position. Rates are reported for the data before and after the children reached an MLU of 2. However, since there were fewer utterances with 3 or more constituents before than after the children reached this point, utterances from Bastian's earlier transcripts (Age 3;0 to 3;3, MLU=1.63) were added to the analysis, together with matched data from Leo, in order to increase the sample size.

Rates of subject-verb agreement errors

Rates of subject-verb agreement errors were established by identifying all finite verbs that occurred with 3 or more constituents including an overt 1sg, 2sg, 3sg or 3pl subject and calculating the rate at which the child used a verb with incorrect person or number marking in a 1sg, 2sg, 3sg or 3pl context. Separate error rates are reported for each of these contexts.

Rate of OI's per verb in the child's speech and rate of infinitives per verb in the input

Rates of OI's in the child's speech were also calculated on a verb-by-verb basis, together with the rates of infinitives per verb in the input. The rates of OI's per verb in the child's speech are based on all of the utterances with 3 or more constituents including an overt subject that Bastian produced between 3;0 and 4;6 and on the matching data from Leo. The rates of infinitives in the input are based on all the maternal utterances containing verbs in each of Bastian's and Leo's corpora. The child data were then used to compare the rate at which OI's occurred with stative (state or change of state), eventive (or agentive) and ambiguous verbs, applying Jordens' (2012) classification, and the child and adult data were used to assess the relation between the relative frequency with which verbs occurred in infinitive versus finite form in the input and the rate at which they occurred as OI's in the child's speech.

Reliability

The reliability of the coding of subject-verb agreement errors and verb-placement errors was assessed by having a second independent coder (who is a native speaker of German) code 48.32% of Bastian's and Leo's utterances. The Cohen's Kappa coefficient for subject-verb agreement was 0.89 and the Cohen's Kappa coefficient for verb-placement errors was 0.91, indicating a high level of agreement.

2.2 Results

The aim of the present study was to use data from two rich corpora of early child German, one from a child with DLD: Bastian, and one from a typically developing child: Leo, to test the predictions of two different accounts of the pattern of verb-marking deficit in DLD: the EOI hypothesis and the Dual-Factor model. In the first analysis, we focus on the question of whether there is a stage in Bastian's development in which he produces OI's at higher rates than Leo at equivalent MLUs. The second and third analyses focus on the question of whether Bastian and Leo make verb-placement and subject-verb agreement errors in their speech – and whether such errors are more common in Bastian's speech. In a final analysis, we focus on the question of whether Bastian's and Leo's tendency to produce OI's with particular verbs is predicted by the relative frequency with which those verbs occur as infinitive versus finite forms in their input.

Does Bastian produce OI's at higher rates than would be predicted on the basis of his MLU?

A key prediction of the EOI hypothesis is that there will be a stage in the development of German-speaking children with DLD in which they produce OI's at higher rates than typically developing children at equivalent MLUs. In contrast, the Dual-Factor model predicts that, since OI's reflect a process of building syntactic knowledge from the right edge of the utterance, the rate of OI's in both groups will be primarily determined by the length of the utterances that the child is able to produce. There will therefore be no difference in the rate of OI's at equivalent MLUs. These predictions were tested by computing the rate of OI's versus correct finite forms in utterances with 3 or more constituents in MLU-matched samples of Bastian's and Leo's speech. Table 1 shows examples of Bastian and Leo's use of correct finite forms and OI's. In line with Rice et al. (1997), compounds such as modal + infinitive constructions were not included in the analysis.[4]

Table 1: Examples of correct finite forms and OI's in Bastian's and Leo's speech.

Bastian	
Correct finite forms	OI's
Igel macht alle (3;1)	Mama auch machen (3;0)
Hedgehog empties all	Mama also do-INF
Hexe schläft da (3;4)	Bastian Haus mal(e)n (3;4)
Witch sleeps there	Bastian house draw-INF
Sonne scheint Möwe (3;6)	Omi auch kleben (3;6)
Sun shines seagull	Grandma also stick-INF
Leo	
Correct finite forms	OI's
Eichi fliegt mit (2;2)	Oma Brücke bauen (2;2)
Eichi flies with	Grandma bridge build-INF
Da hält der Zug (2;4)	Papa mit Eisenbahn spielen (2;3)
There stops the train	Daddy with train play-INF
Der Sägefisch kriegt auch ein Pflaster (2;5)	Du auch was finden (2;5)
The sawfish gets also a plaster	You also what find-INF

---

4 Note that since periphrastic structures were not included in this analysis, Leo's lower rates of OI's reflect the production of a higher proportion of finite lexical verbs. A breakdown of Bastian's and Leo's use of OIs, finite lexical verbs and periphrastic structures is provided in Appendix A. This shows that Leo and Bastian produced periphrastic structures at roughly similar rates over the period in question and confirms that the main difference between the two children was the rate at which they produced OI's and finite lexical verbs.

The results of this analysis are plotted in Figure 2 from which it can be seen that there is a stage between 3;6 and 3;11 during which Bastian produces OI's substantially more frequently than Leo at equivalent MLUw's. The differences in rates at all of the points between 3;6 and 3;11 were analysed using Chi-square or Fisher's Exact tests. With the exception of the difference at 3;6, (X^2 = 3.30, p = .069), all of these differences were statistically significant (all X^2s > 8.00, all ps < .005).

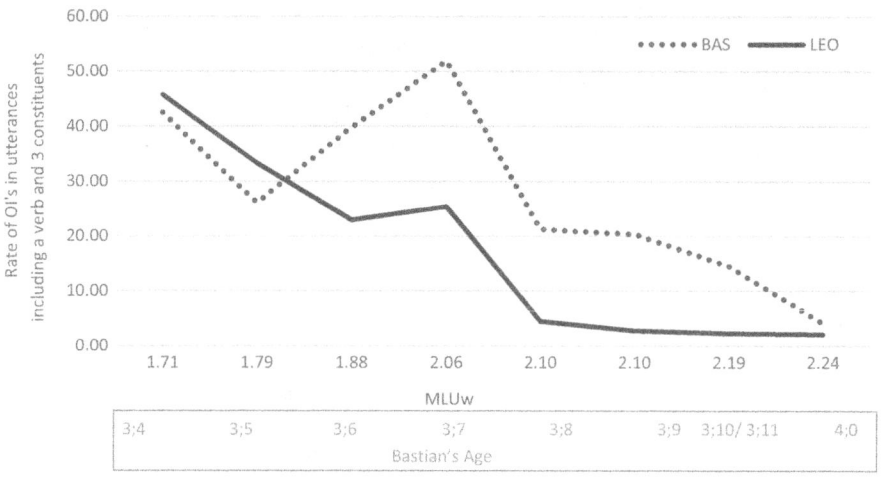

Figure 2: Rates of OI's produced by Bastian and Leo at equivalent MLUw's.

However, it is also clear from Figure 2 that the stage during which the relevant effect can be seen is restricted to a very narrow MLU range (from 1.88 to 2.19), with Bastian's rate of OI's decreasing to less than 5% at the next MLU point (2.24), which is not significantly different from Leo's (p = .6025 by Fisher's Exact).

These results provide some support for Rice et al.'s claim that there is a stage during which German-speaking children with DLD produce OI's at higher rates than MLU-matched controls. However, they also suggest that this stage is much shorter than that reported for English-speaking children – who show MLU-matching effects at much higher MLUs – and hence that it is much shorter than would be predicted by the EOI hypothesis.

An alternative possible interpretation of the data, that is broadly consistent with the Dual-Factor model, is that the MLUw values reported in Figure 2 hide differences between the two children in the average length of their utterances including verbs (MLUv) – and that it is these differences rather than differences in MLUw that predict the differences in the children's rates of OI's. This possibility was investigated by computing the average length of utterances including verbs (MLUv) across the MLU range and comparing these values across the two children.

The results of this analysis are reported in Figure 3 and show that, although the average length of utterances including verbs increases for both children (by around 2 words for Leo and 1 word for Bastian over the period in question), it is always higher in Leo than Bastian at equivalent MLUw's. This difference is statistically significant using a paired sample t-test (t = 4.71, p = .002).

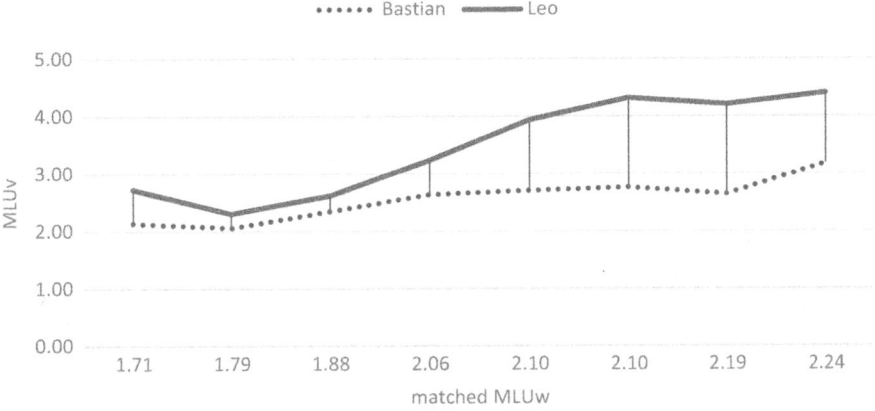

Figure 3: Comparison of MLUv's for Bastian and Leo, when matched on MLUw.

In view of this difference, we conducted an additional analysis in which we compared Bastian and Leo's rates of OI's at the three points at which they had similar MLUv's.[5] The results of this analysis are plotted in Figure 4 and show that the two children produce OI's at similar rates at the first two data points (Both X^2s < .60, both ps > .479), but that at the third data point Bastian's rate of OI's is actually significantly lower than Leo's (X^2 = 7.74, p = .005). In short, there is no evidence that Bastian produces OI's at higher rates than Leo when we control for the average length of his utterances including verbs.

When taken together with the results presented in Figure 2, these results suggest that there is little real evidence for a stage in which Bastian produces more OI's than would be predicted on the basis of the length of the utterances that he produces – or at least on the basis of the length of his utterances including verbs. The data are therefore broadly consistent with the prediction of the

---

[5] Note that for Bastian there are two data points at which his MLUv was 2.64. Bastian's rate of OI's at MLUv = 2.64 was therefore calculated by collapsing across these two data points.

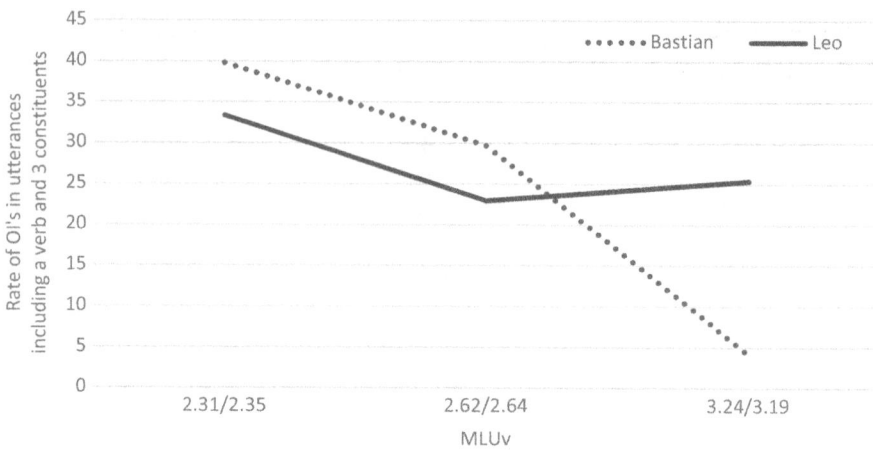

Figure 4: Rates of OI's produced by Bastian and Leo at equivalent MLUv's.

Dual-Factor model that the rate at which German-speaking children with DLD produce OI's is primarily determined by the length of the utterances that they are able to produce.

Does Bastian make verb-placement errors – and are these errors more common in Bastian's than in Leo's data?

The EOI hypothesis predicts that, although German-speaking children with DLD will produce OI's at high rates, they will rarely produce placement errors in which they use infinitives in second position (e.g. *Oma gucken Haus – *Grandma look-INF house) or finite verbs in utterance-final position (e.g. *hier Onkel passt – *Here uncle fits-3sg present). The Dual-Factor model, on the other hand, predicts placement errors when children with DLD (and to a lesser extent typically developing children) default to the most frequent form of the verb in their input.

These predictions were tested on Leo's and Bastian's data by looking at transcripts before and after the children reached an MLU of 2 (Figure 5). Both children made placement errors, particularly before MLU 2, when they both produced infinitives in second position at relatively high rates (32.4% for Bastian and 23.3% for Leo). However, Bastian made significantly more errors than Leo both before MLU 2 ($X^2(1, N=396) = 11.03$, $p = .001$) and after MLU 2 ($X^2(1, N=887) = 49.02$, $p < .001$), with Leo's rate of placement errors decreasing to close to zero at the later measurement point.

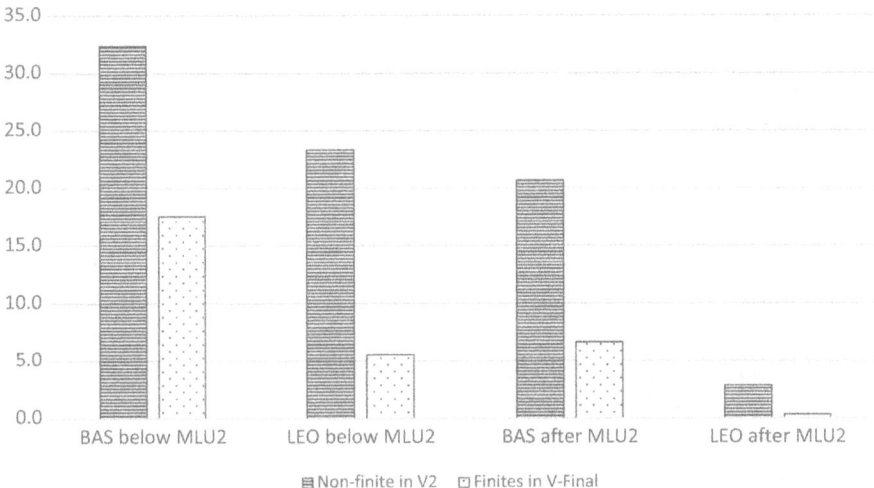

Figure 5: Rates of placement errors in Bastian and Leo.

These results count directly against the predictions of the EOI account that German-speaking children with DLD will not make placement errors, and in favour of the predictions of the Dual-Factor model. Moreover, given that the most common type of error in Bastian's speech appears to be placement errors that reflect the use of infinitives in second position, they are also consistent with the view that these errors reflect a process of defaulting to the form of the verb that occurs most frequently in utterance-final position in the input (see Table 2 for examples).

Table 2: Examples of Bastian's and Leo's verb-placement errors.

Bastian		Leo	
Finite forms in final position	Infinitives in finite position	Finite forms in final position	Infinitives in finite position
Da Puzzle fehlt (3;8) There puzzle is missing	Auto gehen nicht (3;7) Car work-INF not	S-Bahn nach Möckern fährt (2;2) S-Bahn to Möckern drives	Große Eistüte bauen hier (2;2) Big ice-cream cone build-INF here
Maus nicht schläft (3;9) Mouse not sleeps	Tierpark bauen ich wieder gleich (3;11) Zoo build-INF I again soon	Erni was so alles macht (2;2) Erni what so all does	Elefant alle Mäuse malen Himmel (2;2) Elephant all mice paint-INF heaven
Hubschrauber das hier kommt (3;11) Helicopter this here comes	Mama spielen heute mal Karten (4;2) Mummy play-INF today some cards	Noch die malt (2;1) Also this paints	Auto fahren Schaf (2;2) Car drive-INF sheep
Das Mädchen dreckig Teller leckt (4;0) The girl dirty plate licks		Ein Zug nur Sommer fährt (2;4) A train only summer drives	

Does Bastian make subject-verb agreement errors – and are these errors more common in Bastian's than in Leo's data?

A further prediction of the EOI hypothesis is that children with DLD and typically developing children will rarely produce subject-verb agreement errors in which a finite form of the verb is used in the wrong person/number context. The Dual-Factor model, on the other hand, predicts that children with DLD (and to a lesser extent typically developing children) will sometimes default to the most frequent form of the verb in the input and hence produce subject-verb agreement errors. Table 3 shows the rate of subject-verb agreement errors in Bastian's and Leo's speech. This analysis was done on all finite verbs that occurred with an overt 1sg, 2sg, 3sg or 3pl subject and 3 or more constituents in Bastian's transcripts from 3;0 to 4;6 and Leo's matching transcripts.

Table 3: Rate of subject-verb agreement errors in Bastian's and Leo's speech.

Form		all forms	correct forms	incorrect forms	error in %	error type
1st Singular	Bastian	171	135	36	21.1	3rd Person Singular (N=36)
	Leo	10	10	0	0	
2nd Singular	Bastian	33	33	0	0	
	Leo	8	8	0	0	
3rd Singular	Bastian	310	310	0	0	
	Leo	207	207	0	0	
3rd Plural	Bastian	18	17	1	5.7	3rd Person Singular
	Leo	34	31	3	8.8	3rd Person Singular (N=3)

It is clear from Table 3 that subject-verb agreement errors are extremely rare in Leo's data (only three instances of 3sg forms in 3pl contexts). However, it can also be seen that Bastian makes a relatively large number of errors (37 in total), particularly in 1sg contexts, where the error rate is over 20%. Interestingly, all of Bastian's errors reflect the incorrect use of the 3sg (suffix –t) form (e.g. *Ich hat das Fenster – *I has the window; *Ich holt zwei Zettel – *I gets two notes). These errors count directly against the predictions of the EOI hypothesis and are consistent with the view that German-speaking children with DLD make subject-verb agreement errors that reflect a process of defaulting to the highest frequency form of the verb in the input.

Do Bastian and Leo tend to produce OI's with particular verbs in a way that reflects the relative frequency with which those verbs occur as infinitive versus finite forms in their input?

According to the EOI hypothesis, the pattern of verb marking error in the language of German-speaking children with DLD reflects a maturationally-determined difference in the child and the adult's underlying grammar. Therefore, the EOI hypothesis predicts no relation between children's tendency to produce OI's with particular verbs and the rate at which those verbs occur in particular forms in the input. However, input-driven models like the Dual-Factor model predict that both typically developing children and children with DLD will be more likely to produce OI's with eventive than stative verbs (including changes of state) and that the rate at which OI's occur with particular verbs will reflect the relative frequency with which those verbs are used in infinitive versus finite form in the input.

These predictions were tested, first, by classifying all the verbs produced by Bastian and Leo as stative, eventive or ambiguous, in line with Jordens' (2012) classification, and comparing the rate at which these verbs occurred as OI's as opposed to correct finite forms in each of the children's speech; and, second by correlating the rate at which children produced particular verbs as OI's and the rate at which those verbs occurred as infinitives versus finite forms in the child's input.

Table 4 presents the mean rates of OI's in Bastian and Leo for eventive, ambiguous and stative verbs. Analysis of these data using one way analysis of variance revealed a significant effect of verb type in both children ($F(2,29) = 30.14$, $p < .001$ for Bastian and $F(2,42) = 10.69$, $p < .001$ for Leo). In both cases, the rate of OI's was significantly higher for eventive than stative verbs and significantly higher for eventive than ambiguous verbs ($p < .001$ and $p = .003$, respectively for Bastian and $p < .001$, and $p = .042$, respectively for Leo). These results count against the EOI hypothesis and are consistent with the prediction of input-driven models that children tend to produce OI's and correct finite utterances with semantically different sets of verbs.

Table 4: Mean rates (+ SDs) of OI's for eventive, ambiguous and stative verbs for Bastian and Leo.

	%Eventive (SD)	%Ambiguous (SD)	%Stative (SD)
Bastian	80.0 (15.4)	41.5 (17.8)	19.1 (25.6)
Leo	76.5 (34.0)	38.6 (16.7)	27.6 (35.8)

Figures 6 and 7 present scatterplots of the relation between the rate at which the two children produced particular verbs as OI's and the rate at which those verbs occurred as infinitives versus finite forms in their input. In both cases there is a significant positive correlation between the two variables (r(40) = .69, p < .001 for Bastian and r(86) = .49, p < .001 for Leo).

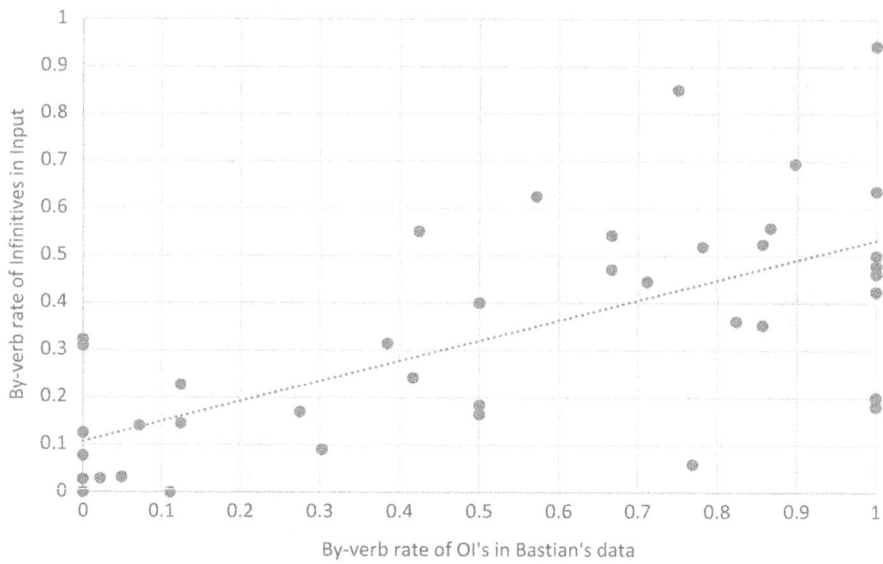

Figure 6: The relation between the by-verb rate of OI's in Bastian's data and the by-verb rate of infinitives in Bastian's input.

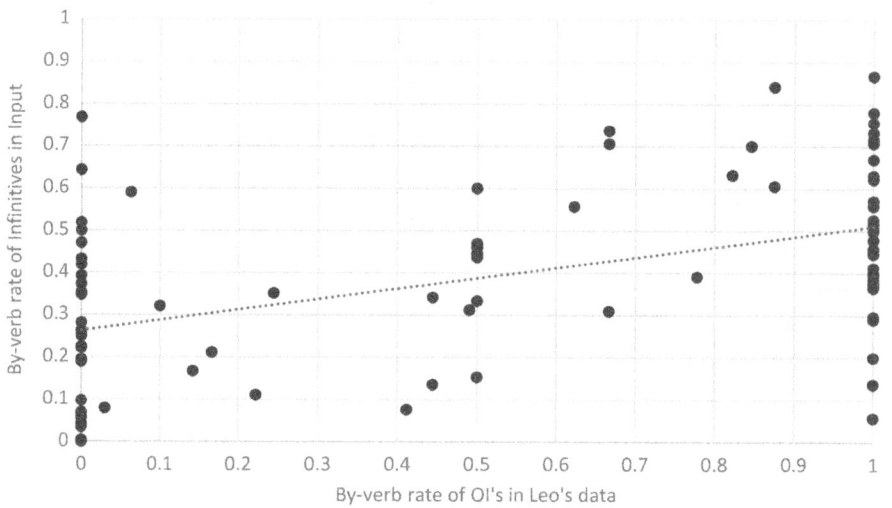

Figure 7: The relation between the by-verb rate of OI's in Leo's data and the by-verb rate of infinitives in Leo's input.

These results provide further support for an input-driven account of the pattern of OI's in German-speaking children and suggest that the semantic-conditioning of OI's in these children's speech reflects the way that semantically different sets of verbs are used in the child's input. It may also be tempting to take the higher correlation in Bastian's data as evidence that Bastian is more strongly influenced by the input than his typically developing counterpart. However, caution should be exercised here since the difference between the two correlations is not significant (p > .10)

3 Discussion

The aim of this study was to use rich corpus data from a German-speaking child with Developmental Language Disorder (Bastian) and a typically developing language-matched control child (Leo) to compare two different models of the verb-marking deficit in DLD: the EOI hypothesis and the Dual-Factor model.

In a first analysis, we focused on the question of whether there was a stage in Bastian's development during which he produced OI's at higher rates than Leo at equivalent MLUs. In line with the EOI hypothesis, our analysis did reveal such a stage. However, this stage was relatively short-lived, with the rate of OI's in both children's speech dropping to less than 5% before they reached an MLU of 2.5. These results provide some support for the EOI hypothesis, but they also raise doubts about its potential to explain the pattern of error across languages, since English-speaking children with DLD appear to show MLU-matching effects much further up the MLU range. For example, Rice et al. (1995) report significant differences in rates of OI's between English-speaking children with DLD and MLU-matched controls at MLUs ranging from 2.78 to 4.44. Our results are broadly consistent with the Dual-Factor model, which predicts that the rate at which German-speaking children produce OI's will be primarily determined by the length of the utterances that they are able to produce. Interestingly, further exploratory analysis revealed that even in speech samples matched for MLU in words, there was a tendency for Bastian's utterances with verbs to be shorter on average than those of Leo, suggesting that matching for MLU in words may not fully control for differences in the complexity of the speech of children with DLD and typically developing children.

In a second analysis, we focused on the question of whether Bastian and Leo made verb-placement errors in their speech – and whether such errors were more common in Bastian's than in Leo's data. Contrary to the predictions of the EOI hypothesis, both Bastian and Leo did make verb-placement errors in their speech, including the use of infinitives in verb second position and the use of finite forms in utterance-final position. There are some alternative explanations in the literature for the production of finite forms in utterance-final position. For example, they could reflect the fact that the child is at a preliminary stage in the acquisition of subordination and is trying to produce a subordinated clause with the conjunction *weil* (because) omitted (Rothweiler, 1993; Müller & Penner, 2009). Alternatively, the children could be trying to produce a participle construction, but omitting the auxiliary and reducing the prefix *ge-* (Marcus, Brinkmann, Clahsen, Wiese & Pinker; 1995), which would result in a form that looks like a finite verb. However, infinitives in verb second position were more common than finite forms in utterance-final position, and Bastian made significantly more errors than Leo, who made virtually no verb-placement errors after MLU 2. These results count directly against the predictions of the EOI hypothesis, and are in line with the predictions of the Dual-Factor model. Moreover, given that the most common type of error in Bastian's speech is the use of infinitives in second position, they are also consistent with the view that these errors reflect a process of defaulting to the form of the verb that occurs most frequently in utterance-final position in the input. Another possible explanation of the relatively high rate of infinitives in verb second position is Jordens' suggestion that such errors may reflect the addition of a constituent to a correctly-formed utterance as an afterthought aimed at providing additional information. For example, an utterance such as *Mama spielen Ball – Mummy play-INF ball*, could be interpreted as *Mama spielen. Ball – Mummy play-INF Ball* with the infinitive *spielen* in utterance-final position and the object *Ball* added to the utterance as an afterthought to provide additional information about what the child wants the mother to play with. Some of the placement errors in our analysis might be explained in this way. For example, the *hier* in Leo's utterance: *Große Eistüte bauen hier – big ice cream cone build-INF here* might plausibly be interpreted as an afterthought aimed at providing additional information about where the child wants to build the cone. However, there are also instances of infinitives in verb-second position that cannot be explained in this way, such as Bastian's utterances: *Tierpark bauen ich wieder gleich – Zoo build-INF I again soon* and *Auto gehen nicht – Car work-INF not*. These utterances are consistent with the idea that Bastian substitutes infinitives into verb-second position when the correct finite form is only weakly represented in his system, as the Dual-Factor model would predict. In future work, prosodic analysis could be used to investigate whether such utterances are ellipses on the part of the child – which could explain their apparently non-target-like word order.

In a third analysis, we focused on the question of whether Bastian and Leo made subject-verb agreement errors in their speech. Although such errors were extremely rare in Leo's data, they were relatively common in Bastian's data, particularly in first person singular contexts. Interestingly, all of these errors involved the incorrect use of the 3sg present tense form in a non-3sg context. This pattern is consistent with the claim that, contrary to the predictions of the EOI hypothesis, German-speaking children with DLD do have problems with subject-verb agreement (Clahsen & Rothweiler, 1993; Rothweiler et al., 2012). It is also consistent with the assumption of the Dual-Factor model that these problems reflect a tendency to default to the highest frequency form of the verb in the input, when the correct form of the verb is only weakly represented in the child's system (Freudenthal et al., 2015a and in prep.).

In a final analysis, we focused on the question of whether Bastian and Leo tended to produce OI's and correct finite forms with semantically different sets of verbs, and whether this tendency could be explained in terms of the relative frequency with which those verbs occurred as infinitive versus finite forms in their input. In both children, the rate of OI's was significantly higher for eventive than stative and ambiguous verbs. This finding counts against the prediction of the EOI Hypothesis that OI's and correct finite forms will occur in free variation in the child's speech, and is consistent with the claim that finite and non-finite verb forms tend to occur in complementary distribution, with OI's occurring in modal contexts, in which eventive verbs like 'play' or 'buy' are used to express desired or intended actions, and finite forms occurring in non-modal contexts in which stative verbs such as 'sit' or resultative verbs such as 'fall' are used to make assertions about states or changes of state (e.g. Jordens, 1990; Ingram & Thompson, 1996). In both children, there was also a significant correlation between the rate at which they produced OI's with particular verbs and the relative frequency with which those verbs occurred as infinitive versus finite forms in their input. This finding suggests that the semantic conditioning of OI's in the children's speech reflects the way that semantically different sets of verbs pattern in the child's input.

When taken as a whole, the results of these analyses provide little support for the EOI hypothesis, and are broadly consistent with the Dual-Factor model and other input-driven accounts of the pattern of verb-marking error in children with DLD (e.g. Jordens, 2012; Leonard et al., 2015). Of course, one obvious limitation of the study is that it is based on only one child with DLD and one language-matched control, and therefore needs to be replicated on a larger number of children. On the other hand, it is also important to recognize that, because it is based on two very rich longitudinal corpora, the amount of data that each child provides is much larger than that analysed in most previous studies. Moreover, it is also worth noting that, although inconsistent with the EOI hypothesis, the results of the present study are actually quite consistent with the results of previous research in the area in the following respects.

First, the finding that the MLU-matching effect in German DLD is relatively short-lived actually mirrors the pattern of results in Rice et al.'s own study, where an MLU-matching effect was only observed at the first measurement point (Rice et al., 1997). In this study the rate of OI's had dropped to less than 10% a year later. The implication is that German-speaking children may only produce large numbers of OI's at low MLUs. Hence, there may be a difference in the rate at which English- and German-speaking children make OI's later in development that the EOI hypothesis cannot explain.

Second, the finding that German-speaking children with DLD do make verb-placement and agreement errors is consistent with the results of a number of studies of DLD in German which suggest that these children have problems with word order and agreement. For example, Leonard (2014) reviews a number of studies of DLD in German and concludes that "word order errors abound in these children" (Leonard, 2014: 100). Furthermore, Rothweiler et al. (2012) compare a group of German-speaking children with DLD and a group of Turkish-German bilingual children and report that both groups struggled with the production of correctly agreeing verb forms. They also note that one possible reason for the discrepancy between their findings and those of Rice et al. (1997) is that Rice et al. only included finite forms with the two affixes, *-t* and *-st* in their agreement analysis.

Finally, the finding that there are semantic-conditioning effects on the rate at which both Bastian and Leo make OI's is consistent with a wealth of cross-linguistic evidence that OI's and finite forms do not occur in free variation in children's speech (Ferdinand, 1996: Ingram & Thompson, 1996; Jordens, 1990; 2012; Josefsson, 2002; Wijnen, 1998). As we have shown, these effects can be explained in terms of the rate at which particular verbs occur as infinitives versus finite forms in the input. This is consistent with two recent studies that document significant input effects in Dutch, English, French, German and Spanish children (Freudenthal, Pine & Gobet, 2010) and French and German children (Laaha & Bassano, 2013). To summarize, the results of the present study are broadly consistent with the results of previous research on OI's in German and other languages, and provide further support for input-driven accounts of these errors. They also support the idea that our understanding of the relation between the pattern of errors in children's speech and the distributional properties of the input could be used to shape therapy for German-speaking children with DLD. A good example of this kind of approach is Fey et al.'s (2017) intervention study, in which they tested a therapy for the verb-marking deficit in English-speaking children with DLD based on Leonard's Competing Sources of Input account (Leonard, 2019).

4 Conclusion

In the present study, we have used rich corpus data from a German-speaking child with DLD and a typically developing language-matched control to compare two different accounts of the verb-marking deficit in children with DLD. Our results provide little support for the EOI hypothesis, and are broadly consistent with the Dual-Factor model and other input-driven accounts of the pattern of verb-marking error in children with DLD (e.g. Jordens, 2012; Leonard et al., 2015). Future research should seek to replicate these results on a larger sample of children.

Appendix

Table A: Bastian's and Leo's rates of finites, OI's and compounds at matching MLU's.

Matching MLU	MLUv		% finites		% OI's		% compounds	
	Bastian	Leo	Bastian	Leo	Bastian	Leo	Bastian	Leo
1.71	2.134	2.722	54.76	52.78	40.48	44.44	4.76	2.78
1.79	2.058	2.307	72.34	56.00	25.53	28.00	2.13	16.00
1.88	2.345	2.622	58.95	72.55	38.95	21.57	2.11	5.88
2.06	2.635	3.241	40.98	65.00	44.26	22.00	14.75	12.00
2.10	2.706	3.936	67.53	85.23	18.18	4.03	14.29	10.74
2.10	2.759	4.315	55.95	77.38	14.29	2.26	29.76	20.36
2.19	2.639	4.208	78.31	86.30	13.25	2.05	8.43	11.64
2.24	3.186	4.407	82.14	92.00	3.57	2.00	14.29	6.00

References

Aguado-Orea, Javier & Julian M. Pine. 2015. Comparing different models of the development of verb inflection in early child Spanish. *PloS One*, 10(3), e0119613.
Behrens, Heike. 2006. The input-output relationship in first language acquisition. *Language and Cognitive Processes*, 21, 2–24.
Bishop, Dorothy V.M., Margaret J. Snowling, Paul A. Thompson, Trisha Greenhalgh & the CATALISE-2 consortium. 2017. Phase 2 of CATALISE: a multinational and multidisciplinary Delphi consensus study of problems with language development: Terminology. *The Journal of Child Psychology and Psychiatry*, 58(10), 1068–1080.
Bittner, Dagmar. 2010. Pronomen: Fallstudie zum Erwerb von Textstrukturierungsfähigkeiten im ungestörten Spracherwerb und bei SSES. *L.O.G.O.S. INTERDISZIPLINÄR*, 5, 46–357.
Bloom, Paul. 1990. Subjectless sentences in child language. *Linguistic Inquiry*, 21, 491–504.

Brown, Roger. 1973. *A first language: The early stages*. Cambridge, MA: Harvard University Press.

Clahsen, Harald, Susanne Bartke & Sandra Göllner, S. 1997. Formal features in impaired grammars: a comparison of English and German SLI children. *Journal of Neurolinguistics*, 10, 151–171.

Clahsen, Harald & Monika Rothweiler. 1993. Inflectional rules in children's grammars: Evidence from German participles. In Geert Booij & Jaap van Marle (Eds.), *Yearbook of Morphology 1992*. 1–34. Dordrecht: Kluwer Academic Publishers.

Ebbels, Susan. 2014. Introducing the SLI debate. *International Journal of Language and Communication Disorders*, 49, 377–380.

Ferdinand, Astrid. 1996. *The development of functional categories: The acquisition of the subject in French*. Doctoral dissertation, University of Leiden, The Netherlands.

Fey, Marc E., Laurence B. Leonard, Shelly L. Bredin-Oja & Patricia Deevy. 2017. A clinical evaluation of the competing sources of input hypothesis. *Journal of Speech, Language, and Hearing Research*, 60, 104–120.

Freudenthal, Daniel, Julian M. Pine, Javier Aguado-Orea & Fernand Gobet. 2007. Modelling the developmental patterning of finiteness marking in English, Dutch, German and Spanish using MOSAIC. *Cognitive Science*, 31, 311–341.

Freudenthal, Daniel, Julian M. Pine & Fernand Gobet. 2009. Simulating the referential properties of Dutch, German and English root infinitives. *Language Learning and Development*, 5, 1–29.

Freudenthal, Daniel, Julian M. Pine & Fernand Gobet. 2006. Modelling the development of children's use of Optional Infinitives in Dutch and English using MOSAIC. *Cognitive Science*, 30, 277–310.

Freudenthal, Daniel, Julian M. Pine & Fernand Gobet. 2010. Explaining quantitative variation in the rate of Optional Infinitive errors across languages: A comparison of MOSAIC and the Variational Learning Model. *Journal of Child Language*, 37, 643–669.

Freudenthal, Daniel, Julian M. Pine, Gary Jones & Fernand Gobet. 2015a. Defaulting effects contribute to the simulation of cross-linguistic differences in Optional Infinitive errors. In David C. Noelle, Rick Dale, Anne S. Warlaumont, Jeffrey Yoshimi, Teenie Matlock, Carolyn D. Jennings & Paul P. Maglio (Eds.), *Proceedings of the 37th Annual Meeting of the Cognitive Science Society*. 746–751. Austin, TX: Cognitive Science Society.

Freudenthal, Daniel, Julian M. Pine, Gary Jones & Fernand Gobet. 2015b. Simulating the cross-linguistic pattern of Optional Infinitive errors in children's declaratives and Wh-questions. *Cognition*, 143, 61–76.

Freudenthal, Daniel, Julian M. Pine, Gary Jones & Fernand Gobet (in prep). Defaulting effects contribute to the simulation of cross-linguistic differences in Optional Infinitive errors: simulating quantitative differences in the rate of OI errors in English, Dutch, German and Spanish.

Hoekstra, Teun & Nina Hyams. 1998. Aspects of root infinitives. *Lingua*, 106, 81–112.

Hyams, Nina. 1996. The underspecification of functional categories in early grammar. In Harald Clahsen (Ed.), *Generative perspectives in language acquisition*, 91–128. Philadelphia: John Benjamins.

Ingram, David & William Thompson. 1996. Early syntactic acquisition in German: evidence for the modal hypothesis. *Language*, 72, 97–120.

Jordens, Peter. 1990. The acquisition of verb placement in Dutch and German. *Linguistics*, 28, 1407–48.

Jordens, Peter. 2012. *Language Acquisition and the Functional Category System*. Berlin: De Gruyter.

Josefsson, Gunlög. 2002. The use and function of nonfinite root clauses in Swedish child language. *Language Acquisition*, 10, 273–320.

Kauschke, Christina. 2012. *Kindlicher Spracherwerb im Deutschen. Verläufe, Forschungsmethoden, Erklärungsansätze*. Berlin: De Gruyter.

Kueser, Justin, Laurence B. Leonard & Patricia Deevy. 2017. Third person singular -s in typical development and specific language impairment: Input and neighbourhood density. *Clinical Linguistics & Phonetics*. 32 (3), 232–248.

Leonard, Laurence B. 2014. *Children with specific language impairment* (2nd Edition). Cambridge, MA: MIT Press.

Leonard, Laurence B. 2019. Reciprocal relations between syntax and tense/agreement morphology in children's interpretation of input: A look at children with specific language impairment. *First Language*, 39(1), 96–110.

Leonard, Laurence B., & Patricia Deevy. 2011. Input distribution influences degree of auxiliary use by children with specific language impairment. *Cognitive Linguistics*, 22, 247–273.

Leonard, Laurence B., Marc E. Fey, Patricia Deevy, & Shelly L. Bredin-Oja. 2015. Input sources of third person singular –s inconsistency in children with and without specific language impairment. *Journal of Child Language*, 42, 786–820.

MacWhinney, Brian. 2000. *The CHILDES project: tools for analyzing talk* (3rd Edition). Mahwah, NJ: Erlbaum.

Pierce, Amy A. 1992. *Language acquisition and syntactic theory: A comparative analysis of French and English*. Kluwer: Dordrecht.

Poeppel, David & Kenneth Wexler. 1993. The full competence hypothesis of clause structure in early German. *Language* 69, 1–33.

Purdy, J. D., Laurence B. Leonard, Christine Weber-Fox & Natalya Kaganovich. 2014. Decreased sensitivity to long-distance dependencies in children with a history of specific language impairment: electrophysiological evidence. *Journal of Speech, Language, and Hearing Research*, 54, 1040–1059.

Radford, Andrew & Ingrid Ploennig-Pacheco. 1995. The morphosyntax of subjects and verbs in child Spanish: a case study. *Essex Reports in Linguistics* 5, 23–67.

Räsänen, Sanna H.M., Ben Ambridge & Julian M. Pine. 2014. Infinitives or bare stems? Are English-speaking children defaulting to the highest frequency form? *Journal of Child Language*, 41, 756–779.

Rice, Mabel L., Karen Ruff Noll, & Hannelore Grimm. 1997. An Extended Optional Infinitive Stage in German-Speaking Children with Specific Language Impairment. *Language Acquisition*, 6, 255–295.

Rice, Mabel L. & Kenneth Wexler. 1996. Toward tense as a clinical marker of specific language impairment in English-speaking children. *Journal of Speech and Hearing Research*, 39, 1239–1257.

Rice, Mabel L., Kenneth Wexler & Patricia L. Cleave. 1995. Specific Language Impairment as a period of extended optional infinitive. *Journal of Speech and Hearing Research*, 38, 850–863.

Rice, Mabel L., Kenneth Wexler & Scott Hershberger. 1998. Tense over time: the longitudinal course of tense acquisition in children with specific language impairment. *Journal of Speech, Language, and Hearing Research*, 41, 1412–1431.

Rizzi, Luigi. 1994. Some notes on linguistic theory and language development: the case of root infinitives. *Language Acquisition*, 3, 371–393.

Rothweiler, Monika. 1993. *Der Erwerb von Nebensätzen im Deutschen*. Niemeyer, Tübingen.

Rothweiler, Monika, Solveig Chilla & Harald Clahsen. 2012. Subject-verb agreement in Specific Language Impairment: A study of monolingual and bilingual German-speaking children. *Bilingualism: Language and Cognition*, 15(1), 39–57.

Theakston, Anna L., Elena V.M. Lieven, Julian M. Pine & Caroline F. Rowland. 2001. The role of performance limitations in the acquisition of verb-argument structure: an alternative account. *Journal of Child Language*, 28, 127–152.

Tomblin, J. Bruce, Nancy L. Records, Paula R. Buckwalter, Xuyang Zhang, Elaine Smith & Marlea O'Brien, M. 1997. Prevalence of Specific Language Impairment in Kindergarten Children. *Journal of Speech, Language, and Hearing Research*, 40(6), 1245–1260.

Valian, Virginia. 1991. Syntactic subjects in the early speech of American and Italian children. *Cognition*, 40, 21–81.

Wexler, Kenneth. 1994. Optional infinitives, head movement and the economy of derivation in child grammar. In Norbert Hornstein & David Lightfoot (Eds.), *Verb Movement*. 305–350. Cambridge: Cambridge University Press.

Wexler, Kenneth. 1998. Very early parameter setting and the unique checking constraint: A new explanation of the optional infinitive stage. *Lingua*, 106, 23–79.

Wijnen, Frank. 1998. The temporal interpretation of Dutch children's root infinitivals: the effect of eventivity. *First Language*, 18, 379–402.

Damaris Bartz
The acquisition of finiteness in *auch*- and *aber*-clauses in DLD. A case study

Abstract: This study investigates the acquisition of *auch*- and *aber*-clauses in the longitudinal data of a German-speaking child with Developmental Language Disorder (DLD) in the age range of 2;5–5;11. *Auch* is produced early and is known as a precursor of finiteness in typical language development and DLD (Dimroth et al., 2003; Jolink, 2005, 2009; Jordens & Dimroth, 2008; Penner et al., 1999, 2000). *Aber* is produced several months after *auch*, but also typically prior to the acquisition of functional finiteness. Previous studies have reported that certain particles support or hamper the realization of finiteness in typical L1- and L2-acquisition, and these effects have been predominantly traced back to information-structural properties of these utterances (Bartz & Bittner, 2018; Bittner & Bartz, 2018; Dietrich & Grommes, 1998; Dimroth, 2002, 2009; Dimroth et al., 2009; Nederstigt, 2003; Penner et al., 2000; Schimke et al., 2008, 2012; Winkler, 2006, 2009). Little is known about the relationship between the acquisition of finiteness and *aber*-clauses in DLD. In her study Skerra (2017) concludes that *aber* can be integrated lexically prior to the acquisition of V2. However, the use of cohesion devices depends to a high degree on morphosyntactic abilities. In the present study, the impact of the acquisition of functional finiteness on the use and structure of *auch*- and *aber*-clauses is explored. In order to investigate particle-specific effects in DLD, the realization of finiteness in *auch*- and *aber*-clauses is analysed and compared to simple main clauses without any particle. In addition, information-structural properties of *auch*- and *aber*-clauses are analysed. Results are compared with the acquisition of *auch*- and *aber*-clauses in typical language development. Deviations are discussed against the background of the assumption of limited working memory capacities in children with DLD.

Keywords: particles, connectives, information structure, discourse, finiteness

Damaris Bartz, Humboldt-Universität zu Berlin; Julius-Maximilians-Universität, Würzburg, e-mail: bartz.damaris@gmail.com

https://doi.org/10.1515/9783110712025-005

1 Introduction

The acquisition of finite clause structure is one of the important milestones in language acquisition and is typically affected in developmental language disorders (DLD, henceforth). Recent research has shown that the acquisition of finiteness is not an all-at-once occurrence, but rather a progressive and structure-dependent development. Westergaard (2009) for example investigates the acquisition of the V2 position in the Tromsø dialect of Norwegian. She suggests that instead of a general setting of a V2 parameter, V2 is acquired construction-specifically, depending on clause type, verb class, type of initial element, and information-structural properties. For example, subject-initial declaratives with focus-sensitive adverbs like in (1) require non-V2 word order, while with modal verbs like in (2), V2 word order is required. Westergaard reports that children take these differences into account from early on.

(1) *Æ bare låne han.*
   I just borrow.PRES him
   'I just borrow him/it.' (Westergaard, 2009: 130)

(2) *Vi kan bare se.*
   We can only look
   'We can just have a look.' (Westergaard, 2009: 130)

Further, studies on L1- and L2-acquisition of German and Dutch show that focus particles affect the realization of finite clause structure. Utterances with the negation particle *nicht* 'not' like example (3) are realized more frequently with a finite verb form in second position compared to utterances not containing a particle (Dietrich & Grommes, 1998; Dimroth, 2009; Penner et al., 2000; Schimke et al., 2012; Winkler, 2006).

(3) *Anna mag nicht schaukeln.*
   Anna likes not swinging

In contrast, utterances with the additive particle *auch* 'too/also' exhibit a finite verb form in V2 less frequently (Dimroth, 2002, 2009; Nederstigt, 2003; Penner et al., 2000; Schimke et al., 2008, 2012). Instead, the verb is either omitted (4), used in a non-finite form in final position (5), or is inflected but not in second position (6).

(4) *Anna auch Eis.*
   Anna too ice-cream

(5) *Anna   auch   Eis   essen.*
    Anna   too   ice-cream   eat

(6) *Anna   auch   isst   Eis.*
    Anna   too   eats   ice-cream

Schimke et al. (2008) and Dimroth et al. (2009) show in L2-acquisition of Dutch and German that clauses with *wieder* 'again' also less frequently exhibit a finite verb form in V2 compared to particle-free clauses.

In the studies investigating particle-specific effects, finiteness is analysed in terms of finite verb forms realized in V2 position. However, following Jordens (2012), it should be noted that the use of finite verb forms in V2 does not serve as evidence of the acquisition of finiteness as a functional category. That is, finite verb forms in second position are already used as unanalysed lexical items prior to the acquisition of 'functional finiteness', i.e. finiteness as it is "realised by the finite component of the verb".[1] The acquisition of finiteness as a functional category is part of a developmental process that leads to a reorganization of the grammatical system with consequences beyond verb inflection. As Jordens' model on the acquisition of functional finiteness is applied in the present study, its key assumptions are briefly summarized[2]:

At the initial stage of language acquisition, the 'lexical stage', verbs are used in complementary distribution according to their semantics: state and change-of-state verbs are realized with finite forms in V2 position; action verbs are realized with infinite forms in utterance-final position. With the acquisition of functional finiteness, two new positions emerge in the grammar of the child: a V2 position for finite verb forms, both lexical and functional, and an initial topic-position that is open to adverbial, nominal, and pronominal constituents. The availability of both positions characterizes the 'functional stage'. It allows for the functional expression of contextual cohesion. At the lexical stage, the use of finite verb forms in V2 is restricted to modal verbs, the copula, and lexical state and change-of-state verbs. In addition, word order is rigid in the sense that the initial position is restricted to nominal elements and deictic adverbials. As argued in Jordens (2012), the emergence of the functional stage seems indicated by the use of:

---

[1] 'Finiteness' is a concept of information structure. It serves to express "that the situation described by the utterance indeed obtains" (Klein, 1998: 227). Functional finiteness is finiteness as it is "realized by the finite component of the verb" (Klein, 1998: 237).
[2] The acquisition of functional finiteness is described in detail in Chapter 1 of this volume.

1. auxiliary constructions (*habe*n 'have' + past participle):
   Anna hat ein Eis gegessen.
   Anna has an ice-cream eaten
   'Anna has eaten an ice cream.'

2. lexical action verbs in V2:
   Anna isst ein Eis.
   Anna eats an ice-cream
   'Anna is eating an ice cream.'

3. agentive particle verbs with V2 and the separated particle in clause-final position:
   Anna isst ihr Eis auf.
   Anna eats her ice-cream up
   'Anna finishes her ice cream.'

4. OVS word order:
   Ein Eis isst Anna.
   An ice-cream eats Anna
   'It is an ice cream that Anna is eating.'

In addition, *functional* elements like determiners and anaphoric pronouns emerge. To conclude, according to Jordens (2012), the acquisition of functional finiteness is clearly indicated by the use of auxiliary verbs and inflected action verbs (with or without a verbal particle) in V2 position. Furthermore, it is also indicated by non-verbal function words and word order variation.

Applying Jordens' (2012) model of the acquisition of functional finiteness, Bittner & Bartz (2018) showed that finite clause structure emerges later in clauses with the adversative particle/connective *aber* 'but' compared to particle-free clauses and even *auch*-clauses. In this case study, the acquisition of *auch*- and *aber*-clauses is analysed in the longitudinal data of a child with DLD. *Aber* does not belong to the class of focus particles that have been the subject of previous studies. However, recent analyses highlight strong parallels between *auch* and *aber* and suggest that *aber* is focus-sensitive as well (Saebø, 2003; Umbach, 2005).

Before the study is described in more detail, syntactic and semantic properties of German *auch* and *aber* are summarized in Section 1.1. Findings from previous studies on the acquisition of *auch* and *aber* in typically developing (TD) children are described in Section 1.2. Here, the focus is on particle-specific effects on the realization of finite clause structure. In Section 1.3, previous findings on the acquisition of *auch*- and *aber*-clauses in DLD are summarized.

1.1 Syntactic and semantic properties of German *auch* and *aber*

Auch is a focus particle with additive meaning. The structural integration of focus particles into the utterance is crucial for the meaning of the utterance. *Auch* can associate either with the topic of the utterance like in (7) or with (parts of) the comment like in (8). The associated constituent is also called the domain of application, DoA henceforth (Dimroth, 2004).

(7) *Anna will AUCH schaukeln*
 Anna wants too to swing
 'Anna wants to swing, too.'

(8) *Anna will auch SCHAUkeln.*
 Anna wants also to swing
 'Anna also wants to swing.'

In (7), *auch* associates with 'Anna' and implies that someone else other than Anna wants to swing – Tim for example. Here, *auch* is stressed and used in what Dimroth (2009) refers to as the *contrastive topic case*. In (8), *auch* associates with 'schaukeln' and implies that Anna does or wants to do something else other than swinging, e.g. climbing. *Auch* is unstressed and used in what Dimroth (2009) refers to as the *neutral topic case*. In the contrastive topic case, *auch* and its DoA are typically in non-adjacent position. In the neutral topic case, *auch* and its DoA are in adjacent position.

Klein (2012) suggests an alternative analysis of *auch*. The particle expresses that another proposition (ALIUD) is true and compatible with the proposition realized in the *auch*-clause (HOC). Thus, *auch* marks a so-called *secondary assertion*. Stressed and unstressed *auch* are accounted for by a single analysis. Independent of the stress pattern of *auch*, the particle divides the utterance into a non-scope part to its left and a scope part to its right. The non-scope part defines the topic of HOC and ALIUD, while the scope part constitutes their comment. Depending on the location of the deviation of the two propositions in the topic or in the comment, it is expressed that different topic situations share the same property, like in (9), or the same topic situation has different properties, like in (10). The deviant information is underlined in both examples. The stress on *auch* is seen as a result of deaccenting consistent information following the particle.

(9) <u>Max</u> will schaukeln. <u>Anna</u> will AUCH schaukeln.
    Max wants to swing   Anna wants too   to swing
    'Max wants to swing.' 'Anna wants to swing, too.'

(10) Anna will <u>schaukeln</u>. Anna will auch <u>rutschen</u>.
     Anna wants to swing   Anna wants also to slide
     'Anna wants to swing.' 'Anna also wants to slide.'

In contrast to the initially introduced analyses, contrastive topics per se do not lead to complex scope relations according to Klein's analysis. However, lexical verbs in second position may cause complications, as the lexical content of the predicate as part of the scope part (*schaukeln*) and morphosyntactic finiteness marking have to merge. As a consequence, the surface structure of the utterance in (11) no longer mirrors the underlying structure of 'non-scope part – *auch* – scope part'.

(11) Max schaukelt. Anna schaukelt AUCH.
     Max swings   Anna swings   too
     'Max swings.' 'Anna swings as well.'

Aber has adversative meaning and is classified as a conjunction, an adverb, or a particle in the literature. While most analyses of *aber* focus on its use as a conjunction in monologues, the present study investigates its use in dialogues. As shown by Gülzow et al. (2018), children typically take up someone else's utterance with *aber* rather than their own. Thus, this conjunction plays a minor role in the study of children's spontaneous speech.

Regarding the semantics of *aber*, Sæbø (2003), Umbach (2005), and Brauße (1998) suggest a uniform analysis of its different uses.[3] Sæbø (2003) analyses *aber* in parallel to *auch*. He states that "*aber* introduces a presupposition that can be encoded in a meaning definition differing minimally from the one for *auch*" (Sæbø, 2003: 264). He defines the presupposition "in terms of **topic alternatives** and **negation**" (Sæbø, 2003: 257, emphasis in original). The similarities can be demonstrated by the examples (12) to (16). In order to generate a well-formed *auch*-clause, only a new topic is required, as demonstrated in (12a). *Aber* on the other hand requires some kind of negation as can be seen by contrasting the examples (12b) and (12c). Alternatively, a deviation from the context in

---

[3] Other accounts, suggesting different types of *aber*, are not discussed in this paper (see for example Lakoff, 1971).

the comment part of the utterance can be expressed by a lexical contrast as in example (12d). If negation is already realized in the context, *aber*-clauses with bare contrastive topics are possible like in (13). If no contrast is realized in the topic of the utterance, it is realized in the comment part (14). Again, in contrast to *auch*, *aber* requires a more complex contrast, including (explicit or implicit) negation. Besides the explicit contrast realization as in (12)–(14), the contrast in *auch*- and *aber*-clauses can also be realized implicitly like in (15) and (16). In these cases, a third proposition has to be inferred (*someone with fear of heights does not like climbing frames; someone who likes to play outside does so only in dry weather*). As pointed out by Umbach (2005), even the whole *aber*-clause can be contrasted like in (16).

(12) *Max will schaukeln.* (a) *Anna will AUCH schaukeln. / Anna AUCH.*
 'Max wants to swing.' 'Anna wants to swing, too.'
 (b) **Anna will aber schaukeln. / *Anna aber.*
  *'But Anna wants to swing.'
 (c) *Anna will aber nicht schaukeln. / Anna aber nicht.*
  'But Anna doesn't want to swing.'
 (d) *Anna will aber rutschen. / Anna aber rutschen.*
  'But Anna wants to slide.'

(13) *Max will nicht schaukeln.* *Anna will aber schaukeln. / Anna aber.*
 'Max doesn't want to swing.' 'But Anna wants to swing.'

(14) *Max will schaukeln.* (a) *Er will auch rutschen.*
 'Max wants to swing.' 'He also wants to slide.'
 (b) **Er will aber rutschen.*
  *'But he wants to slide.'
 (c) *Er will aber nicht rutschen.*
  'But he doesn't want to slide.'

(15) *Max hat Höhenangst.* (a) *Anna mag AUCH keine Klettergerüste.*
 'Max has a fear of heights.' 'Anna doesn't like climbing frames either.'
 (b) *Aber er mag das neue Klettergerüst.*
  'But he likes the new climbing frame.'

(16) *Max will schaukeln.* *Es regnet aber in Strömen.*
 'Max wants to swing.' 'But it's pouring.'

Brauße (1998) characterizes *aber* as negated *und* ('and') and emphasizes that the appropriateness of *aber* or *und* depends on the question under discussion.[4] *Aber* is used when two propositions cannot be combined under the same (implicit) question under discussion.

In contrast to *auch*, *aber* cannot be stressed. Regarding its structural integration into the utterance, *aber* is flexible. Without affecting the meaning of the utterance, *aber* can be used in utterance-initial position like in (17) as well as in utterance-internal position like in (18). In fact, *aber* can be located in front of every constituent and even in utterance-final position. However, some authors suggest that the position of *aber* affects the information structure of the utterance and thereby the reading of the *aber*-clause (Breindl, 2004; Lang, 2004; Lang & Adamíková, 2007). According to Lang (2004) and Lang & Adamíková (2007), *aber* in utterance-internal position leads to a concessive reading, an assumption that is rejected by Umbach (2005, 2001). Nevertheless, Umbach (2005) highlights the importance of information structure for the analysis of *aber*-clauses. She suggests that *aber* is focus-sensitive in the sense that the contrast expressed in the *aber*-clause depends on the focus in the utterance. Thus, Umbach observes close similarities between *aber* and focus particles like *auch*.

(17) Aber Anna will schaukeln.
But Anna wants to swing

(18) Anna will aber schaukeln.
Anna wants but to swing

The relevant analyses presented above suggest that adversative *aber* and additive *auch* show several parallels. However, *aber* is semantically more complex, while *auch* is more restricted regarding its structural integration into the utterance.

1.2 The acquisition of *auch* and *aber* in typically developing children

Typically developing children start to produce *auch* very early, usually before their second birthday. Most typically, stressed *AUCH* emerges prior to unstressed *auch* (Müller et al., 2009; Nederstigt, 2003; Penner et al., 2000) and prior to the acquisition of finiteness. Penner et al. (1999, 2000) suggest that *auch* functions as

---

4 Von Stutterheim & Klein (2002) speak of the *quaestio*.

a syntactic precursor in the acquisition of finiteness. It bootstraps syntactic structure above the VP. The hypothesis is that *auch* "projects an Affect Configuration, opening a complement slot for the VP and a specifier position" (Penner et al., 2000: 155). The suggested structure of this resulting focus particle phrase (FPP) is shown in Figure 1.

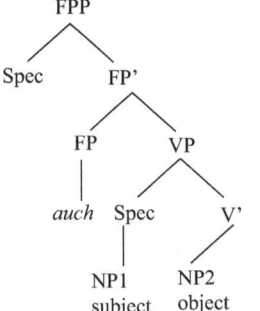

Figure 1: Structure of the focus particle phrase (Penner et al., 2000: 155).

Dimroth et al. (2003) and Jordens & Dimroth (2008) suggest that *auch* serves as a precursor of finiteness in the sense that the particle is used in the same position with the same function as finite verbs in the target grammar. This holds for L1- and L2-acquisition. Early learner utterances follow the order: topic – comment. *Auch*, like other so-called lexical linking elements, specifies the semantic relation between the topic and the comment. As a linking element, *auch* overtly asserts that the information given in the comment holds for the topic. With the acquisition of finiteness, this function of assertion is exerted by the finite verb in V2 position.

Despite the important role attributed to *auch* with respect to the acquisition of finiteness, finite verb forms in V2 are comparatively rare in utterances with *auch* (Dimroth, 2009; Nederstigt, 2003; Penner et al., 2000; Winkler, 2009). Penner et al. (2000) only state that they "assume that the underlying 'minimal' Affect Configuration (with a Focus Phrase governing a VP) tends to remain unchanged during early grammar" (Penner et al., 2000: 155). Other authors attribute this fact to information-structural properties of *auch*-clauses (Dimroth, 2002, 2009; Dimroth et al., 2009; Schimke et al., 2008; Winkler, 2009). Dimroth (2009) provides the most comprehensive explanation, focusing on the comparison of *auch*- and *nicht*-clauses. While *auch* is typically used with contrastive topics (see example 19), *nicht* is mainly used with neutral topics (20).

(19) *Max will schaukeln.*   *Anna will AUCH schaukeln.*
     Max wants to swing   Anna wants too to swing
     'Max wants to swing.' 'Anna wants to swing, too.'

(20) *Anna will schaukeln. Sie möchte nicht rutschen.*
Anna wants to swing   she wants not to slide
'Anna wants to swing.'   'She doesn't want to slide.'

Dimroth (2009) argues that in the contrastive topic case, scope relations are more complex than in the neutral topic case and considers three challenges for the realization of finite verbs in second position. First, the particle and its DoA (*Anna* in (19)) are in non-adjacent position as soon as a verb appears in second position. In the neutral topic case, the particle and its element in scope (*rutschen* in (20)) are always in adjacent position. Second, learners start to use *auch* in a cluster of 'topic+*auch*'. This cluster must be broken up in order to insert a verb in V2. Third, Dimroth suggests that the anaphoric property of particles that associate with the topic may play a role. As they anaphorically refer to an earlier assertion, where the same statement was made for another topic, learners could assume that anaphoric assertion marking is sufficient and thus morphological finiteness marking is redundant. Winkler (2009) follows Dimroth's assumption of information-structural complexity as the primary factor and assumes that children fall back on earlier acquired (non-finite) clause structures in order to reduce production effort.

Bartz (in prep.) applies Jordens' (2012) stage model of the acquisition of finiteness as a functional category. She shows that at the lexical stage, i.e. as long as functional finiteness is not yet acquired, finite verb forms in second position are less frequently realized in utterances with *auch* compared to simple main clauses. At the functional stage, evidence for functional finiteness emerges immediately but stepwise. Verbs tend to be omitted more frequently, but only one in five children shows a stronger preference for non-finite forms in *auch*-clauses. Information-structural patterns of *auch*-clauses are comparable at both stages, including the use of *auch* with contrastive topics (stressed *auch*) and with neutral topics (unstressed *auch*), the explicit and implicit contrast realization,[5] and the use of *auch* in adjacent as well as in non-adjacent position relative to its DoA.

The production of *aber* starts several months later than that of *auch*, i.e. around the second birthday. However, it typically emerges one to two months prior to the acquisition of functional finiteness (Bittner & Bartz, 2018). Bittner & Bartz (2018) investigated the morphosyntactic properties of *aber*-clauses in the first 12 months of *aber* production with 4 typically developing children by applying Jordens' (2012) acquisition model of functional finiteness. Despite considera-

---

[5] Examples of explicit *auch*-clauses are given in (12a) and (14a). An example of an implicit *auch*-clause is given in (15a).

ble individual variation, they found a common developmental process. Compared to simple main clauses, the regular production of all four structures indicating functional finiteness (see 1. to 4. on p. 166) was 2–6 months later in *aber*-clauses. Furthermore, the acquisition of *aber*-clauses was found to proceed in three stages (see Table 1): the 'pre-finiteness stage', the 'external finiteness stage', and the 'internal finiteness stage'. The pre-finiteness stage includes all *aber*-productions prior to the acquisition of functional finiteness in simple main clauses. *Aber*-clauses at this stage are characterized by the omission of obligatory constituents, i.e. mainly the verb, but also verb arguments. The external finiteness stage covers all *aber*-clauses that are produced after the emergence of functional finiteness in simple main clauses but prior to the use of finiteness in *aber*-clauses. They are characterized by the use of finite verb forms and are generally syntactically well-formed. The use of functional finiteness in *aber*-clauses is only found in the last stage: the internal finiteness stage.

Table 1: Three stages in the realization of functional finiteness in *aber*-clauses (Bittner & Bartz, 2018).

	Pre-finiteness stage	External finiteness stage	Internal finiteness stage
Simple main clauses	no	yes	yes
Aber-clauses	no	no	yes

Like in *auch*-clauses, the four structures indicating functional finiteness emerge stepwise in *aber*-clauses. The following order seems to be most typical: lexical verbs expressing an action predicate in V2 position, OVS word order, auxiliary constructions (*haben* 'have' + past participle), and clause-final position of verbal particles expressing action predicates. Concerning the information-structural properties of *aber*-clauses, the contrast can be alternatively located in the topic as in (12c) and (13), in the comment as in (14c), or in the topic and in the comment as in (12d). Bartz & Bittner (2018) revealed an early preference for topic-including contrasts over comment-located ones and for explicit over implicit contrast realization.[6] It is argued that children initially concentrate on the realization of the complex content relations including the information-structural alignment of the contrasted constituents and the anticipation of an implicit proposition and fall back on non-finite clause structures until the involved processes are automatized.

---

6 Examples of explicit *aber*-clauses are given in (12c), (12d), (13), and (14c). Examples of implicit *aber*-clauses are given in (15b) and (16).

1.3 The acquisition of *auch* and *aber* in children with DLD

So far, little is known about the acquisition of *auch-* and *aber*-clauses in children with DLD. Penner et al. (1999) analyse the data of three German speaking late talkers. They assume that *auch* has a bootstrapping function in the acquisition of finiteness in delayed language acquisition, too. Similarly, Jolink (2005, 2009) shows that Dutch monolingual children with DLD like typically developing children use particles like *ook* (Dutch equivalent to German *auch*) as lexical linking devices and thus as a precursor of morphosyntactic finiteness marking. Dimroth & Lindner (2005) investigate the acquisition of finiteness in L2-learners and children with DLD. In both groups, they observe an intermediate stage in which the production of light verbs, modal verbs like in (21), copulas, and auxiliaries exceeds the use of lexical verbs (see example 22).

(21) Anna   will   ein   Eis   essen.
      Anna   wants   an   ice-cream   eat
      'Anna wants to eat an ice cream.'

(22) Anna   isst   ein   Eis.
      Anna   eats   an   ice-cream.
      'Anna is eating an ice cream.'

They conclude that the integration of the lexical content of the verb and the morphosyntactic expression of finiteness is difficult for these learners. For the L2-learners they report that during this stage, *auch*-clauses more frequently exhibit non-finite utterance structures.

Studies on the acquisition of *aber* mainly focus on its frequency and appropriate use at school age. Tribushinina et al. (2015, 2017) investigated the production of *i* 'and' and *a* 'and/but' in Russian monolingual children with DLD. Both studies show that the frequency of use as a connective by children with DLD at early school age does not differ from that of children without DLD at the same age, but the frequency of inappropriate use is higher in children with DLD. Skerra (2017) investigated the acquisition of cohesive devices in German monolingual children with DLD (age range 5;1–10;11), including the comprehension and production of *aber* as a connective in narratives. In comprehension tasks, children with DLD ignored *aber*. Nevertheless, *aber* is available for production. Skerra suggests that connectives like *aber* are integrated into the utterance lexically as long as finite clause structure is not acquired. While V2 acquisition stagnates, the use of connectives is limited and conceptually restricted. Only after the acquisition of a generalized V2 can *aber* be integrated formally.

To conclude, *auch* is produced early and is seen as a precursor of functional finiteness in typical language development and DLD. *Aber* is produced several months after *auch*, but also typically prior to the acquisition of functional finiteness. Adversative *aber* is semantically more complex than additive *auch*, a fact that can explain its later emergence in language production at least partially. However, it is unclear whether semantic complexity is the only reason for its later emergence. The syntactic integration of *aber* into the utterance is not expected to be challenging. As a particle, *aber* can easily be structurally integrated into the utterance. Even as a connective, Skerra (2017) assumes that *aber* can be integrated lexically, meaning that no advanced syntactic structures are required. Nevertheless, in her study Skerra also concludes that morphosyntactic abilities play a decisive role regarding the availability of cohesion devices in children with DLD. Given that *aber* relates an utterance to the previous discourse and discourse anchoring is the main function of finiteness (Jordens, 2012, this volume), the acquisition of finite clause structure might be relevant for the use of *aber*.

The following questions will be addressed in the present study:

1. How does the structure of *auch*- and *aber*-clauses develop in DLD and what is the impact of the acquisition of functional finiteness on this process?
2. What is the effect of *auch* and *aber* on the realization of finite clause structure in DLD?
3. Are the observed deviations from the acquisition of *auch*- and *aber*-clauses in TD children in line with the assumption of limited working memory capacities in children with DLD as suggested by Jordens (this volume)? The results of the study will be compared with those reported for TD children in the discussion.

2 The study

2.1 Database and coding

The study is based on the longitudinal data of the Bastian corpus, collected under the supervision of Dagmar Bittner (Bittner, 2010). It includes four to nine recordings per month between ages 1;8 and 5;4 and one to four recordings between ages 5;5 and 6;9. Transcriptions were carried out according to the CHILDES transcription guidelines (MacWhinney, 2000). All *auch*- and *aber*-clauses up to age 4;11 were selected using the kwal-command in CHILDES CLAN. Due to the small number of *aber*-clauses up to age 4;11, analyses of *aber*-clauses were extended for another 12 months until age 5;11. As shown in Tables 2 and 3, the data contained 847 *auch*-clauses and 90 *aber*-clauses in total.

Table 2: Number of documented and analysed *auch*-clauses in Bastian's data.

Age	Number of *auch*-productions	Number of analysed *auch*-clauses	Age	Number of *auch*-productions	Number of analysed *auch*-clauses
2;05	47	40	3;09	27	22
2;06	34	29	3;10	15	12
2;07	69	61	3;11	21	15
2;08	39	30	4;00	15	11
2;09	23	21	4;01	7	7
2;10	11	10	4;02	20	12
2;11	17	14	4;03	26	25
3;00	13	8	4;04	37	28
3;01	52	40	4;05	26	23
3;02	36	28	4;06	19	18
3;03	24	12	4;07	22	19
3;04	32	22	4;08	2	1
3;05	30	26	4;09	43	32
3;06	52	46	4;10	2	1
3;07	33	31	4;11	31	25
3;08	19	16			

*Total number of **auch**-productions: 847*
*Total number of analysed **auch**-clauses: 685*

Table 3: Number of documented and analysed *aber*-clauses in Bastian's data.

Age	Number of *aber*-productions	Number of analysed *aber*-clauses	Age	Number of *aber*-productions	Number of analysed *aber*-clauses
3;10	2	1	5;00	9	8
3;11	2	1	5;01	1	1
4;02	2	2	5;02	1	0
4;03	0	0	5;03	5	5
4;04	6	5	5;04	4	3
4;05	7	7	5;05	7	4
4;06	8	8	5;06	3	3
4;07	6	6	5;07	1	1
4;08	2	2	5;08	3	3
4;09	5	4	5;09	0	0
4;10	0	0	5;10	8	6
4;11	6	6	5;11	2	2

*Total number of **aber**-productions: 90*
*Total number of analysed **aber**-clauses: 78*

The following criteria led to the exclusion of a data point from analysis:
- bare *aber-* or *auch*-production
- formulaic expression (songs, nursery rhymes, etc.)
- imitation
- identical self-repetition
- completely unintelligible utterance
- occurrence in question
- occurrence in subordinated clause
- utterance containing *noch* (still, even), *schon* (already), *wieder* (again), or *und* (and) in addition to *auch/aber*

A total number of 685 *auch*-clauses and 78 *aber*-clauses remained for analysis. In order to investigate the emergence of functional finiteness, they were coded for the following criteria:
a. realization of the verb: no verb, non-finite form, in/correctly inflected or in/correctly placed finite verb form
b. realization of the verb in an obligatory context: yes/no
c. type of finite verb form: copula, modal, auxiliary, lexical verb expressing a state/action predication
d. position of the finite verb form: V2, V3
e. structures indicating functional finiteness: (1) auxiliary constructions: *haben* 'have' + past participle (yes/no); (2) lexical action verbs in V2 (yes/no); (3) agentive particle verbs with V2 and the separated particle in clause-final position (yes/no); (4) OVS word order (yes/no) (see Section 1).

For the investigation of information-structural properties of the *auch*-clauses, the database was reduced to utterances produced from 3;0 onwards. 481 *auch*-clauses and 78 *aber*-clauses were further coded for:
f. the location of the contrast:
    auch-clauses: T = Contrast in the topic ('contrastive topic case')
                              C = Contrast in the comment ('neutral topic case')
    aber-clauses: Tp = Contrast in the topic and change in polarity (see 12c and 13)
                              TC = Contrast in the topic and in the comment (see 12d)
                              C = Contrast in the comment (see 14c and 15b)
                              S = Contrast of the whole *aber*-clause (see 16)
g. the syntactic position of *auch/aber*:
    auch: its position in relation to the contrast: adjacent/non-adjacent
    aber: its position within the utterance: initial/internal/final
h. the explicitness of the contrast-relation: explicit/implicit (see 15 and 16).

The coding of the information-structural properties was mainly based on context information. If the information structure remained ambiguous, the stress pattern of the utterance was checked in the video. In the case of *auch*, the contrast was located in the topic if it was located to the left of *auch* and in the comment if it was located to its right. Only in the case of a contrast on the finite verb form (*Anna SCHAUkelt auch /'Anna also swings'*) was the contrast located in the comment in spite of its occurrence to the left of *auch*. In the case of *aber*, topic was assigned to the initial constituent. In the case of incomplete or elliptical *aber*-clauses, the position of negation or other particles in relation to the relevant constituent within the *aber*-clause was consulted. If negation was realized in the first conjunct instead, its position in relation to the alternative of the doubtful constituent was considered. In the order X+negation, X was considered as the topic constituent. In the order negation+X, X was considered as the focus. In the absence of other particles, the *aber*-clause was coded as "unclear" and deleted from the specific analysis. Implicit contrast realization was assigned to *auch*- and *aber*-clauses if the relevant *auch*- or *aber*-clause referred to something not expressed verbally or to an utterance in the context where a third proposition had to be inferred, like in the examples (15) and (16) (see Section 1.1).

In order to find out whether *auch* and *aber* lead to specific developmental processes, simple main clauses were analysed at ages 3;6, 3;11, and 4;6. Coding of simple main clauses was conducted for criteria (a) to (e) in order to compare the realization of finite clause structure in *auch*- and *aber*-clauses with that in simple main clauses, i.e. main clauses with no particle or connective. The comparison was based on the data of three months: 3;6 is several months before the acquisition of functional finiteness in the grammar, 3;11 is the month where functional finiteness emerges, and 4;6 is several months after the acquisition of functional finiteness.

For 3;11 and 4;6, 200 utterances for each month were analysed, accounting for 30% to 36% of all utterances recorded in each month. For 3;6, 250 utterances were analysed due to the high number of recordings, representing about 10% of all utterances. Utterances were selected randomly and excluded from analysis if one of the following criteria was met:
- the utterance solely consists of *ja* 'yes', *nein* 'no', *doch* (no match in English), or *bitte* 'please'
- utterance contains a particle like *auch* 'also/too', *nicht* 'not', *nur* 'only', *noch* 'still/even', or a connective like *und* 'and', *aber* 'but', *oder* 'or'
- question
- unclear verb type due to unintelligible parts of the utterance
- formulaic expression

2.2 Results

2.2.1 Production of *auch* compared to *aber*

One use of *auch* is documented at age 2;2, followed by two *auch*-utterances at age 2;4, only consisting of the particle or an additional unintelligible word. A regular production of *auch* in two-word utterances is observed from age 2;5 on. The production of *aber* starts at age 3;10.[7] As shown in Figure 2, the relative frequency of *auch* between ages 2;5 and 4;11 roughly ranges from 1% to nearly 5% with a mean of 2%. The relative frequency of *aber* between ages 3;10 and 5;11 ranges from 0% to roughly 2% with a mean of 0.5%. During the months of parallel analyses of *aber* and *auch* between ages 3;10 and 4;11, the mean relative frequency of *auch* with 2.10% is considerably higher compared to that of *aber* with 0.38%. For the frequency of *auch*- and *aber*-productions and the number of analysed *auch*- and *aber*-clauses per month, see Tables 2 and 3 in Section 2.1.

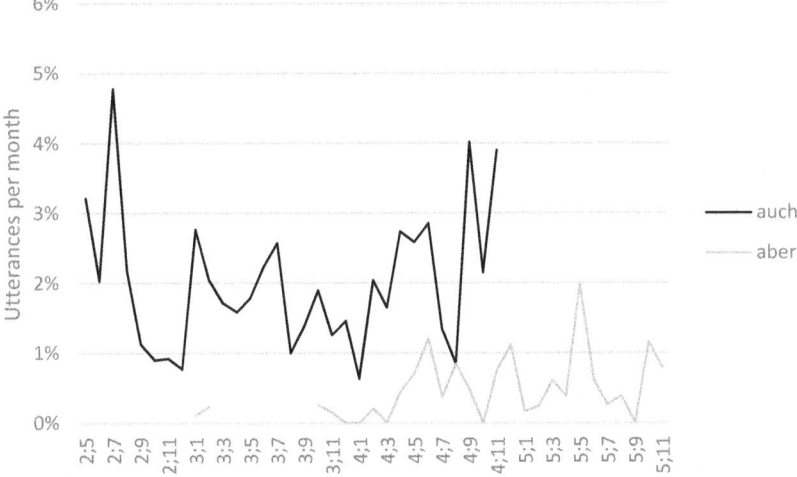

Figure 2: Relative frequency of *auch*- and *aber*-production in the recordings of Bastian.

---

[7] Four occurrences of *aber* between ages 3;1 and 3;2 are not regarded as productive because the utterance is always the same and the next *aber*-production does not occur until 7 months later.

2.2.2 Finite clause structure

Emergence of finite clause structure in Bastian's simple main clauses
First, the emergence of both finite verb forms, including unanalysed and analysed forms, and structures unambiguously indicating functional finiteness is described on the basis of Bastian's simple main clauses, i.e. main clauses with no particle or connective at ages 3;6, 3;11, and 4;6. It serves as a baseline for later comparisons of the effects of *auch* and *aber* on the realization of finite clause structure.

Results show a significant increase in finite verb forms between ages 3;6 and 3;11 (from 25% to 46%, $\chi^2(1) = 20.416$, $p < .001$). Non-finite forms (infinitives and bare participles) and verbless utterances both decrease as depicted in Figure 3. No significant changes in the distribution of finite verb forms in V2, non-finite forms, and verbless utterances take place between ages 3;11 and 4;6 ($\chi^2(2) = 0.796$, $p = .67$). After excluding verbless utterances, the increase in the use of finite verb forms in V2 is still highly significant between ages 3;6 and 3;11 ($\chi^2(1) = 17.456$, $p < .001$).

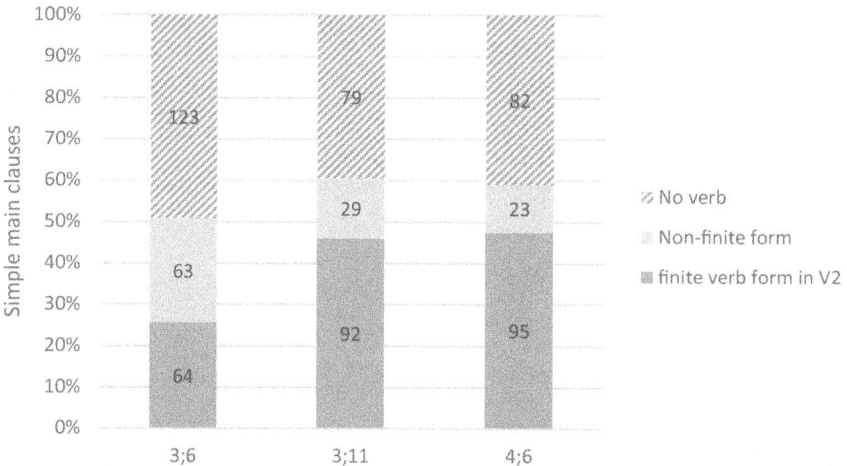

Figure 3: Distribution of no verbs, non-finite forms (infinitives and bare participles), and finite verb forms in Bastian's simple main clauses at ages 3;6, 3;11, and 4;6.

Taking a closer look at the verb types (Table 4), qualitative changes are observed between ages 3;6 and 3;11. Evidence for the acquisition of functional finiteness is hardly documented at age 3;6. Only three instances of lexical action verbs with a finite verb form are produced with two different verbs. At age 3;11, auxiliary constructions as well as lexical action verbs with a finite verb form are produced several times. Further evidence suggesting the emergence of functional finiteness are agentive particle verbs with V2 and the separated particle in clause-final position (henceforth: separated agentive particle verbs). Their first occurrence is at age 3;11 and there is no further increase (see Table 5). OVS word order, indicating the availability of a functional prefield in the grammar, is not documented throughout the analysed subset (see Table 5). After considering all utterances produced at ages 3;11 and 4;0, first instances of OVS word order are documented at age 4;0.

Table 4: Number and proportion of verb types in Bastian's simple main clauses at ages 3;6, 3;11, and 4;6.

	No verb	Non-finite form	Copula	Modal verb	LexV state predicate	LexV action predicate	LexV light verb	Aux: *sein* 'be' + PP	Aux: *haben* 'have' + PP
3;6	123 (49%)	63 (25%)	6 (3%)	5 (2%)	38 (15%)	3 (1%)	12 (5%)	–	–
3;11	79 (39%)	29 (15%)	20 (10%)	14 (7%)	32 (16%)	14 (7%)	6 (3%)	–	6 (3%)
4;6	82 (41%)	23 (11%)	24 (12%)	19 (10%)	18 (9%)	10 (5%)	8 (4%)	2 (1%)	14 (7%)

Table 5: Number and proportion of OVS word orders and separated agentive particle verbs in Bastian's simple main clauses.

	Number of analysed simple main clauses	OVS word order	Separated agentive particle verbs[8]
3;6	250	–	–
3;11	200	–	5 (3%)
4;6	200	–	5 (3%)

To summarize the emergence of finite clause structure in Bastian's grammar, functional finiteness in the form of action verbs in V2, auxiliary constructions, and separated agentive verb particles emerges at age 3;11 and goes hand in hand with a significant increase in the production of finite verb forms in V2. First evidence for a functional prefield in the form of OVS word order emerges at age 4;0.

---

[8] Light verbs like forms including a form of *machen* 'to make' are excluded.

Emergence of finite clause structure in Bastian's *auch-clauses*

In Bastian's *auch*-clauses, evidence for a structural V2 position emerges at age 3;11 as finite verb forms expressing an action predicate (see 24a), followed by an auxiliary construction at age 4;0 (24b). The number and proportion of all verb types produced each month are shown in Table A in the Appendix.

OVS word order as evidence for a functional prefield emerges at age 4;2 (24d). After an absence of four months, OVS structures are regularly produced from age 4;7 on, when separated particles with agentive particle verbs also start to appear (24g). The number and proportion of OVS structures and separated agentive particle verbs per month can be found in Table 6.

Table 6: OVS word order and separated agentive particle verbs in Bastian's *auch*-clauses.

	Number of analysed *auch*-clauses	OVS structures	Separated agentive particle verbs
2;05 – 4;0	494	–	–
4;01	7	–	–
4;02	12	3 (25%)	
4;03	25	–	–
4;04	28	–	–
4;05	23	–	–
4;06	18	–	–
4;07	19	5 (26%)	1 (5%)
4;08	1	–	–
4;09	32	3 (9%)	–[9]
4;10	1	–	–
4;11	25	2 (8%)	2 (8%)

Concerning the realization of finite verb forms in V2, qualitative changes are observed at ages 3;11 and 4;6. At age 3;11 utterances with only non-finite forms in final position (infinitives or bare perfect participles) disappear for the first time. After sporadic occurrences between ages 4;3 and 4;5, these utterances disappear at age 4;6 for the rest of the analyses (see Figure 4). Throughout the analysed period, finite verb forms occur in V2 position except for three instances produced prior to 3;11, where the verb is used in V3 ("Das auch kann das." (3;8.25)).

---

[9] One example with a separated particle was excluded from analysis due to the presence of the connective 'and'.

The development of the use of verb forms in obligatory contexts is depicted in Figure 5. The omission of the verb can lead to a well-formed ellipsis like in example (23c). These instances are excluded in Figure 5. At age 4;6, verb omissions in obligatory contexts disappear for the rest of the analyses with three exceptions.

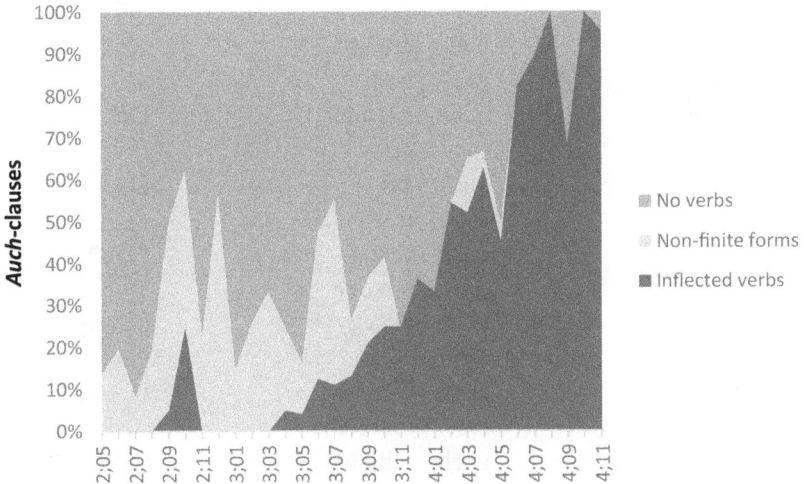

Figure 4: Development of finite verb forms in Bastian's *auch*-clauses.

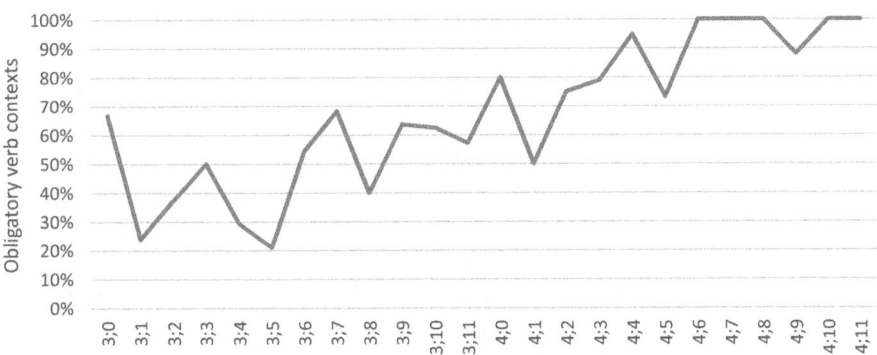

Figure 5: Development of the realization of the verb in obligatory contexts in *auch*-clauses.

The following examples show typical *auch*-clauses prior to the acquisition of functional finiteness (examples 23a–p) and after the acquisition of functional finiteness (examples 24a–g).

(23) *Auch*-clauses prior to the acquisition of functional finiteness

a)	papa			auch	hier		(2;5.24)
	daddy			too	here		
b)	meine			auch			(2;5.00)
	mine			too			
c)	oma			auch			(2;7.06)
	granny			too			
d)	will			auch	gucken		(2;10.06)
	want			too	look		
e)	mama			auch	machen		(3;0.21)
	mummy			too	do		
f)	ente			auch	kalt		(3;1.13)
	duck			too	cold		
g)	mama			auch	wegmachen		(3;4.04)
	mummy			too	remove		
h)	hat	baby		auch	creme		(3;4.06)
	has	baby		too	cream		
i)	mama			auch	regenschirm		(3;5.08)
	mummy			too	umbrella		
j)				auch	schlafen		(3;5.08)
				too	sleep		
k)	frosch			auch	nabel		(3;6.09)
	frog			too	navel		
l)	mama			auch	eisenbahn	haben	(3,6.13)
	mummy			too	railway	have	
m)	jenny			auch	puzzle		(3;8.25)
	jenny			too	puzzle		
n)	ich	will		auch	ein	anrufen	(3;9.06)
	I	want		too	one	call	
o)	ich	brauch		auch			(3;9.24)
	I	need		too			
p)	unten	ist	kleine	auch			(3;10.28)
	beneath	is	small	too			

(24) *Auch*-clauses after the acquisition of functional finiteness

a)	spiel(e)	auch	(3;11.20)
	play	too	

b)	urlaub	hab(e)n		auch	an(g)eguckt	(4;0.03)
	holiday	have		too	looked at	
c)	denise	war		auch	da	(4;1.14)
	denise	was		too	there	
d)	das	hat	julie	auch	gemalt	(4;2.28)
				too	painted	
e)	hier			auch		(4;3.12)
	here			too		
f)	oma	manchmal		auch		(4;4.06)
	granny	sometimes		too		
g)	das	mal(e)	ich	auch mal	ein bisschen aus	(4;7.13)
	this	paint	I	too *(particle)*	a little out	

Emergence of finite clause structure in Bastian's *aber*-clauses

In Bastian's *aber*-clauses, evidence for a structural V2 position emerges at age 4;5 in the form of an auxiliary construction with *haben* (see example 25c). From age 4;9 on, lexical action verbs are sporadically documented like in example (25e). All verb types are listed in Table B in the Appendix.

OVS word order as evidence for the acquisition of a functional prefield is only documented once at age 5;11 (25i). An additional analysis of the adverbs produced in the functional prefield showed that only deictic expressions like *da* 'there' or *jetzt* 'now' are produced. Whether or not this might be evidence for a functional prefield is not clear. Separated agentive particle verbs are not documented throughout the analysed period.

Aber-clauses almost always exhibit a finite verb form in V2 position. In other positions they are not observed.[10] After age 3;10, there is only one utterance with just an infinitive and, at age 5;3, there is only one case of a verb missing in an obligatory context. All other verbless *aber*-clauses are verbal ellipses like in (25f).

---

10 At age 4;7 a finite verb form is produced in utterance-final position, but it remains unclear whether a sub-ordinating conjunction has been omitted: *CHI: Der [: die] [*] das aber braucht (4;07.21).

(25) *Aber*-clauses
   a) da   rutscht   aber   (4;2.18)
      there   slips   but
   b) ich   möchte   das   aber   (4;4.23)
      I   want   that   but
   c) papa   hat   aber   gekauft   (4;5.02)
      daddy   has   but   bought
   d) schmeckt   aber   (4;5.13)
      tastes   but
   e) jetzt   schummelst   du   aber   (4;9.26)
      now   cheat   you   but
   f) aber   ich   (5;4.01)
      but   I
   g) aber die   0*schmecken mir   nicht   (5;3.01)
      but   these 0*taste   me   not
   h) aber ich   war   draußen   (5;3.27)
      but   I   was   outside
   i) das   solltest   du   aber gar nicht   (5;11.13)
      this   ought   you   but   at all not

Comparing finite clause structure in *auch*-, *aber*-, and simple main clauses
As soon as a structural V2 position has been established in simple main clauses at age 3;11, *auch*-clauses showing clear evidence for a structural V2 position are going to emerge. In *aber*-clauses, evidence for a structural V2 position is documented at 4;5, i.e. with a delay of 6 months. In simple main clauses, all three structures – as listed in Section 2.1 under e. (1–3) – indicating the acquisition of a structural V2 position are documented at age 3;11. In *auch*- and *aber*-clauses, these structures emerge stepwise. In *aber*-clauses it takes more time for these structures to be documented. However, as shown in Table 7, the order in which these structures emerge is similar in both *auch*- and *aber*-clauses:

   Auch-clauses: LexV action predicate < Aux ('have' + PP) < separated agentive particle verbs
   Aber-clauses: Aux ('have' + PP) < LexV action predicate < separated agentive particle verbs

A functional prefield is proven in *auch*-clauses 2 months later than in simple main clauses, but OVS word order remains very rare until age 4;6 in both clause types.

In *aber*-clauses, OVS word order is documented at age 5;11 with a delay of nearly 2 years. Taking into account all four structures indicating functional finiteness, the following order of emergence applies to Bastian's *auch*- and *aber*-clauses: Aux ('have' + PP) / LexV action pred. < OVS < separated agentive particle verbs

Table 7: Emergence of functional finiteness in simple main, *auch*-, and *aber*-clauses.

	Simple main clauses	*Auch*-clauses	*Aber*-clauses
Aux: 'have' + PP	3;11	4;0	4;5
LexV action predicate	3;11	3;11	4;9
Separated agentive particle verbs	3;11	4;7	–
OVS word order	4;0	4;2	5;11

In order to investigate the effect of *auch* and *aber* on the realization of finite verb forms in second position, the proportions of utterances with finite verb forms, no verbs, and non-finite forms are compared in *auch*-, *aber*-, and simple main clauses at ages 3;6, 3;11, and 4;6. Due to the late beginning of their production and a single *aber*-clause at age 3;11, only *aber*-clauses produced at age 4;6 can be considered in this analysis. Figure 6 shows that at age 3;6 the proportion of finite verb forms in second position is significantly smaller in *auch*-clauses compared to simple main clauses ($\chi^2(1)=8.024$, $p < .005$), but not at age 3;11 ($\chi^2(1)=1.144$, $p = .285$). At age 4;6, it is even higher in *auch*-clauses compared to simple main clauses ($\chi^2(1)=7.613$, $p < .01$), while all *aber*-clauses exhibit a finite verb form in V2 position.

If a verb is used, non-finite forms prevail prior to the acquisition of functional finiteness in *auch*-clauses and are more frequently used in *auch*-clauses compared to simple main clauses (89% vs. 50%, $\chi^2(1)=9.81$, $p < .005$). After the acquisition of functional finiteness, at ages 3;11 and 4;6, non-finite forms are still documented in simple main clauses (24% and 19%), but not in *auch*- and *aber*-clauses. The number of analysed *auch*-clauses at age 3;11 is small. Nevertheless, only 5 out of all 74 verb-containing *auch*-clauses analysed between 3;11 and 4;6 exhibit a non-finite form, accounting for 7% and thus confirming the lower proportion of non-finite forms after the acquisition of functional finiteness in *auch*-clauses. However, *auch*-clauses at age 3;11 are more frequently verbless than simple main clauses ($\chi^2(1)=4.45$, $p < .05$). In most cases the omission of the verb leads to a well-formed ellipsis. However, even after excluding verbal ellipses, the verb is more frequently missing in *auch*-clauses than in simple main clauses: 2 (33%) vs. 13 (10%) (see Table 8). Due to the low number of *auch*-clauses, statistical tests were not calculated. However, in the following 3 months the omission of verbs in obligatory contexts is still comparatively high in *auch*-clauses with 20% to 40%.

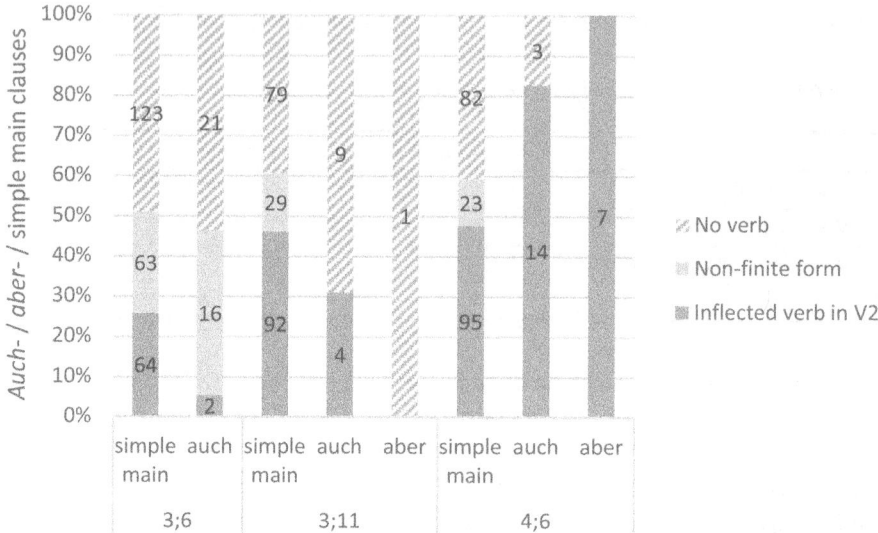

Figure 6: Proportion of finite verb forms in V2 position in *auch*-, *aber*- and simple main clauses.

Table 8: Finite verb forms in V2 position, non-finite forms, and no verbs in obligatory contexts in *auch*- and simple main clauses at age 3;11.

	Auch-clauses	Simple main clauses
Finite verb forms in V2	4 (67%)	92 (69%)
Non-finite forms	–	29 (21%)
No verbs	2 (33%)	13 (10%)

Figure 7 provides a closer look at the distribution of verb types. It shows that after the acquisition of functional finiteness, *auch*- and *aber*-clauses occur with modal verbs to a higher degree (50–57%) as observed in simple main clauses. Considering all *auch*- and *aber*-clauses produced between ages 3;11 and 4;11, the proportion of modal verbs fluctuates. Nevertheless, the average proportion of modal verbs in *auch*-clauses with 35% and *aber*-clauses with 38% is higher than in simple main clauses with a maximum of 16%.

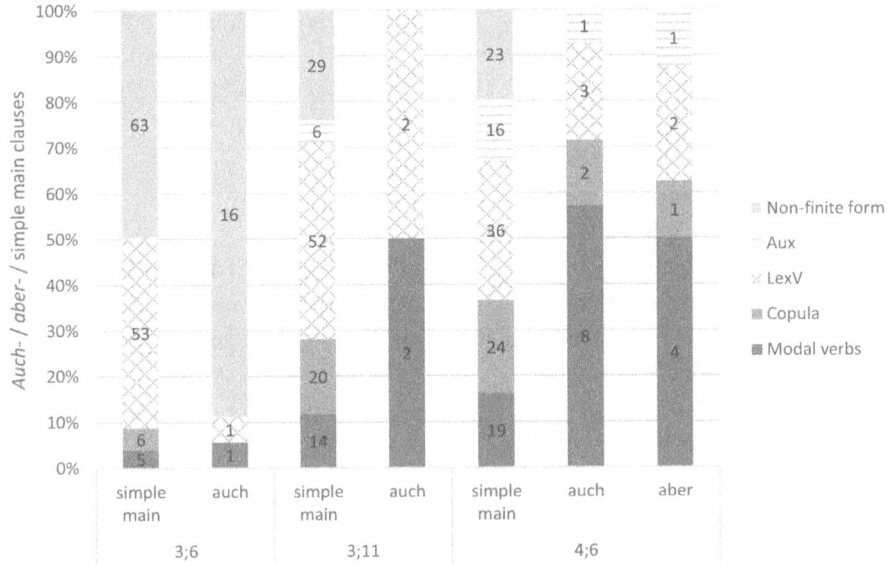

Figure 7: Verb types in *auch*-, *aber*-, and simple main clauses (verbless utterances excluded).

2.2.3 Information-structural properties

Information-structural properties of *auch*-clauses

Examples of *auch*-clauses prior to and after the acquisition of functional finiteness are given in (26) and (27).

(26) *Auch*-clauses prior to the acquisition of functional finiteness
    a) *CHI: Evi AUCH tasse   (3;0.29)
              Evi too cup   ('Evi has a cup, too')
    b) *MOT: da ist der Hund lieb und schläft, auf dem gelben Sofa.
                                         ('Here, the dog is good and sleeps on
                                         the yellow sofa.')
       *CHI: hier AUCH lieb   (3;1.13)
              here too good   ('here the dog is good as well')
    c) *CHI: papa nass (. . .)   ('Daddy is wet')
       *CHI: mama AUCH   (3;2.01)
              mummy too   ('Mummy as well')

  d) *CHI: hier kann laufen ('this one can walk')
    *CHI: hier AUCH laufen   (3;6.08)
       here too walk ('this one can walk as well')
  e) *CHI: Mama rückfahren ('Mummy should drive back')
       (...)
    *CHI: Mama auch xx   (3;6.24)
       KINdergarten
       Mummy also xx ('Mummy should drive to the
       kindergarten   kindergarten as well')
  f) *MOT: der ist bestimmt mit dem bus ('He certainly came by bus')
       gekommen.
    *CHI: bus gefahrt.   ('came by bus')
    *CHI: Papa auch LAUfen.   (3;7.19)
       Daddy also walk ('Daddy can walk as well')
  g) *MOT: der kleine vogel kann das ('the small bird can do this')
    *CHI: das AUCH kann das   (3;8.25)
       this too can that ('this one can do it as well')
  h) *The child's mother is speaking on the phone*
    *CHI: Ich will AUCH ein anrufen   (3;9.06)
       I want too (some)one call ('I want to call someone as
                  well')

(27) *Auch*-clauses after the acquisition of functional finiteness
  a) *MOT: pferd geht schnell weg ('the horse hurries away')
       (...)
    *CHI: ich möchte AUCH schnell   (3;11.20)
       durch   ('I want to pass through
       I want too quickly through quickly, too')
  b) *MOT: timmy ist dein freund (...) ('Timmy is your friend')
    *CHI: melvin AUCH mein freund   (4;2.08)
       melvin too my friend ('Melvin is my friend as well')
  c) *MOT: evi, das ist rot   ('Evi, this is red')
    *CHI: hier ist AUCH rot   (4;4.12)
       here is too red   ('here is red as well')

d)	*CHI:	nee, schwarz	('no, black')	
	*CHI:	ich möchte auch WEISS haben		(4;7.21)
		I want too white have	('I want to have white as well')	
e)	*CHI:	ich hab bloss bababab gemacht (...)	('I was just doing bababab')	
	*CHI:	dann hat die evi AUCH bababab gemacht		(4;11.10)
		then has the evi too bababab done	('then Evi was doing bababab as well')	
f)	*CHI:	evi möchte nicht stuhl abwechseln	('Evi doesn't want to take turns with the chair')	
	*CHI:	dann hat evi auch geÄRgert		(4;11.29)
		then has evi also teased	('Then Evi also teased me')	

Throughout the whole analysed period, *auch* is mainly used with contrastive topics like in examples (26a, b, c, d, g, h) and (27a, b, c, e). The use of *auch* with neutral topics like in (26e, f) and (27d, f) remains occasional. The proportion of *auch* with contrastive and neutral topics is depicted in Figure 8. Both variants are produced prior to the acquisition of functional finiteness.

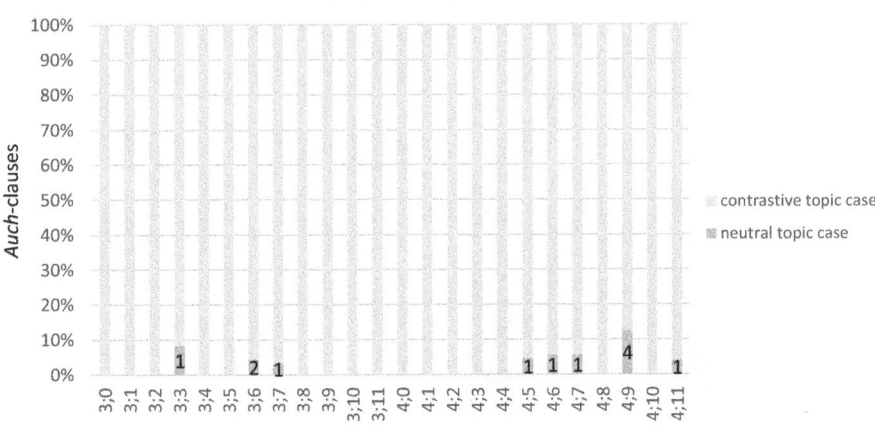

Figure 8: The use of *auch* in the contrastive and neutral topic case.

In the contrastive topic case, *auch* can be used in adjacent position to the topic like in (26a, b, c, d, g) and (27b) and in non-adjacent position like in (26h) and (27a, c). Adjacency occurs if AUCH is used with a contrastive topic and no verb in

V2 position. In the neutral topic case, *auch* and its DoA are in adjacent position regardless of the realization of a verb in V2 (see 26e, f and 27d, f).

As shown in Figure 9, the use of *auch* in non-adjacent position as in (26h) is present from early on and increases with age. At age 3;6 it is produced on a regular basis.

The contrast in *auch*-clauses is realized explicitly, as in (26b–d, f, g) and (27a–e), as well as implicitly (26h and 27f) from early on. Figure 10 shows that the proportion of implicit contrast realizations slightly increases after the acquisition of functional finiteness from 25% (age 3;0–3;10) to 34% (age 3;11–4;11). The increase is statistically not significant ($\chi^2(1)=2.507$, p = .113).

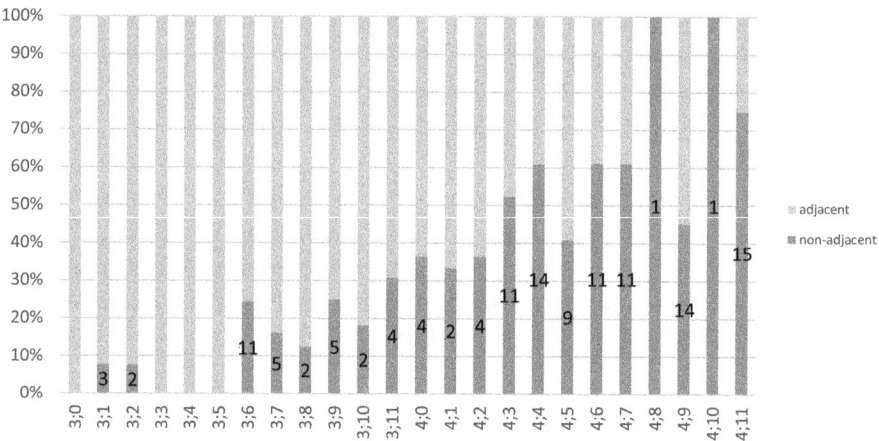

Figure 9: Development of non-adjacency of *auch* and its DoA in Bastian's *auch*-clauses.

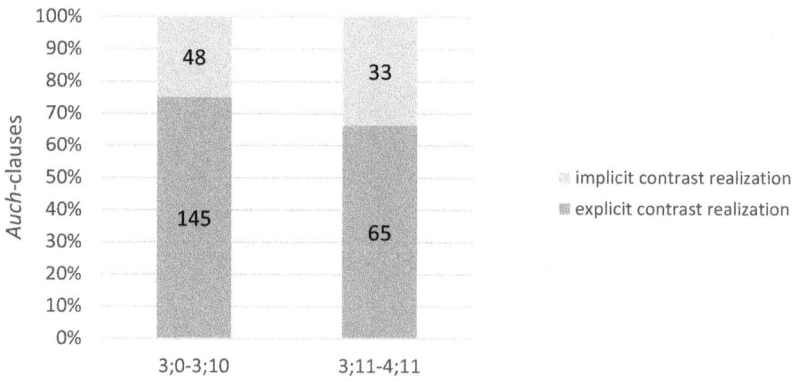

Figure 10: Implicit and explicit contrast realization in Bastian's *auch*-clauses.

To summarize, between ages 3;0 and 3;10, *auch* is predominantly used adjacent to a contrastive topic. The contrast is typically realized explicitly. After the acquisition of functional finiteness between ages 3;11 and 4;11, the non-adjacent position of *auch* relative to its domain of application (DoA) increases. Furthermore, explicit contrast still prevails.

Information-structural properties of *aber*-clauses
As argued before, even when finiteness seems to be established it may not occur yet in *aber*-clauses. The relevant stage is termed the 'external finiteness' stage. As soon as finiteness is used in *aber*-clauses too, the relevant stage is termed the 'internal finiteness' stage. Examples of *aber*-clauses in the 'external finiteness' stage and the 'internal finiteness' stage are given in (28) and (29) respectively.

(28) *Aber*-clauses in the external finiteness stage
    a) *CHI: ich male hier ('I am drawing here')
        *CHI: mama hier kratzt aber, weisst du? ('Mummy, but it's scratching here, you know?') (4;2.14)
        Mummy here is scratching but, know you?
    b) *MOT: und hatte ganz lustige ohren ('and had funny ears')
        *CHI: da rutscht aber (4;2.28)
        there slips but ('but they slipped')
    c) *SIS: rauf legen ('put it here')
        *CHI: nicht alles aber (4;4.16)
        not everything but ('but not everything')
    d) *MOT: da kannst du ihm das zeigen ('here you can show him')
        *CHI: schnell aber (4;4.23)
        quickly but ('but quickly')
    e) *MOT: Du willst nicht essen. Du willst nicht trinken.
        (*addressing the child's sister:* 'You don't want to eat. You don't want to drink.')
        *CHI: ich kriege aber alles, joghurt (4;4.16)
        I get but everything, yoghurt ('but I get to have everything, even yoghurt')

(29) *Aber*-clauses in the internal finiteness stage
    a) *MOT: nee, gibt es nicht. ('you won't get it')
        *CHI: doch. ('I will')

	*CHI:	papa hat aber gekauft.	(4;05.02)
		Daddy has but bought	('but Daddy bought it')
b)	*MOT:	die mama hat noch gar nichts gegessen	('Mummy has not eaten yet')
	*CHI:	papa hat aber gegessen	(4;6.02)
		daddy has but eaten	('but Daddy has already eaten')
c)	*MOT:	evi du hattest gestern den drachen	('Evi you had the kite yesterday')
	*CHI:	ich möchte aber heute	(4;6.29)
		I want but today	('but I want it today')
d)	*MOT:	du darfst kein feuer machen	('you are not allowed to make a fire')
	*CHI:	nein, da aber	(4;7.26)
		no, there but	('no, but over there')
e)	*CHI:	du darfst nicht baden, bastian	('you are not allowed to take a bath')
	*CHI:	aber wir	(4;8.16)
		but we	('but we are')
f)	*CHI:	jenny hat zwei schneckenhäuser	('Jenny has two snail shells')
	*CHI:	aber ich habe bloss eine gemacht	(4;11.24)
		but I have only one made	('but I have only made one')
g)	*MOT:	bastian, setz dich mal bitte da rüber	('please change your seat over there, bastian')
	*CHI:	ich möchte aber heute mehr hier sitzen	(5;1.18)
		I want but today more here sit	('but I rather want to sit over here today')

Aber-clauses initially show a preference for contrast type C, i.e. with the contrast established in the comment part of the utterance. Examples like: *Max will schaukeln. Er will aber **nicht rutschen*** are given in (28a–d) and (29g). Contrast type Tp, i.e. with a contrastive topic and a change in polarity as, for example, in ***Max** will **nicht schaukeln**. **Anna** will aber **schaukeln***, occurs in (29b, d, e). As shown in Figure 11, utterances of type Tp are used productively when functional finiteness has been established in *aber*-clauses. Contrast type Tp is first produced at age 4;6 and constitutes the dominant type for the following 12 months.

Contrast type TC, i.e. with the contrast in the topic and in the comment as, for example, in ***Max** will **schaukeln**. **Anna** will aber **rutschen***, occurs in (28e) and (29c, f). It is produced only sporadically. The same is true for contrast type S, i.e. contrast of the whole *aber*-clause as, for example, in **Max will schaukeln. Es regnet aber in Strömen**. An example is given in (29a). The development of the different types of contrast is depicted in Figure 11.

Within the first *aber*-clauses the contrast is realized implicitly as in (28a–d) and (29a) and explicitly as in (28e) and (29b, c, e, f, g). Explicit contrast realization becomes more frequent at age 4;6 (see Figure 12).

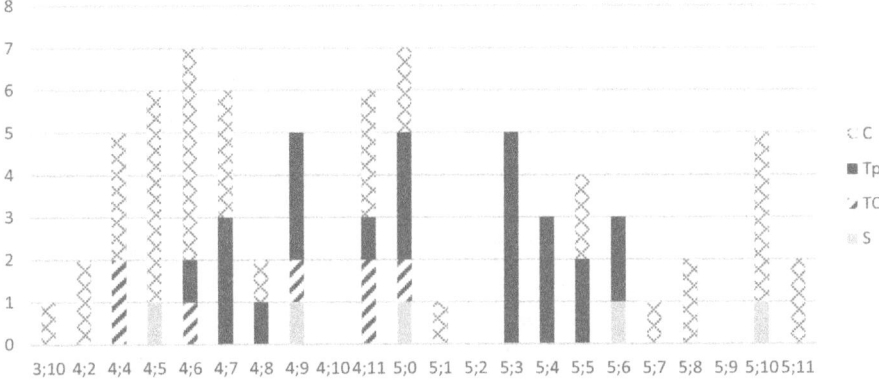

Figure 11: Contrast types in Bastian's *aber*-clauses: C (contrast in the comment), Tp (contrastive topic and change in polarity), TC (contrast in the topic and comment), S (contrast of the whole proposition).

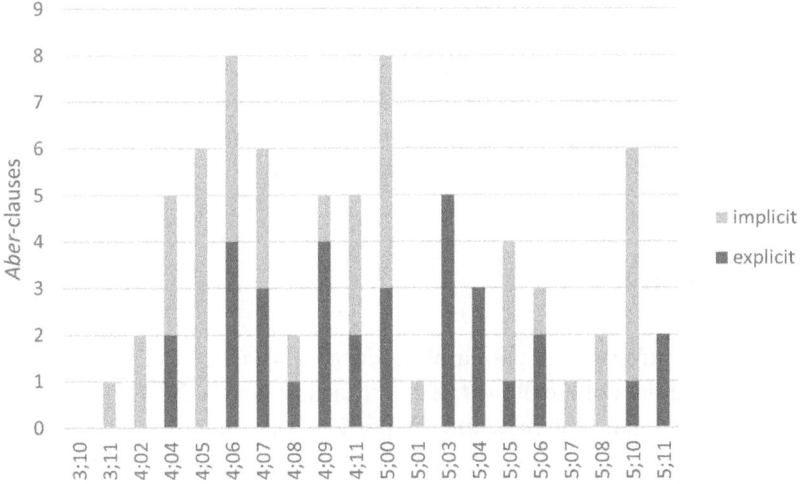

Figure 12: Number of implicit and explicit contrast realizations in *aber*-clauses.

Until age 4;4, *aber* mainly occurs in utterance-final position (see 28a–d). After 4;5, *aber* occurs in utterance-final (29d), utterance-internal (29a, b, c, g), and utterance-initial position (29e, f), see Figure 13.

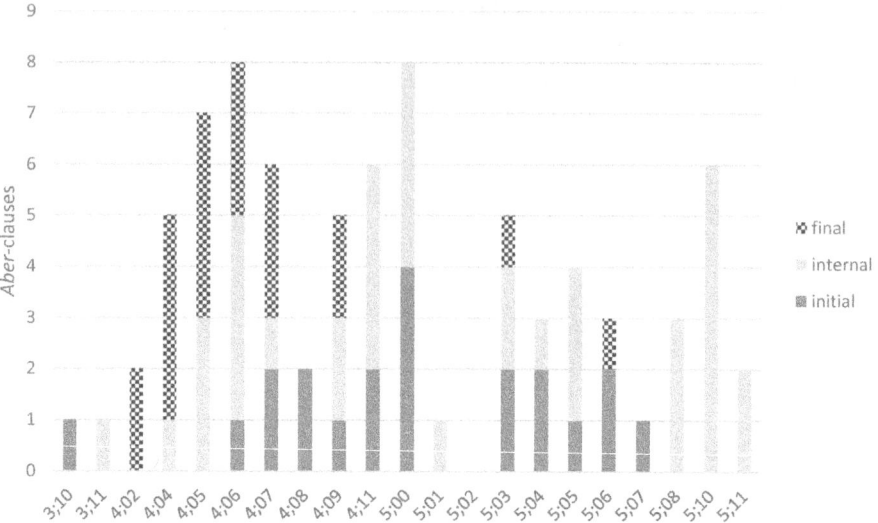

Figure 13: Production of *aber* in utterance-final, -internal, and -initial position.

To summarize, in *aber*-clauses between 3;11 and 4;04, i.e. prior to the emergence of functional finiteness in *aber*-clauses, there is a contrast relation in the comment part with *aber* in internal/final position. Examples are given in (28). As soon as *aber*-clauses are going to express functional finiteness, more variable *aber*-clauses emerge regarding the contrast type, i.e. contrastive comment and contrastive topic, and the position of *aber* within the utterance, i.e. utterance-internal and utterance-initial. Examples are given in (29).

3 Discussion

The present study investigates the early production of *auch-* and *aber*-clauses in the longitudinal data of a child with DLD. It focuses on the interaction of the acquisition of functional finiteness and the particles *auch* and *aber*. The results are compared with the acquisition of *auch-* and *aber*-clauses in typically developing children (Bartz, in prep.; Bartz & Bittner, 2018; Bittner & Bartz, 2018). Furthermore, the compatibility of the results with Jordens' (this volume) assumption of DLD as a computational problem will be discussed. According to Jordens, children with DLD have limited working memory capacities, leading to a delay in the ability to express contextual cohesion. According to this account, a delayed but parallel acquisition process in DLD compared to typical language development is expected.

Impact of functional finiteness on auch- *and* aber-*production*

The regular production of *auch*-clauses starts at age 2;5, 18 months prior to the acquisition of functional finiteness. All types of *auch*-uses, including the contrastive and the neutral topic case (e.g. 26a and 26e), the adjacent and non-adjacent position of *auch* (e.g. 26a and 26h), and explicit as well as implicit *auch*-clauses (e.g. 26b and 26h) are produced prior to the acquisition of functional finiteness. After the acquisition of functional finiteness at age 3;11 (in *auch*- and simple main clauses simultaneously), the non-adjacent position of *auch* relative to its DoA further increases (e.g. 27a).

The production of *aber*-clauses starts one month prior to the acquisition of functional finiteness, at age 3;10. As long as functional finiteness is not applied in *aber*-clauses, they show a rigid pattern: *aber* is mainly used in utterance-final position (e.g. 28a). The contrast is predominantly realized implicitly and the contrast is regularly established in the comment part of the *aber*-clause (e.g. 28a). Once functional finiteness is also expressed in *aber*-clauses, the use of *aber* in initial position (e.g. 29e) and of contrastive topics (e.g. 29b) begins, breaking up the initially stereotypical pattern of *aber*-clauses.

The simultaneity of the developmental process of *aber*-production and the acquisition of the functional features of finiteness suggests that the informational function of finiteness serves as the driving force. A similar interaction between *auch*-production and the acquisition of functional finiteness is not observed.

Effect of auch *and* aber *on the realization of finite clause structure*

The question of the impact of *auch* and *aber* on the realization of finite verb forms in V2 and on the acquisition of functional finiteness must be answered differently for each particle.

Auch hampers the realization of finite verb forms in V2, but this effect is limited to the period prior to the acquisition of functional finiteness. Thus, at age 3;6, finite verb forms in V2 are significantly less frequently realized in *auch*-clauses compared to simple main clauses (5% vs. 25%). This difference disappears after the acquisition of functional finiteness at age 3;11. At age 4;6, finite verb forms in second position are even more frequently realized in *auch*-clauses compared to simple main clauses. This strongly supports the assumption that similarly to in TD, *auch* serves as a precursor of morphosyntactic finiteness marking (Dimroth & Lindner, 2005; Jolink, 2005, 2009). After the acquisition of functional finiteness, the DLD child manages to integrate the finite verb forms in second position between topic and particle. This result speaks against challenges in realizing contrastive topics and *auch* in non-adjacent position (*Anna will AUCH Eis essen*) as suggested for TD children (Dimroth, 2009) and might be explained in different ways:

First, the long experience in the production of *auch*-clauses prior to the acquisition of functional finiteness might be an advantage for the DLD child. Second, the comparatively high proportion of modal verbs in *auch*-clauses might play a role. In contrast to Dimroth (2009), Klein (2012) assumes that complex scope relations in *auch*-clauses arise with the use of lexical verbs in V2 (*Anna isst AUCH ein Eis*, see Section 1.1). This analysis is also suggested by Bartz (in prep.) to explain the pattern of the *auch*-clauses produced by the TD children. Third, the results might be caused by the application of Jordens' (2012) acquisition model of functional finiteness with the distinction between the use of finite verb forms and the acquisition of finiteness. Applying the same model, Bartz (in prep.) confirmed a hampering effect of *auch* on the realization of finite verb forms in V2 after the acquisition of functional finiteness for only one of five children.

However, *auch*-clauses after the acquisition of functional finiteness tend to lack the verb more frequently. The use of *auch* as an anaphoric assertion marker as suggested by Dimroth (2009) is able to account for this pattern, as well as the acquisition of target-like verbal ellipses as suggested by Bartz (in prep.) for typical language acquisition.

The use of functional finiteness in *auch*-clauses is delayed for most but not all structures. *Auch*-clauses with lexical action verbs in V2 are documented as soon as functional finiteness is acquired in the grammar at age 3;11. Auxiliary constructions ('have' + PP), OVS word order, and separated agentive particle verbs are delayed for 1 to 8 months compared to simple main clauses.

Aber rather promotes the use of finite verb forms in V2 once regularly produced. Yet all structures indicating the acquisition of functional finiteness emerge delayed in *aber*-clauses. First evidence for the acquisition of functional finiteness emerges 6 months later than in simple main and *auch*-clauses, at age 4;5. Like in *auch*-clauses, the delay in *aber*-clauses is most pronounced for OVS word order and action verbs in V2 with separated particles. However, the delay is much longer in *aber*-clauses. OVS word order first emerges at age 5;11 with a delay of 23 months compared to simple main clauses, and action verbs with separated particles are not documented until age 5;11 at all.

Comparison of* auch- *and* aber-*production in DLD and TD
Comparison of these results with those reported for typically developing children (see Section 1.2) reveals similarities as well as differences. Thus, the order of acquisition of *auch* before *aber* holds equally for the TD children and the DLD child. This also holds for the fact that the acquisition of functional finiteness co-occurs with the onset of *aber*-production. Nevertheless, the difference between the onset of *auch*- and *aber*-production is much larger for the DLD child, with 17 months compared to TD children with 1 to 9 months. Furthermore, the presence of an 'external finiteness stage' in the acquisition of *aber*-clauses, as described by Bittner & Bartz (2018) for TD children, is confirmed in the data of the DLD child. The same is true for the stepwise emergence of the structures indicating the acquisition of functional finiteness in *auch*- and *aber*-clauses. In *auch*-clauses, the temporal distance between the documentation of the first evidence for functional finiteness and further evidence for the remaining structures is comparable in both populations. For *aber*-clauses, the temporal distance is much longer in the data of the DLD child, especially for OVS word order and separated particle verbs. Only auxiliary constructions emerge with a comparable delay.

The use of finite verb forms in V2 position in the *auch*- and *aber*-clauses of the DLD child is comparable to that in TD children. That is, in both cases the rare use of finite verb forms in *auch*-clauses compared to simple main clauses is mainly restricted to *auch*-clauses produced prior to the acquisition of functional finiteness. Furthermore, in both populations, *auch*-clauses tend to omit the verb more frequently after the acquisition of functional finiteness. In *aber*-clauses, the use of finite verb forms is supported once functional finiteness is acquired.

Significant developmental differences between TD children and the DLD child are not observed in the acquisition of *auch*-clauses. At the beginning of *aber*-production, however, these children behave differently. TD children produce all the kinds of *aber*-clauses from early on, although they show a preference for explicit contrast realizations of contrast type Tp, i.e. of *aber*-clauses with a contrastive topic and change in polarity (e.g. 29b, d, e). The DLD child, on the other hand, starts with the use of *aber*-clauses of the contrast type C only, i.e. of *aber*-clauses with a neutral topic and the contrast in the comment part. After this initial phase, this child's *aber*-clauses resemble those produced by typically developing children at their initial stage. The relevant *aber*-clauses are characterized by a preference for contrast type Tp and a variable position of *aber* within the utterance.

To summarize, comparing the acquisition data of *auch*- and *aber*-clauses in the DLD child and in typically developing children, similarities prevail. These include:
– the earlier acquisition of *auch* compared to *aber*

- the co-occurrence of the use of *aber* and the acquisition of functional finiteness
- the late acquisition of functional finiteness in *aber*-clauses and the presence of an 'external finiteness stage'
- the stepwise emergence of the structures showing the acquisition of functional finiteness in *auch*- and *aber*-clauses
- the hampering effect of *auch* on the use of finite verb forms in V2 position prior to the acquisition of functional finiteness
- the more pronounced tendency of verb omission in *auch*-clauses after the acquisition of functional finiteness
- the development of utterance structure in *auch*-clauses depending on features of information structure.

Differences in the acquisition of *auch*- and *aber*-clauses between the DLD child and the TD-children include:
- a larger difference between the onset of *aber*-production and that of *auch*-production
- a stronger delay in the emergence of OVS word order and separated agentive particle verbs
- a limited means initially to express contrast in *aber*-clauses

The similar but delayed production of *auch*- and *aber*-clauses by the DLD child is consistent with Jordens' (this volume) assumption of DLD as a computational problem. Interestingly, the regular production of *aber* starts 21 to 27 months later compared to that of the TD children but nevertheless coincides with the acquisition of functional finiteness. This finding suggests that the onset of the production of *aber*-clauses is closely related to the acquisition of functional finiteness. Variable use of contrast in *aber*-clauses only starts at the 'internal finiteness stage', i.e. when in *aber*-clauses the functional features of functional finiteness are used too. The results are consistent with Skerra (2017). She shows that the development of cohesion devices like connectives depends on the acquisition of morphosyntax. The use of these devices is limited and conceptually restricted as long as the development of the grammatical system stagnates.

The particularly long delay in the realization of OVS word order and separated particle verbs in the *aber*-clauses of the DLD child further supports the assumption of a computational problem in DLD. The higher demands of these structures on the working memory compared to auxiliary constructions and lexical action verbs add to the complexity of *aber*-clauses (see Section 1.1). The findings suggest that a certain degree of practice and automation of the involved processes is necessary in order to apply them within the same utterance.

The question remains of why the DLD child starts to produce *aber*-clauses in a way that is unlike the previously analysed TD children. These TD children produce all types of *aber*-clauses from early on, while they typically show an initial preference for the use of *aber*-clauses with a contrastive topic and a change in polarity as, for example, in (29b) (type Tp). The DLD child, however, produces *aber*-clauses exclusively with the contrast in the comment part of the utterance as in (28a) (type C), where the contrast is mainly realized implicitly. The early production of *aber*-clauses is rather surprising as in the data of the TD children the use of *aber*-clauses of type C with implicit contrast increases with age. However, the untypical use of *aber* in utterance-final position by the DLD child is less surprising and might reveal difficulties in the syntactic integration of *aber* into the utterance. While Skerra (2007) suggests, as also observed in the TD children (Bartz, in prep.), that *aber* can be lexically integrated into the *aber*-clause in initial position prior to the acquisition of functional finiteness, it seems that the DLD child attaches *aber* only after the production of the utterance is complete. In doing so, the utterance is marked as adversative afterwards. The initial use of implicit *aber*-clauses of contrast type C might be traced back to the DLD child's more advanced cognitive development. That is, when he starts to produce *aber*-clauses, he is roughly two years older compared to the TD children. However, due to the late onset of the production of *aber*-clauses, it seems very likely that his lexical development is more advanced at that time. Contrasts established in the comment part of the *aber*-clause typically refer to actions or properties, as they add new and contrastive information to an already established topic. The expression of these contrasts thus requires the use of newly introduced lexical elements that are acquired comparatively late. Contrastive topics, on the other hand, are typically expressed with deictic elements, proper names, or nouns, which are acquired early. It seems reasonable that children with DLD initially stick with one arbitrary pattern of *aber*-clauses possibly until they are able to use the features of functional finiteness within *aber*-clauses. The fact that the DLD child begins the production of *aber*-clauses with only one of the possible uses seems to mirror the high complexity of the acquisition process. This complexity is not only due to the relevant semantic, syntactic, and information-structural features involved, but also to the variable ways in which *aber* can be used.

4 Conclusion

The present study provides new insights into the interaction between the acquisition of finite clause structure and the particles *auch* and *aber*. It once again shows that DLD can function as a magnifier in the study of language acquisition when developmental processes run quickly in typically developing children (Dimroth & Lindner, 2005). However, limitations of this study due to the nature of case studies and the infrequent production of *aber* by the DLD child must be considered. In addition, the higher proportion of *auch*- and *aber*-clauses with modal verbs relative to simple main clauses might have contributed to the late emergence of lexical action verbs in V2 position and separated agentive particle verbs. This is because these constructions are mutually exclusive. However, if this is assumed to be the case, the emergence of OVS word order still needs to be explained.

Appendix

Table A: Verb types in Bastian's *auch*-clauses.

	No verb	Infinitive	Copula	Modal verb	LexV state predicate	LexV action predicate	LexV light verb	Aux: *sein* 'be' + PP	Aux: *haben* 'have' + PP	Unclear
2;05	31 (78%)	5 (13%)	–	–	–	–	–	–	–	4 (10%)
2;06	20 (69%)	5 (17%)	–	–	–	–	–	–	–	4 (14%)
2;07	53 (87%)	5 (8%)	–	–	–	–	–	–	–	3 (5%)
2;08	21 (70%)	5 (17%)	–	–	–	–	–	–	–	4 (13%)
2;09	10 (48%)	9 (43%)	–	1 (5%)	–	–	–	–	–	1 (5%)
2;10	3 (30%)	3 (30%)	–	2 (20%)	–	–	–	–	–	2 (20%)
2;11	10 (71%)	3 (21%)	–	–	–	–	–	–	–	1 (7%)
3;00	3 (38%)	4 (50%)	–	–	–	–	–	–	–	1 (13%)
3;01	28 (70%)	5 (13%)	–	–	–	–	–	–	–	7 (18%)
3;02	17 (61%)	6 (21%)	–	–	–	–	–	–	–	5 (18%)
3;03	6 (50%)	3 (25%)	–	–	–	–	–	–	–	3 (25%)
3;04	15 (68%)	4 (18%)	–	–	1 (5%)	–	–	–	–	2 (9%)
3;05	20 (77%)	3 (12%)	–	–	1 (4%)	–	–	–	–	2 (8%)
3;06	21 (46%)	14 (30%)	–	1 (2%)	3 (7%)	–	1 (2%)	–	–	6 (13%)
3;07	12 (39%)	12 (39%)	–	1 (3%)	1 (3%)	–	1 (3%)	–	–	4 (13%)
3;08	11 (69%)	2 (13%)	–	1 (6%)	1 (6%)	–	–	–	–	1 (6%)
3;09	12 (55%)	3 (14%)	1 (5%)	1 (5%)	2 (9%)	–	–	–	–	3 (14%)
3;10	7 (58%)	2 (17%)	2 (17%)	1 (8%)	–	–	–	–	–	–
3;11	9 (60%)	–	–	2 (13%)	1 (7%)	1 (7%)	–	–	–	2 (13%)

Table A (continued)

4;00	7 (64%)	–	–	–	2 (18%)	1 (9%)	–	1 (9%)	–
4;01	4 (57%)	–	1 (14%)	1 (14%)	–	–	–	–	1 (14%)
4;02	5 (42%)	–	3 (25%)	2 (17%)	–	–	–	1 (8%)	1 (8%)
4;03	8 (32%)	3 (12%)	3 (12%)	2 (8%)	6 (24%)	–	–	1 (4%)	2 (8%)
4;04	9 (32%)	1 (4%)	2 (7%)	10 (36%)	2 (7%)	2 (7%)	1 (4%)	–	1 (4%)
4;05	11 (48%)	1 (4%)	2 (9%)	6 (26%)	1 (4%)	–	–	1 (4%)	1 (4%)
4;06	3 (17%)	–	2 (11%)	8 (44%)	3 (17%)	–	–	1 (6%)	1 (6%)
4;07	2 (11%)	–	1 (5%)	10 (53%)	2 (11%)	2 (11%)	1 (6%)	1 (5%)	–
4;08	–	–	–	1 (100%)	–	–	–	–	–
4;09	10 (31%)	–	6 (19%)	4 (13%)	6 (19%)	4 (13%)	–	2 (6%)	–
4;10	–	–	–	–	–	–	–	1 (100%)	–
4;11	1 (4%)	–	2 (8%)	7 (28%)	1 (4%)	5 (22%)	2 (9%)	5 (20%)	2 (8%)
Total	369 (54%)	98 (14%)	25 (4%)	61 (9%)	33 (5%)	15 (2%)	6 (1%)	14 (2%)	64 (9%)

Table B: Verb types in Bastian's *aber*-clauses.

	No verbs	Non–finite form	Copula	Modal verb	LexV state predicate	LexV action predicate	LexV light verb	Aux: *sein* 'be' + PP	Aux: *haben* 'have' + PP	Unclear
3;10	–	1 (100%)	–	–	–	–	–	–	–	–
3;11	1 (100%)	–	–	–	–	–	–	–	–	–
4;02	–	–	–	–	2 (100%)	–	–	–	–	–
4;04	2 (40%)	–	–	1 (20%)	2 (40%)	–	–	–	–	–
4;05	1 (15%)	–	–	4 (57%)	1 (14%)	–	–	–	1 (14%)	–
4;06	–	–	–	4 (50%)	2 (25%)	–	–	–	1 (12%)	1 (13%)
4;07	4 (67%)	–	–	–	2 (33%)	–	–	–	–	–
4;08	1 (50%)	1 (50%)	–	–	–	–	–	–	–	–
4;09	1 (20%)	–	–	–	–	2 (40%)	–	–	1 (20%)	1 (20%)
4;11	1 (17%)	–	–	2 (33%)	2 (33%)	–	–	–	1 (17%)	–
5;00	3 (37%)	–	–	1 (13%)	4 (50%)	–	–	–	–	–
5;01	–	–	–	1 (100%)	–	–	–	–	–	–
5;03	3 (60%)	–	1 (20%)	–	1 (20%)	–	–	–	–	–
5;04	2 (67%)	–	–	1 (33%)	–	–	–	–	–	–
5;05	1 (25%)	–	2 (50%)	–	–	1 (25%)	–	–	–	–
5;06	1 (34%)	–	–	–	1 (33%)	1 (33%)	–	–	–	–
5;07	–	–	–	1 (100%)	–	–	–	–	–	–
5;08	–	–	1 (34%)	1 (33%)	–	–	–	–	–	1 (33%)
5;10	–	–	3 (50%)	1 (17%)	2 (33%)	0	–	–	–	–
5;11	–	–	–	2 (100%)	–	–	–	–	–	–
Total	21 (27%)	2 (3%)	7 (9%)	19 (24%)	19 (24%)	4 (5%)	–	–	4 (5%)	3 (4%)

References

Bartz, Damaris. in prep. *Partikelspezifische Effekte von 'auch' und 'aber' auf die Finitheitsrealisierung im Deutschen L1-Erwerb*. Doctoral dissertation.

Bartz, Damaris & Dagmar Bittner. 2018. Contrast relations in the early *aber*-clauses of German-speaking infants. *Linguistics Vanguard* 4(s1). https://doi.org/10.1515/lingvan-2016-0102.

Bittner, Dagmar. 2010. Pronomen: Fallstudie zum Erwerb von Textstrukturierungsfähigkeiten im ungestörten Spracherwerb und bei SSES. *L.O.G.O.S. INTERDISZIPLINÄR* 5.

Bittner, Dagmar & Damaris Bartz. 2018. Finiteness in early but-clauses in German L1-acquisition. *First Language* 38(4), 337–358. https://doi.org/10.1177/0142723717747470.

Brauße, Ursula. 1998. What is adversativity? 'But' or 'and'? (Opposites, semantic contrast). *Deutsche Sprache* 26(2), 138–159.

Breindl, Eva. 2004. Relationsbedeutung und Konnektorbedeutung: Additivität, Adversativität und Konzessivität. In Hardarik Blühdorn, Eva Breindl & Ulrich H. Waßner (eds.), *Brücken schlagen. Grundlagen der Konnektorensemantik*, 225–253. Berlin/New York: De Gruyter.

Dietrich, Rainer & Patrick Grommes. 1998. 'nicht'. Reflexe seiner Bedeutung und Syntax im Zweitsprach-erwerb. In Heide Wegener (ed.), *Eine zweite Sprache lernen: Empirische Untersuchungen zum Zweitspracherwerb*, 173–202. Tübingen: Gunter Narr Verlag.

Dimroth, Christine. 2002. Topics, assertions, and additive words: How L2 learners get from information structure to target-language syntax. *Linguistics* 40(4), 891–923. https://doi.org/10.1515/ling.2002.033.

Dimroth, Christine. 2004. *Fokuspartikeln und Informationsgliederung im Deutschen*. Tübingen: Stauffenburg.

Dimroth, Christine. 2009. Stepping stones and stumbling blocks. Why negation accelerates and additive particles delay the acquisition of finiteness in German. In Christine Dimroth & Peter Jordens (eds.), *Functional Categories in Learner Language*, 137–170. Berlin/New York: De Gruyter.

Dimroth, Christine, Petra Gretsch, Peter Jordens & Clive Perdue. 2003. Finiteness in Germanic languages: A stagemodel for first and second language development. *Information Structure and the Dynamics of Language Acquisition* 26, 65–93.

Dimroth, Christine & Katrin Lindner. 2005. Was langsame Lerner uns zeigen können. *Zeitschrift Für Literaturwissenschaft Und Linguistik*, 35(4), 40–60.

Dimroth, Christine, Sarah Schimke & Josje Verhagen. 2009. Is verb-raising influenced by information structure? [Poster]. 19th European Second Language Association Conference (EuroSLA), Cork, Ireland. https://www.researchgate.net/profile/Christine_Dimroth/publication/46721643_Is_verb-raising_influenced_by_information_structure/links/0c96052eb8a07ac041000000.pdf.

Gülzow, Insa, Victoria Bartlitz, Milena Kühnast, Felix Golcher & Dagmar Bittner. 2018. The adversative connectives aber and but in conversational corpora. *Journal of Child Language* 45(5), 1212–1226. https://doi.org/10.1017/S0305000917000630.

Jolink, Anke. 2005. Finite linking in normally developing Dutch children and children with specific language impairment. *Zeitschrift Für Literaturwissenschaft Und Linguistik* 35(4), 61–80.

Jolink, Anke. 2009. Finiteness in children with SLI. A functional approach. In Christine Dimroth & Peter Jordens (eds.), *Functional categories in learner language*, 235–260. Berlin/New York: De Gruyter.

Jordens, Peter. 2012. *Language Acquisition and the Functional Category System*. Berlin/New York: De Gruyter.
Jordens, Peter & Christine Dimroth. 2008. Finiteness in children and adults learning Dutch. In Natalia Gagarina & Insa Gulzow (eds.), *The Acquisition of Verbs and their Grammar: The Effect of Particular Languages*, 173–198. Dordrecht: Springer Netherlands. https://doi.org/10.1007/978-1-4020-4335-2_8.
Klein, Wolfgang. 1998. Assertion and finiteness. In Norbert Dittmar & Zvi Penner (eds.), *Issues in the theory of language acquisition: Essays in honor of Jürgen Weissenborn*, 225–245. Bern: Lang.
Klein, Wolfgang. 2012. Assertion-related particles in German. In Katharina Spalek & Rainer Dietrich (eds.), *Sprachliche Variationen, Varietäten und Kontexte: Beiträge zu psycholinguistischen Schnittstellen: Festschrift für Rainer Dietrich*, 13–38. Tübingen: Stauffenburg.
Lakoff, Robin. 1971. If`s, and`s and but`s about conjunction. In Charles J. Fillmore & D. Terrence Langendoen (eds.), *Studies in linguistic semantics*, 115–149. New York: Holt, Rinehart & Winston.
Lang, Ewald. 2004. Schnittstellen bei der Konnektoren-Beschreibung. In Hardarik Blühdorn, Eva Breindl & Ulrich H. Waßner (eds.), *Brücken schlagen. Grundlagen der Konnektorensemantik*, 45–92. Berlin/New York: De Gruyter.
Lang, Ewald & Marcela Adamíková. 2007. The lexical content of connectors and its interplay with intonation. An interim balance on sentential connection in discourse. In Andreas Späth (ed.), *Interfaces and Interface Conditions*, 199–230. Boston: De Gruyter.
MacWhinney, Brian. 2000. *The CHILDES project: The database* (Vol. 2). Psychology Press.
Müller, Anja, Barbara Höhle, Michaela Schmitz & Jürgen Weissenborn. 2009. Information structural constraints on children's early language production: The acquisition of the focus particle auch ('also') in German-learning 12- to 36-month-olds. *First Language* 29(4), 373–399. https://doi.org/10.1177/0142723709105314
Nederstigt, Ulrike. 2003. *Auch and noch in Child and Adult German*. Berlin: Walter de Gruyter.
Penner, Zvi, Rosemarie Tracy & Jürgen Weissenborn. 2000. Where Scrambling Begins: Triggering Object Scrambling at the Early Stage in German and Bernese Swiss German. In Susan M. Powers & Cornelia Hamann (eds.), *The Acquisition of Scrambling and Cliticization*, 127–164. Dordrecht: Springer Netherlands. https://doi.org/10.1007/978-94-017-3232-1_6.
Penner, Zvi, Rosemarie Tracy & Karin Wymann. 1999. Die Rolle der Fokuspartikel 'auch' im frühen kindlichen Lexikon: Eine Studie zum Erwerb des Deutschen im Vergleich mit dem doppelten Erstspracherwerb Deutsch-Englisch und dem verspäteten Sprechbeginn. In Jörg Meibauer & Monika Rothweiler (eds.), *Das Lexikon im Spracherwerb*. Tübingen/Basel: Francke.
Saebø, Kjell Johan. 2003. Presupposition and contrast: German *aber* as a topic particle. *Proceedings of Sinn Und Bedeutung* 7, 257–271.
Schimke, Sarah, Josje Verhagen & Christine Dimroth. 2008. Particules additives et finitude en néerlandais et allemand L2. Étude expérimentale. *Acquisition et interaction en langue étrangère* 26, 191–210.
Schimke, Sarah, Josje Verhagen & Giuseppina Turco. 2012. The different role of additive and negative particles in the development of finiteness in early adult L2 German and L2 Dutch. In M. Watorek, S. Benazzo, & M. Hickmann (eds.), *Comparative Perspectives on Language Acquisition: A Tribute to Clive Perdue*, 73–91. Bristol: Multilingual Matters.

Skerra, Antje. 2017. *Verfügbarkeit von Kohäsionsmitteln für Kinder mit einer Sprachentwicklungsstörung* [Humboldt-Universität zu Berlin]. https://edoc.hu-berlin.de/handle/18452/19323.

Tribushinina, E., Dubinkina, E., & Sanders, T. 2015. Can connective use differentiate between children with and without specific language impairment? *First Language* 35(1), 3–26.

Tribushinina, Elena, Willem M. Mak, Elizaveta Andreiushina, Elena Dubinkina & Ted Sanders. 2017. Connective use in the narratives of bilingual children and monolingual children with SLI. *Bilingualism: Language and Cognition* 20(1), 98–113.

Umbach, Carla. 2005. Contrast and Information Structure: A Focus-Based Analysis of but. *Linguistics* 43(1), 207–232. https://doi.org/10.1515/ling.2005.43.1.207.

Umbach, Carla. 2001. Contrast and contrastive topic. *Proceedings of Esslli 2001 Workshop on Information Structure, Discourse Structure and Discourse Semantics: University of Helsinki*, 175–188.

von Stutterheim, Christiane & Wolfgang Klein. 2002. Quaestio and L-perspectivation. In Carl Friedrich Graumann & Werner Kallmeyer (eds.), *Perspective and Perspectivation in Discourse*. Amsterdam/Philadelphia: John Benjamins Publishing.

Westergaard, Marit Richardsen. 2009. *The Acquisition of Word Order: Micro-cues, Information Structure, and Economy*. John Benjamins Publishing.

Winkler, Stefanie. 2006. *Finiteness in first and second language acquisition*. Annual Report; Max-Planck-Institut für Psycholinguistik, Nijmegen.

Winkler, Stefanie. 2009. The acquisition of syntactic finiteness in L1 German. A structure-building approach. In Christine Dimroth & Peter Jordens (eds.), *Functional Categories in Learner Language*, 97–134. Berlin/New York: Mouton de Gruyter.

Index

action 4–5, 17–18, 22–23, 27, 31, 47, 71, 78–79, 90–98, 101, 105–106, 109, 111–115, 126
Agent first 25, 30, 47, 70, 99, 103, 105–106, 119
agentive predicate 16, 47, 92–93, 102, 105, 106
agentive utterance 30–33, 70–71, 90, 98, 106
agreement errors (subject-verb) 141–144, 147–148, 154, 160
ambiguous verbs 148, 155, 159
anaphoric pronouns 2–5, 109, 123
assertion 1, 23–24, 35, 44, 51, 72, 81, 124, 137, 168, 173–174, 200
attentional capacity 83, 85–86
auxiliary verb 35–40, 102–104, 107, 110–111

basic language system /variety 5, 14, 19, 22, 34, 47, 67, 69, 101, 123–124, 126, 128–129
Bates, Elizabeth B. 91
Bishop, Dorothy V.M. 56, 83–85, 138
bootstrapping 176

case marking 62, 73, 76–78
change of state 17, 18, 22–23, 27, 32, 47, 70–71, 79, 90, 92, 96–98, 105–107, 115, 121, 126
Clahsen, Harald 30, 56–66, 75–81, 85–86, 141, 158–159
complementary distribution 5, 15–16, 94, 105
computational demands 85–86, 89, 123, 125–126
computational difficulty 81, 84–86
computational limitations 132
computational problem 81, 199, 202
conflicting constraints 30, 48
contextual cohesion 1, 3, 33–34, 46–47, 55, 73–74, 80, 85, 89, 123–125, 130–131, 165, 167, 177, 199, 202
contextual inflection 75–78, 80
contrastive topic 169–171, 173–174, 179, 193, 195–201, 203

control (CTL) 17–18, 22–24, 47, 89, 92, 99–100, 121, 124
control agreement 55, 59, 61–64, 66, 75, 80, 86

defaulting (errors) 143–144, 153–154, 158
definiteness 46, 73–74, 109
developmental progress 1, 3, 46, 67
Dimroth, Christine 14, 165–167, 169, 173–174, 176, 200, 204
domain of application (DoA) 169, 174, 194–195, 199
driving force 72, 116, 199
Dual-Factor Model 137, 143–144, 149, 152, 154–155, 158–159
Duinmeijer, Iris 83–85, 125
dummy auxiliary verb 50

eventive (agentive) verb 142, 143, 148, 155, 159
Extended Optional Infinitive 137, 141, 155, 157, 159
external argument 17, 22–23, 27, 29, 35, 47–48, 63, 70, 90–92, 96–97, 100, 102–103, 105, 116, 124, 128–129, 131
external finiteness stage 175, 195, 201–202

finite verb form 5, 7–8, 15, 58–59, 61–62, 77–78, 91–92, 102, 110
finite vs. infinite 3, 5, 103
finiteness functional 174–175, 177, 179–180, 182, 189, 195, 198–203
finiteness morphological 5, 36, 67, 110
finiteness semantic 1, 3, 34–37, 44, 48, 51, 60, 72–74, 81, 86, 110, 124
finiteness 102–103, 109, 131
focalization 34, 42, 44, 49, 127, 129
Focus expression last 129
focus particle 166, 168–169, 172–173
focus-sensitive adverb 166, 168, 172
Freudenthal, Daniel 137, 142–143, 159, 160
functional category system 3, 34, 46–47, 56, 60, 81, 85–86

functional category 1, 3–4, 33–35, 46, 55–56, 58–60, 75, 81, 85–86
functional prefield 2, 51, 72, 102–103, 124, 183–184, 187–188
functional projection 34–35, 37, 44, 46, 51
functional topic position 40, 44, 127
functional V2 position 37, 107, 109, 112–113, 115, 117
functional-grammatical deficit 58

gender marking 57, 59, 62, 66–67
grammatical agreement deficit 57, 59, 60, 66
Grimm, Hannelore 90

Håkansson, Gisela 65
Hamann, Cornelia 59
hat, hab + Vpp 103–105
head-complement (structure) 22–23, 47
head-final 7
head-initial 7, 16
Hyams, Nina 140

impaired inflection 61, 64
inchoative aspect 126–127
infinite verb form 6–7, 58, 91, 102
inflectional morphology 5, 34, 57, 61, 64, 75–80, 102
information structure 1, 27, 47, 51, 67, 72, 167, 172, 180, 202
informativeness 100, 108
internal finiteness stage 175, 195, 202
inversion (subject-verb) 1, 34, 56, 58, 102, 103, 107, 109

Klein, Wolfgang 1–3, 23, 25–27, 34, 48, 60, 77, 169, 170, 172, 200
Kolk, Herman 81–82, 84, 125

language disorder 55–56, 82, 89, 107, 123
Lebeaux, David 81
left-dislocated 99, 107, 120, 128–129, 131
Leonard, Laurence B. 55–56, 58–60, 80–81, 86, 89, 143–144, 160–161
lexical aspect 105, 126, 131–132
lexical learner system 2, 6, 66
lexical linking 173, 176

lexical projection 2, 5, 17–18, 33, 35, 45–46, 48
Lindner, Katrin 59, 176, 200, 204
linguistic deficit 55, 56, 73, 81, 85, 89, 123, 125

MacWhinney, Brian 90, 145
Master Tree 45–46
Minimalist Program 45
Missing Agreement Hypothesis 55, 59–60, 66
modal/aspectual head 8–9, 11, 15, 17, 22–24, 47–48, 70
morphological deficit 56, 59
morpho-syntactic deficit 55, 58, 61–62, 66, 86
morpho-syntactic finiteness 170, 176, 200
MOSAIC (Model of Syntax Acquisition) 143

neutral topic 169, 173–174, 179, 193–194, 199, 201
non-agentive predicate 16, 47, 91–93, 102, 105
non-agentive utterances 17, 23–25, 27, 30, 32–33, 70–71, 90, 92, 98, 105–106, 128
noun plurals 64

object scrambling 24
Optional Infinitive 58, 137, 139–141, 155
Organic Grammar 45
Overlap Hypothesis 8

participle inflection 55, 57, 64, 66
particle verbs 19–22, 49, 96–97, 11
particle-specific effects 165, 167–168
Penner, Zvi 59, 158, 165–166, 172–173, 176
Perdue, Clive 25, 27, 30
perfect aspect 105, 126
Pine, Julian 137–138, 143–144, 160
Poeppel, David 8, 19, 58, 137, 139–140
pre-finiteness stage 175
presentatives 27–29, 100–102, 119, 121–122
progressive aspect 105, 126–127

Reilly, Judy 82, 84–85
result state 76, 105, 107, 114

Rice, Mabel 58, 60, 137, 139, 141–142, 145–147, 149–150, 157, 160
right dislocation 126, 130–132
right-dislocated 131
Rizzi, Luigi 140
root infinitive 6–9
Rowland, Caroline 138

scope 169–170, 174, 200
separated-particle verb 20, 22, 96, 168, 179, 183–184, 200–202
Siegmüller, Julia 90–91
stage model 46, 67
state 4–5, 17–19, 22–23, 27, 32, 47, 70–71, 79, 90, 92, 94–98, 102, 105–107, 111, 114, 142, 148, 155, 159
subject 23, 25–27, 30–32, 44, 47, 57, 59, 65, 71–73, 77, 85, 102, 107–109, 116–117, 119–121, 127, 130
subject-verb agreement 1, 46, 56, 59, 61, 63, 73–74, 76–79, 83, 86, 109, 110, 116

tense marking 5, 63, 66, 77, 84
theme 17–18, 20, 22–23, 25–28, 30, 32–33, 47, 70–71, 89–90, 92, 96–98, 102–103, 105–106, 116–117, 119, 124, 128, 133
Topic first 25–26, 30, 35, 48, 107
topic situation (TS) 25–26, 34, 44, 48–49, 51, 65, 67, 72, 74, 77, 81, 86, 109, 120, 124, 127
topic time (TT) 77, 81
topicality 1, 48, 72–73, 81, 102–103, 109, 124–125, 131

topicalization 3, 30, 34, 42, 44, 49, 74, 99, 117, 124, 126–130
topicalized 48, 65, 98–99, 117

Umbach, Carla 168, 170–172

Vainikka, Anne 45–46
verb movement 3–4, 8, 34, 60, 63–64, 67, 73–75, 80–81, 85–86, 102–103, 109, 111, 113, 116, 124
verb second 1, 3, 34, 36, 48, 60, 63–66, 74, 81, 103, 107, 109, 124
verbal particle 5, 12–15, 68, 130–131
verb-placement errors 137, 141, 143–144, 147–148, 152–153, 157–158, 160

Wexler, Kenneth 8, 19, 58, 60, 137, 139–140
wh-elements 26, 43, 49
wh-question 26, 34, 55, 58, 83, 102, 109, 120
Winkler, Stefanie 165–166, 173–174
word order 1–5, 24–25, 46–47, 63, 65–67, 70, 74, 83, 98, 101–102, 105, 107
working memory 46, 55, 82, 85, 89–90, 125–126, 128–129, 131–132, 165, 177, 199, 202

yes/no-question 3, 26, 34, 42–43, 49, 102, 109, 120
Young-Scholten, Martha 45–46

www.ingramcontent.com/pod-product-compliance
Lightning Source LLC
Chambersburg PA
CBHW031312150426
43191CB00005B/191